THE 1896 OLYMPIC GAMES

THE 1896 OLYMPIC GAMES

Results for All Competitors in All Events, with Commentary

by
Bill Mallon
and Ture Widlund

RESULTS OF THE EARLY MODERN OLYMPICS, 1

McFarland & Company, Inc., Publishers
Jefferson, North Carolina, and London

British Library Cataloguing-in-Publication data are available

Library of Congress Cataloguing-in-Publication Data

Mallon, Bill.
   The 1896 Olympic Games : results for all competitors
in all events, with commentary / by Bill Mallon and Ture
Widland.
       p.   cm. — (Results of the early modern Olympics ; 1)
   Includes bibliographical references and index.
   ISBN 0-7864-0379-9 (library binding : 50# alkaline paper) ∞
   1. Olympic Games (1st : 1896 : Athens, Greece)   2. Olympics —
Records.   I. Widland, Ture.   II. Title.   III. Series: Mallon,
Bill.   Results of the early modern Olympics ; 1.
   GV721.8.M32   1998
   [GV722   1896]
   796.48 s
   [796.48] — DC21   97-26356
                                                                  CIP

Manufactured in the United States of America

McFarland & Company, Inc., Publishers
   Box 611, Jefferson, North Carolina 28640

To the memory
of Erich Kamper

Table of Contents

Introduction

The modern Olympic Games are more than a century old; in the summer of 1996, the world celebrated the centennial games in Atlanta. The modern Olympic Games began in 1896 in Athens, Greece, through the efforts of the Frenchman Baron Pierre de Coubertin, who made it his life's work to resurrect the Olympic dream that had first begun in ancient Greece several centuries before the common era.

It is reasonable to ask, why an unofficial report of an Olympic Games which ended more than 100 years ago? This book began as one of a series of monographs attempting to resurrect the results of the earliest games. Complete records of the results of the earliest Olympics do not exist, unlike more recent Games, in which computers and the media dissect each event with almost surgical precision. While corresponding with each other we found that we were both working on the same project of unearthing the records of the 1896 Games, which led to our collobration on this project.

We are primarily trying to present in detail the most complete results ever seen of the 1896 Olympic Games. Thus the emphasis here is on the statistics, and we have not intended to present new political or sociological analyses of the first modern Games. We will leave that to our academic colleagues. We have included a short synopsis of the Sorbonne Congress, the Organization, and the details of the 1896 Olympics. In addition, we have included some reprints of rather famous articles describing the 1896 Olympics. These are often referenced in academic works and are the best descriptions of the 1896 Olympics in English, but they are not always easy to find, especially for Europeans looking for sources.

We have provided extensive references for the results and statistics. This effort is primarily meant to note that we have looked at all sources and that we wish to correct previously published errors. In noting errors in more recent works, it is not our intent to denigrate the original authors, but to let the reader know that we are aware of any discrepancy between our data and those of other authors, and then to present our sources and the reasons for our conclusions. In all cases, we have tried to use 1896 sources, of which we have been able to identify several, by examining works in a number of languages. (Note from Mallon: these 1896 sources, at least 18, were unearthed primarily through the excellent research of Widlund.) We did not succeed in finding complete results of all events, although we have come close.

This work is the first in a series published by McFarland on the earliest Games, detailing the very nearly complete records of the poorly documented Olympics from 1896 through 1920.

There has been a rebirth of interest in the history of the Games. The authors of this book, along with five other Olympic historians (Ian Buchanan, Stan Greenberg, Ove Karlsson, Peter Matthews, and David Wallechinsky), were founding members of the International Society of Olympic Historians (ISOH), which was created on 5 December 1991. Much of this work has been reviewed and edited by members of ISOH. In addition, much of the work has used material contributed by other ISOH members. We are thankful to all of them for their efforts.

We give special thanks to the following: Tony Bijkerk [NED], Ian Buchanan [GBR], Jim Crossman [USA/SHO], Konstantinos Georgiadis [GRE], Heiner Gillmeister [GER/TEN], Volker Kluge [GER], Jiří Kössl [CZE], Hans Agersnap Larsen [DEN], Karl Lennartz [GER], Wolf Lyberg [SWE/many sports], Athanasios Tarasouleas [GRE], Walter Teutenberg [GER], and David Wallechinsky [USA/many sports].

Finally, we both acknowledge our debt to the late Erich Kamper of Austria, who was the pioneer of all Olympic historians and statisticians. Erich was the motivating force behind the founding of ISOH and served as its honorary president in its first Olympiad of existence. He died in late 1995. This book is dedicated to his memory.

Bill Mallon
Durham, North Carolina

Ture Widlund
Stockholm, Sweden

October 1997

Abbreviations

General

A	athletes competing
AB	abandoned
AC	also competed (place not known)
bh	behind
C	countries competing
d.	defeated
D	date(s) of competition
DNF	did not finish
DNS	did not start
DQ	disqualified
E	entered
est	estimate(d)
f	final
F	format of competition
h	heat
km.	kilometer(s)
m	meter(s)
NH	no-height
NM	no mark
NP	not placed
OR	Olympic Record
r	round
T	time competition started
wo	walkover (won by forfeit)
WR	World Record

Sports

ATH	Athletics (Track & Field)
CYC	Cycling
FEN	Fencing
GYM	Gymnastics
ROW	Rowing & Sculling
SHO	Shooting
SWI	Swimming
TEN	Tennis (Lawn)
WAP	Water Polo
WLT	Weightlifting
WRE	Wrestling (Greco-Roman)

Nations

AUS	Australia
AUT	Austria
BUL	Bulgaria
CHI	Chile
DEN	Denmark
EGY	Egypt
FRA	France
GBR	Great Britain and Ireland
GER	Germany
GRE	Greece
HUN	Hungary
ITA	Italy
SMY	Smyrna
SUI	Switzerland
SWE	Sweden
USA	United States

References

with Their Abbreviations as Cited in Text

Primary Sources from 1896

AATM   *Arms and the Man*. American shooting magazine from 1896.

Akrp   *Akropolis*. Greek (Athens) newspaper from 1896.

Argy   Argyros, A. *Diethneis olympiakoi agones tou 1896*. Athens, 1896.

ASZ   *Allgemeine Sport-Zeitung*. Austrian weekly sporting newspaper from 1896.

BDP   *Birmingham Daily Post*. British newspaper from 1896.

Berg   Bergman, Johan. *På klassisk mark*. Stockholm, 1896.

Bici   *La Bicicletta*. Italian (Milan) sporting newspaper, 1896.

Boland   Boland, John Pius. *Collected Diaries of John Pius Boland*. Unpublished.

Butler   Butler, Maynard. "The Olympic Games," *Outlook 53* (30 May 1896): 993–995.

Chrysafis   Chrysafis, Ioannis. *Oi protoi diethneis olympiakoi agones en Athinais to 1896*. Athens 1896.

Coubt   Coubertin, Baron Pierre de. "The Olympic Games of 1896," *Century Magazine 53*, 31 (November 1896): 39–53.

Epth   *Epitheorisis*. Greek (Athens) newspaper from 1896.

Gagalis   Gagalis, Athanasiou; Kazis, Milt.; Ioannidis, Georg. *Perifrafi ton en Athinais proton diethnon olympiakon agonon*. Athens 1896.

Gavrilidou Gavrilidou, V. *I Ellas kata tous olympiakous agonas tou 1896*. Athens 1896.

Grigoriou   *Grigoriou*. Greek (Athens) newspaper from 1896.

Guth   Guth-Jarkovský, Jiří. "Die olympischen Spiele in Athen 1896." In *Zeitschrift für die Österreichischen Gymnasien*. 1896.

Hüppe   Hüppe, Ferdinand. "Griechenland und die jetzigen und einstigen olympischen Spiele." A series of articles in *Allgemeine Sport-Zeitung*, November 1896–January 1897.

NS   *Nea Smyrna*. Greek (Athens) newspaper from 1896.

OR   Official Report of the 1896 Olympic Games — the actual bibliographic information is as follows: The Baron de Coubertin; Philemon, Timoleon; Lambros, Spiridon P.; and Politis, Nikolaos G., editors. *The Olympic Games 776 B.C.–1896 A.D.; With the approval and support of the Central Council of the International Olympic Games in Athens, under the Presidency of H.R.H. the Crown Prince Constantine.* Athens:

Charles Beck, 1896. This was issued in various versions, including several in parallel texts, as follows: Greek/English; Greek/French; Greek/French/English; and German/English. Also, multiple reprints of this first Official Report have been produced, most notably a 1966 edition with English/French/Greek parallel texts published by the Hellenic Olympic Committee, and also a 1971 German edition entitled *Die olympischen Spiele 1896: Offizieller Bericht*, published by the Carl-Diem-Institut in Cologne, Germany. Finally, see "KL96" below, which is a German reprint of the Official Report, supplemented with articles on the 1896 Olympics by various Olympic historians, and also containing reprints of various primary documentary material from 1896.

Plng   *Palingenesia.* Greek (Athens) newspaper from 1896.

Pron   *Pronoia.* Greek (Athens) newspaper from 1896.

Prsk   Paraskevopoulos, K. *To dekaimeron ton olympiakon agonon.* Athens 1896.

Roberts   Robertson, George Stuart. "The Olympic Games by a Competitor and Prize Winner," *Fortnightly Review* 354 (1 June 1896): 944–957.

Rufus   Richardson, Rufus. "The New Olympian Games," *Scribner's Magazine* 20, 3 (September 1896): 267–286.

RW   *Rad-Welt.* German cycling magazine from 1896.

Salpigx   *Salpigx.* Greek (Athens) newspaper from 1896.

SiB   *Sport im Bild.* German sporting newspaper from 1896.

Smnds   *Simeonidis.* Greek (Athens) newspaper from 1896.

SS   *Schwimmsport.* German swimming magazine from 1896.

SV   *Sport-Világ.* Hungarian sporting newspaper from 1896.

TfI   *Tidning för Idrott.* Swedish sporting newspaper from 1896, containing a series of articles written by Viktor Balck (Swedish IOC member) entitled, "De olympiska Spelen i Athen 5–14 April 1896."

TF   *The Field.* British sporting newspaper from 1896.

ToA   *To Asty.* Greek (Athens) newspaper from 1896.

Velo   *Le Vélo.* French sporting newspaper from 1896.

Waldst   Waldstein, Charles. "The Olympian Games at Athens," *The Field,* May 1896.

Olympic Historical and Statistical Works after 1896

CD   Diem, Carl. *Ein Leben für den Sport.* Düsseldorf: no year.

Chrysafis   Chrysafis, Ioannis E. *Hoi protoi diethnais olympiakoi agones en Athenais 1896.* Athens: Biblioteke tes Epitropes ton Olympiakon Agonon, 1926 and 1930.

Coub1   Coubertin, Pierre de. *Une Campagne de vingt-et-un ans (1887–1908).* Paris: Librairie de l'Education Physique, 1909.

Coub2   Coubertin, Pierre de. *Mémoires olympiques.* Aix-en-Provence: 1931.

Curtis   Curtis, Thomas P. "High Hurdles and White Gloves," *The Sportsman* 12, 1 (July 1932): 60–61.

DW   Wallechinsky, David. *The Complete Book of the Olympics.* First edition, Middlesex, England: Penguin Books, 1983. Second edition, New York: Viking Penguin, 1988. Third edition, London: Aurum, 1991. Fourth edition, New York: Little, Brown, 1996.

EK   Kamper, Erich. *Enzyklopädie der olympischen Spiele.* Dortmund: Harenberg, 1972. Parallel texts in German, French, and English. American edition issued as *Encyclopaedia of the Olympic Games* by McGraw-Hill (New York) in 1972.

EzM   zur Megede, Ekkehard. *Die olympische Leichtathletik*. Bands 1–3. Darmstadt: Justus von Liebig Verlag, 1984.

FM   Mező, Ferenc. *The Modern Olympic Games*. Budapest: Pannonia Press, 1956. Multiple editions were issued in English, French, German, Spanish, and Hungarian.

FW   Wasner, Fritz. *Olympia-Lexikon*. Bielefeld, Germany: Verlag E. Gunglach Aktiengesellschaft, 1939.

Georgi   Georgiadis, Konstantinos. "Die Geschichte der ersten olympischen Spiele 1896 in Athen — ihre Entstehung, Durchführung und Bedeutung." Unpublished diplomarbeit, Johannes Gutenberg Universitat Mainz, 1986/87.

Gynn   Gynn, Roger. *The Guinness Book of the Marathon*. London: Guinness, 1984.

Henry   Henry, Bill. *An Approved History of the Olympic Games*. Last three editions edited by Henry's daughter, Patricia Henry Yeomans. First edition, New York: G.P. Putnam, 1948. Second edition: New York: G.P. Putnam, 1976. Third and fourth editions, Sherman Oaks, Calif.: Alfred Publishing, 1981 and 1984.

KL96   Lennartz, Karl, ed. *Die olympischen Spiele 1896 in Athen: Erläuterungen zum Neudruck des Offiziellen Berichtes*. Agon Sportverlag, 1996.

KLWT   Lennartz, Karl, and Teutenberg, Walter. *Die deutsche Olympia-Mannschaft von 1896*. Kassel: Kasseler Sportverlag, 1992.

Levy   Levy, E[dward] Lawrence. *Autobiography of an Athlete*. Birmingham, England: J.G. Hammond & Co., 1913.

Lyberg   Lyberg, Wolf. *The History of the IOC Sessions. I. 1894–1930*. Lausanne: International Olympic Committee, Oct. 1994.

MacAl   MacAloon, John J. *This Great Symbol: Pierre de Coubertin and the Origins of the Modern Olympic Games*. Chicago: University of Chicago Press, 1981.

Mallon   Mallon, Bill. *The Olympic Games 1896, 1900, 1904, and 1906. Part I: Track and Field Athletics*. Durham: author, 1984.

Mandell   Mandell, Richard D. *The First Modern Olympics*. Berkeley: University of California Press, 1976.

Mantk   Manitakis, P. *100 chronia neoellinikou athlitismen 1830–1930*. Athens, 1962.

Olympiadebogen   Andersen, Peder Christian, and Hansen, Vagn. *Olympiadebogen. De olympiske Lege 1896–1948*. København: 1948.

ORev   Lovesey, Peter. "The First Olympic Hurdles," *Olympic Review 121–122* (November–December 1977): 722.

OTAF   *Olympic Track and Field*. Editors of *Track & Field News*. Los Altos, Calif.: Tafnews Press, 1979.

PIX   Kluge, Volker, ed. *1896 Athens: The Pictures of the First Olympiad*. Parallel texts in German, English, French, and Spanish. Brandenburgisches Verlaghaus, 1996.

Pointu   Pointu, Raymond. *42,195 km.: Grandeurs et misères des marathons olympiques*. Paris: Éditions du Seuil, 1979.

Sinn   Sinn, U. "Neue Erkenntnisse zu den letzten olympischen Spielen in der Antike — ein Neufund aus Olympia." *Antike Welt* 26, 2 (1955): 155.

SG   Greenberg, Stan. *The Guinness Book of Olympics Facts & Feats*. Enfield, Middlesex, England: Guinness, 1983. Second edition issued as *Olympic Games: The Records*, same publisher, 1987. Third edition issued as *The Guinness Olympics Fact Book*, same publisher, 1991.

Tara   Tarasouleas, Ath[anassios]. *Olympic Games in Athens 1896–1906*. Athens: author, 1988.

TMF   Martin, David E., and Gynn, Roger W. H. *The Marathon Footrace*. Champaign, Ill.: C.C. Thomas, 1979.

Tsolak   Tsolakidis, Elias. "Die olympischen Spiele von 1896 in Athen: Versuch einer Rekon-
              struktion." Unpublished diplomarbeit, Deutsche Sporthochschule Köln, 1987.
VK   Kluge, Volker. *Die olympischen Spiele von 1896 bis 1980.* Berlin: Sportverlag, 1981.
Young   Young, David C. "Demetrios Vikelas: First President of the IOC." In *Stadion* (1988),
              pp. 85–102.

National Olympic Histories

Buchanan, Ian. *British Olympians: A Hundred Years of Gold Medallists.* London: Guinness, 1991.

Glanell, Tomas, Huldtén, Gösta, et al., editors. *Sverige och OS.* Stockholm: Brunnhages Förlag
      AB, 1987.

Lennartz, Karl. *Geschichte der deutschen Reichsaußchußes für olympische Spiele: Heft 1–Die Beteili-
      gung Deutschlands an den olympischen Spielen 1896 in Athen.* Bonn: Verlag Peter
      Wegener, 1981.

Lennartz, Karl, and Teutenberg, Walter. *Die deutsche Olympia-Mannschaft von 1896.* Frankfurt
      am Main: Kasseler Sportverlag, 1992.

Lester, Gary. *Australians at the Olympics: A Definitive History.* Sydney: Lester-Townsend Pub-
      lishing, 1984.

Mallon, Bill, and Buchanan, Ian. *Quest for Gold: The Encyclopaedia of American Olympians.* New
      York: Leisure, 1984.

Mező, Ferenc. *Golden Book of Hungarian Olympic Champions / Livre d'or des champions olympiques
      hongrois.* Budapest: Sport Lap. És Könyvkiadö, 1955. Parallel texts in English and
      French.

Tarasouleas, At[hanassios]. *Helliniki simmetokhi stis sinkhrones olympiades.* Athens: author, 1990.

1896 Olympic Games — Analysis and Summaries

Dates:	6–15 April 1896 [Julian calendar (Greece): 25 March–3 April 1896]
Site:	Athens, Greece
Official Opening By:	King Georgios I
Countries Competing:	15¹*
Athletes Competing:	*ca.* 245 [245 Men–0 Women]
Sports:	9 [9 Men–0 Women]
Events:	43 [43 Men–0 Women]

Members of the International Olympic Committee in 1896 (Years on IOC in brackets)

Argentina	José Benjamin Zubiaur [1894–1907]
Belgium	Count Maxime de Bousies [1894–1901]
Bohemia	Dr. Jiří Guth-Jarkovský [1894–1943]
France	Ernest Callot [1894–1913]; Treasurer
	Pierre Frédy, Baron Pierre de Coubertin [1894–1925]; Secretary-General
Germany	Karl August Willibald Gebhardt [1896–1909]
Great Britain	Arthur Oliver Russell, Lord Ampthill [1894–1898]
	Charles Herbert [1894–1906]
Greece	Demetrios Vikelas [1894–1897]; President
Hungary	Dr. Ferenc Kémény [1894–1907]
Italy	Duke Riccardo d'Andria Carafa [1894–1898]
New Zealand	Leonard Albert Cuff [1894–1905]
Russia	General Aleksey Butowsky [1894–1900]
Sweden	Major Viktor Gustaf Balck [1894–1921]
United States	Professor William Milligan Sloane [1894–1924]

See Notes on pages 24–25.

1

1896 Organizing Committee

President:	Crown Prince Konstantinos
Secretary-General:	Timoleon J. Filimon
Treasurer:	Paulos Skouzes
Secretaries:	Georgios Melas
	Georgios Streit
	Konstantinos Th. Manos
	Alexandros Mercatis
Members:	Nikolaos Deligiannis
	Leon Delygeorgis
	Alexandros Zaïmis
	Pyrros Karapanos
	Nikolaos K. Metaxas
	Kyriakos Mavromikhalis
	Alexandros Skouzes
	Georgios Typaldos-Kozakis
	Georgios K. Romas
	Alexandros D. Soutsos
	Th. Retsinas

1896 Organizing Sub-Committees

Committee for Nautical Events — President: HRH Prince Georgios. Secretary: Paulos A. Damalas. Members: Dimitrios Kriezis, K. Sakhtouris, Georgios Kountouriotis, Dimitrios Argyropoulos, Konstantinos Kanaris, K. Argyrakis.

Committee for the Rifle Range — President: HRH Prince Nikolaos. Secretary: Ioannis Frangoudis. Members: Dimosthenes Staikhos, Alkibiades Krassas, Ioannis Konstantinidis, Ath. D. Botsaris, Ath. N. Pierrakhos, Georgios Antonopoulos, Stefanos Skouloudis, Alex. Kontostavlos.

Committee for the Preparation of Greek Athletes — President: Andreas Psyllas. Secretary: Spiridon Lambros. Members: Ioannis Khatzidakis, Ioannis Fokianos, Khristos Koryllos, I. Nyder, A. Gerousis, G. Papadiamantopoulos, Konstantinos Papamikhalopoulos, Konstantinos Lomvardos, A. Diomides Kyriakos, A. D. Themistaleas.

Committee for Athletic Events and Gymnastics — President: Ioannis Fokianos. Secretary: Georgios Streit. Members: Ioannis Genisarlis, Loukas Belos, Nikolaos Politis, Charles Waldstein, Dimitrios Aiginitis, Dimitrios Sekkeris, Spiridon Koumoundouros, Konstantinos Manos, Spiridon Antonopoulos.

Committee for Fencing — President: Meleagros Athanasiou. Secretary: St. Rallis. Members: Paulos Skouzes, Khr. Rallis, Epaminondas Ebairikos, Nikolaos Pyrgos, Ekhtor Romanos, Ioannis Delaportas, Konstantinos Komninos-Miliotis, Petros Kanakis, Georgios Kolokhotronis.

Committee for Cycling Events — President: Nikolaos Vlangalis. Secretary: K. Vellinis. Members: Spiridon Mauros, Nikolaos Kontogiannakhis, Mar. Filipp, Iak. A. Theofilas.

Committee for Athletic Games (Lawn Tennis, Cricket, etc.) — President: Ferdinand Serpieris. Secretary: Iakh. Negrepontis. Members: Alexandros Rangavis, Petros Kalligas, Alexandros Merkatis, Leon Melas, Konstantinos Manos, Charles Merlin, Pyrros Karapanos.

Committee for the Preparation and Renovation of the Panathenaeic Stadium — President: An. Theofilas. Secretary: P. Kavvadias. Members: Wilhelm Dörpfeld, C. J. Richardson, Cecil H.

Smith, Ant. Matsas, Fok. Negris, Oth. Lyders, Anastasios Metaxas, L. Pappagos, Th. Limbritis, Alexandros Ambelas.[2]

Reception Committee—President: If. Kokkidis.[3] Secretary: Mikh. Lambros. Members: Mikh. Paparrigopoulos, Markos N. Dragoumis, Periklis Valaoritis, Nikolas Louriotis, Khr. Vournazos, Dimitrios Silyvriotis, Ioannis Doumas, Khr. Khatzipetros. Georgios Valtatzis, Periklhis Ieropoulos, Ang. Metaxas, Georgios M. Averof, Dimitrios M. Kallifronas, Lambros Kalliphronas, Konstantinos Koutsalexis, Nikolaos D. Zakharias, Anastasios Khristomanos, Zaf. Matsas, Trif. Moutsopoulos, Nikolas Khantzopoulos, P. Zafeiriou, L. Feraldis.

The Sorbonne Congress and the Renovation of the Olympic Games

The Modern Olympic Games were revived by a Frenchman, Pierre Frédy, the Baron de Coubertin. Numerous attempts at revival, usually of a local or national nature, had taken place in the 19th century, but Coubertin first publically broached the idea of a revival at a sporting congress held in Paris on 25 November 1892, which celebrated the 5th anniversary of the founding of the Union des Sociétés Françaises de Sports Athlétiques (USFSA). He received little acclaim or support for this idea, but he ended the speech with one of his most famous statements, "Let us export rowers, runners, and fencers; there is the free trade of the future, and on the day when it is introduced within the walls of old Europe the cause of peace will have received a new and mighty stay. This is enough to encourage your servant to dream now about the second part of his program; he hopes that you will help him as you have helped him hitherto, and that with you he will be able to continue and complete, on a basis suited to the conditions of modern life, this grandiose and salutary task, the restoration of the Olympic Games."[4]

Coubertin wrote of the frosty reception he received, "Naturally I had foreseen every eventuality, except what actually happened. Opposition? Objections, irony? Or even indifference? Not at all! Everyone applauded, everyone approved, everyone wished me great success but no one had really understood. It was a period of total, absolute lack of comprehension that was about to start.

"And it was to last a long time."[5]

But he plotted in his mind, not giving up the idea. He noted, "The winter of 1892-1893 went by without the idea causing any stir among the general public. I decided to keep the idea of a Congress, but to use a little deception. Amateurism, an admirable mummy that could be presented as a specimen of the modern art of embalming. Half a century has gone by without it seeming to have suffered in any way from the unceasing manipulations to which it has been submitted. It seemed intact. Not one of us expected it to last so long."[6]

Coubertin travelled to the United States in the fall of 1893, looking to organize support for his Olympic idea. He found a kindred spirit in Professor William Milligan Sloane, a professor of history at Princeton University, but otherwise received little popular support. He also used the trip to study American educational systems and, in particular, sporting organizations. Upon his return to France, he began to organize another sporting congress, this time to be held in 1894. Adolphe de Palissaux had previously suggested a conference on amateurism, and a preliminary program had been approved by the officers of the union on 1 August 1893.[7,8]

Coubertin designed a circular announcing that a congress was to be held from 16 to 24 June 1894. The circular contained a list of officers for the congress and a ten-point program set forth for discussion of the various problems of amateurism. The last points for discussion in the suggested program appeared under the subtitle, "Olympic Games," as follows:

VIII. Possibility of restoring the Olympic Games. Advantages from the athletic, moral, and international standpoints — Under what conditions may they be restored?

IX. Conditions to be imposed on the competitors — Sports represented — Material organization, periodicity, etc.

X. Nomination of an International Committee entrusted with preparing the restoration.[9,10]

Mandell, MacAloon, and Lyberg state that points 8–10 were included on the program prior to the Sorbonne Congress. However, Prof. David Young disagrees,[11] stating that the program which was sent out prior to the Congress contained only point VIII above, and that the last two points were added only after the Congress, and published in the first *Bulletin du Comité International des Jeux Olympiques*.[12] But *Tidning för Idrott* for 26 April 1894 listed the full program and included points IX and X.[13]

In January 1894, Coubertin sent the circular to all the athletic clubs abroad for which he had addresses. The text of the invitation read (translation by MacAloon[14]):

> We have the honor to send you the program of the International Congress which will meet in Paris on June 17 next, under the auspices of the French Union of Athletic Sports Clubs.[15] Its aim is twofold.
>
> Above all, it is necessary to preserve the noble and chivalrous character which distinguished athletics in the past, in order that it may continue effectively to play the same admirable part in the education of the modern world as the Greek masters assigned to it. Human imperfection always tends to transform the Olympic athlete into a circus gladiator. We must choose between two athletic formulae which are not compatible. In order to defend themselves against the spirit of lucre and professionalism that threatens to invade their ranks, amateurs in most countries have drawn up complicated rules full of compromises and contradictions; moreover, too frequently their letter is respected rather than their spirit.
>
> Reform is imperative, and before it is undertaken it must be discussed. The questions which have been placed on the Congress agenda relate to these compromises and contradictions in the amateur regulations. The proposal mentioned in the last paragraph would set a happy seal upon the international agreement which we are as yet seeking not to ratify, but merely to prepare. The revival of the Olympic Games on bases and in conditions suited to the needs of modern life would bring the representatives of the nations of the world face-to-face every four years, and it may be thought that their peaceful and chivalrous contests would constitute the best of internationalisms.
>
> In taking the initiative which may have such far-reaching results the Union is not trying to usurp a position of precedence which belongs to no country and to no club in the republic of muscles. It merely thinks that the clarity of its principles and its attitude, together with the high friendships both in France and abroad upon which it prides itself, justify it in giving the signal for a reform movement the need for which is becoming daily more apparent. It does so in the general interest and without any hidden motive or unworthy ambitions.

Coubertin received solid support from within France but otherwise had a variable response. He received no answers from Switzerland or the Netherlands. His relations with German sporting organizations were strained at best. The German Turner societies were the best organized sporting groups in the world, but their philosophy of physical education was different from the cosmopolitan and elitist attitude espoused by the English, which Coubertin favored.

Coubertin contacted the German military attaché in Paris, Colonel Ernst von Schwartzkoppen. At the latter's recommendation, invitations were sent twice to the president of the Union Sportsclub in Berlin, Viktor van Podbielski. He acknowledged receipt of the invitation, but discarded it.[16] But before the Germans could respond, the leader of the Union des Sociétés Gymnastiques declared that if the Germans were invited, he would support a withdrawal of the French gymnasts. Eventually a German living in London, Baron Christian Eduard von Rieffenstein, attended the congress, but as an "unofficial" observer, which enabled several French officials to participate without loss of face. Germany was not the only nation which caused Coubertin problems in organizing the 1894 congress. The Belgian gymnastic societies denounced Coubertin's plans in circulars which they sent all over Europe.[17]

Somehow, on Saturday, 16 June 1894, at 1615, the congress began in the grand amphitheater of the new Sorbonne with 2,000 in attendance. The meeting is now usually termed "The Sorbonne Congress" by the Olympic family, but the formal term in the invitations and program was "Congrès International de Paris: pour le rétablissement des jeux olympiques."

There were, in all, 78 delegates from 49 societies in 11 countries — Australia, Belgium, Bohemia, France, Great Britain, Greece, Italy, New Zealand, Russia, Spain, Sweden, and the United States.[18] Coubertin later noted that he wished "to please and impress" the delegates and that he wished "not to convince, but to seduce." Accordingly, he was meticulous in creating an atmosphere that would lead the delegates to believe that they themselves were making history.[19]

Baron de Courcel, the French ambassador to Berlin, opened the proceedings with a short, formal speech. Then, after several inspiring speeches came the pièce de résistance, a performance of the "Delphic Hymn to Apollo." MacAloon described it well:

> In 1893, the French School in Athens had discovered tablets inscribed with the ode and what turned out to be musical notation. Theodore Reinach, who was present this evening to provide a commentary, translated the verses, and the celebrated composer Gabriel Fauré wrote a choral accompaniment to the ancient melody. Earlier in the year, the composition had been performed to great acclaim in Athens, Constantinople, Brussels, and Paris. For Coubertin's occasion, Fauré outdid himself. To the rich background of harps and a great choir, Jeanne Remacle of the Opera sang the ode. According to Coubertin, the effect of these magic harmonies echoing through the amphitheater was "immense":
>
> "The two thousand persons present listened in a religious silence to the divine melody risen from the dead to salute the Olympic renaissance across the darkness of the ages.
>
> "The sacred harmony plunged the great audience into the ambiance hoped for. A sort of subtle emotion flowed as the ancient eurythmy sounded across the distance of the ages. Hellenism thus infiltrated the vast enclosure. In these first hours, the Congress had come to a head. Henceforth I knew, consciously or not, that no one would vote against the restoration of the Olympic Games."
>
> The London *Times* concurred. "The plaintive beauty of the chords of the Greek 'Hymn' coming at the close of such constant references to the race that cultivated rhythm and music to the point of excellence beyond the achievement of all others served no doubt as the most constraining of all arguments in favor of the idea on which this Congress is engaged."[20]

Early in the proceedings the congress divided into two committees, in one of which sports administrators discussed amateurism. The other commission, on Olympism, was titularly headed by Demetrios Vikelas (1835–1908), the delegate from Athens. Like Coubertin and Sloane, he was a historian, and also a novelist. Sloane was the vice-chair of the committee on Amateurism.

In actuality, Coubertin had already published an article, "Le Rétablissement des jeux olympiques," in the *Revue de Paris* on 15 June 1894 — that is, during the same time as the congress was held. The specific recommendations that the committee on Olympism eventually agreed upon were these, labelled as points VIII–XIV in the *Bulletin*[21]:

> **VIII.** There is no doubt that there exist advantages to reestablish the Olympic Games, based on athletic, moral, and international considerations, provided that they conform to modern conditions.
>
> **IX.** That, except in the case of fencing, only amateurs would be allowed to compete.
>
> **X.** The International Committee will be responsible for organizing the Games, and will have the right to exclude persons whose previous acts may damage the good name of the institution.
>
> **XI.** No nations had the right to compete using athletes other than its own nationals. In each country, elimination events to choose their Olympic athletes should be held, so that only true champions should take part in each sport.
>
> **XII.** The following sports ought to be represented, if possible: Athletic sports (track & field), Aquatic Sports (rowing, sailing, and swimming), Athletic Games (football, lawn tennis, paume, etc.), Skating, Fencing, Boxing, Wrestling, Equestrian sports, Polo, Shooting, Gymnastics, and Cycling.
>
> There should also be instituted a general athletic championship under the title of pentathlon.
>
> At the occasion of the Olympic Games, an alpinism prize should be awarded to the most interesting climb accomplished since the last edition of the Games.
>
> **XIII.** The modern Olympic Games should take place every four years. After Athens in 1896 and Paris in 1900, they should be organized in a new city every fourth year.
>
> **XIV.** As the Olympic Games can only be successfully organized with the support of governments, the International Committee should make arrangements to see that such assistance is given.[22]

The Vikelas committee was also charged with forming an International Olympic Committee. Coubertin, Sloane, and Vikelas were, of course, to be members. To fill the roster of members of the first IOC, Coubertin provided a list of suitable candidates. The following 13 members formed the first International Olympic Committee: President Demetrios Vikelas (GRE), Secretary-General Pierre de Coubertin (FRA), Treasurer Ernest Callot (FRA), Aleksey de Butowski (RUS), Viktor Balck (SWE), Jiří Guth (BOH), Leonard A. Cuff (NZL), William Sloane (USA), Charles Herbert (GBR), Lord Ampthill (GBR), Ferenc Kemeny (HUN), José Zubiaur (ARG), and Mario Lucchesi Palli (ITA). A presence in Paris or even an interest in the committee was not a necessary prerequisite for eligibility, and only six of these individuals actually were present: Vikelas, Coubertin, Callot, Sloane, Herbet, and Lucchesi Palli.[23] Coubertin informed the others by mail. Some of the members were wealthy men who did not contribute much to the IOC, and later Coubertin called them "une façade."[24]

Near the end of the Congress, the committee members took it upon themselves to select the host city for the first Olympic Games. For some time Coubertin had rather expected and had led everyone to believe that the first Games of the modern era would take place in Paris in 1900 as part of the Universal Exposition. The conference had gone well, but there was concern that waiting the six years that remained until the Universal Exposition in Paris might cause the Olympic Idea to lose momentum.

It was proposed to hold the first Games in 1896. Balck had offered Stockholm as the site of the Games, but not necessarily the first. Many members had proposed London as a possible host city. But perhaps it would be best to consider the original home of the Olympics, Greece. Apparently on 18 or 19 June, Coubertin discussed this possibilty with Vikelas. The two men held a hurried conversation, and Coubertin then arose to make the formal proposal, and the assembly approved it unanimously. Athens would be the site of the first Modern Olympic Games in 1896. The king of Greece had already sent Coubertin a telegram dated 21 June 1894, thanking the members of the congress for "the reestablishment of the Olympic Games."

Pierre de Coubertin seems himself to have been transported into a euphoric state by the atmosphere he created. The final dinner was held in the Jardin d'Acclimatisation on 23 June 1894. Coubertin closed the congress which had re-established the Olympic Games with the following speech:

> We have been brought together in Paris, this grand metropolis, whose joys and anxieties are shared by the whole world to such an extent that one can say that we meet at the nerve center of the world. We are the representatives of international athletics and we voted unanimously (for it appears that the principle is scarcely controversial at all) for the restoration of an idea that is 2,000 years old. But this idea still quickens the hearts of men in whom it stimulates the instincts ... that are the most noble and the most vital. In a great temple of science, our delegates have heard the modern echo of a melody which is also 2,000 years old and was resurrected by a scholarly archaeologist who based his work upon that of preceding generations. And this evening electricity transmitted everywhere the news that the Olympism of ancient Hellas has re-emerged in the world after an eclipse of many centuries....
>
> Some of the adherents of the old school wailed that we held our meeting openly in the heart of the Sorbonne. They knew full well that we are rebels and that we would climax our proceedings by bringing down the structure of their worm-eaten philosophy. That is true, gentlemen! We are rebels and that is why the members of the press, who have always supported beneficial revolutions, have understood us and helped us, for which, by the way, I thank them with all my heart.
>
> I astonish myself and apologize, gentlemen, for having employed rhetoric like this and for having taken you to such lofty heights. If I were to continue, the champagne might evaporate, leaving boredom. Therefore I hasten to propose a toast again. I raise my glass to the Olympic idea which, like a ray of the all-powerful sun, has pierced the mists of the ages to illuminate the threshold of the twentieth century with joy and hope.[25]

After 16 centuries, the Olympic Games were once again a reality.

The Organization of the Games of the 1st Olympiad

On 3 July 1894, Vikelas received a telegram from Lieutenant-Colonel Sapuntzakis, an aide-de-camp of Crown Prince Konstantinos. "The duke of Sparta has noted with great pleasure that the Olympic Games will be inaugurated in Athens. I am certain that the King and the Prince will accord the celebration of these Games their patronage."[26] But Coubertin and Vikelas soon found themselves buried in difficulties. While the Greek nation as a whole enthusiastically embraced the idea of the Games, the Greek political hierarchy was not so moved. Greece was then embroiled in political turmoil and on the verge of bankruptcy, which led the politicians to be more concerned with matters political and financial and less with matters sportive.

At the time Greece was serving as a political battlefield between Charilaos Trikoupis and Theodorus Deligiannis, who for almost 15 years had alternated as prime minister of Greece. In 1894, Trikoupis held the post, and while he did not actively oppose the Olympics, neither did he actively support them.

Vikelas and Coubertin found that an Athenian family named Zappas had left a considerable bequest for the purpose of erecting and administering a large building to be known as the Zappeion, in which athletic demonstrations and contests could be held. As the directors of the Zappas estate were citizens of considerable prominence in Athens, this group was an admirable nucleus around which to build the Organizing Committee, especially since they had control over the Panathenaic Stadium. Vikelas arranged for a meeting of the commission, but before it could convene he was called back to Paris because his wife was dying.[27] With Vikelas back in Paris, Coubertin had to act on his own.

Immersed in his project of reviving the Games, Coubertin thought that the people of Athens would leap at the prospect of being first to revive an event that reflected so much credit on their ancestors. He turned the project over to the directors of the Zappeion and settled back to watch his dream come true. Things began to happen right away, but they were not exactly what Coubertin had anticipated. Imagine his embarrassment when he discovered that the directors of the Zappeion were not major supporters of the Olympic revival.[28]

They were led by Etienne Dragoumis, a political ally of Trikoupis. The Zappeion group seemed favorably inclined toward the Games, but Trikoupis seemingly influenced them otherwise. When Vikelas returned to Paris, the directors of the Zappeion met and in his absence dispatched the following letter to Coubertin:

Athens, Nov. 1, 1894
My dear Baron:
I wish to thank you for the communication you have sent regarding the international Olympic Games.

The choice of Athens for the first celebration of the Games could not fail to produce a feeling of satisfaction and fond recollections in Greece. It is no less true, however, that the choice of our people because of their illustrious past constitutes for these descendants of the ancient founders of the Games a heavy responsibility concerning which I doubt their ability to acquit themselves with the degree of success warranted by this great world celebration voted by the Paris Athletic Congress. Since his recent stay in Athens M. Vikelas has taken note of the hesitation we have felt since the idea of holding the first Games here was known and the official announcement made.

I do not wish to insist on a matter in which our government is particularly interested. How can it think of placing itself at the head of this movement, send out invitations, take the initiative necessary to guarantee success to such a great international festival at a moment when it finds itself facing a great economic crisis at home and facing foreign complications of the most grave nature? The duty that is incumbent upon the government to watch over the dignity of its country and the solicitude it feels toward the great cause we are all so anxious to see revived will probably call for an attitude of extreme reserve.

One could be accused of false pride if he did not admit that in a new country where there still remains much to be accomplished before it attains suitable conditions for the actual existence of a civilized people, the exact thing that you call "athletic sports" does not exist. It is exactly to such a country that, because of its past history, you wish to award the responsibility of presiding over the first celebration of these Games which are founded upon a new and extremely complicated basis and set of regulations.

The great international fair announced as planned for 1900 in France undoubtedly offers much greater possibilities, should you consider holding the first Olympic Games at that time and place. At Paris, with her tremendous resources, the nearness of centers of population and of world tradition, aided by the strongly organized sports societies, the Games would be certain of success. Would it not be prudent to set back the opening date of these peaceful modern struggles? The new Olympics would undoubtedly have the éclat gained by a more significant date of launching, the opening of a new century.

I have given you, my dear Baron, a summary of the opinions expressed at the meeting of our committee. We trust you will understand how great is our regret at being forced to decline an honor so graciously offered our country and at the same time to deprive ourselves of the opportunity to be associated with the high type of men who will preside over the revival of such a beautiful and historic institution as the Olympic Games. Knowing the feebleness of the means at the actual disposal of the Greek people and convinced that the task exceeds our strength, we are left without choice in the matter.

With assurance of highest consideration and my best personal regards, I remain, Sincerely yours,
Etienne Dragoumis[29]

Having been warned by Vikelas that such a response might be forthcoming, Coubertin made appropriate plans. He ensured that the Olympic Games would be held somewhere in 1896 by communicating with Ferenc Kemeny, the Hungarian IOC member, and making contingency plans to switch the Games at a later date, if necessary, to Budapest. Such an event in 1896 would celebrate the 1,000th anniversary of Hungary's existence as a state. But Coubertin also made plans to make a personal visit to Athens to head off, if possible, Dragoumis' attempts to reject the 1896 Olympics.[30]

As the Dragoumis letter made its way to Paris, Coubertin found two messages waiting for him once he arrived in Athens. One was from Dragoumis, and that letter informed Coubertin that Greece was declining the honor of holding the Games. The other was from Ferenc Kemeny, and it gave his assurances that, if necessary, the Hungarians could host the Games.[31]

Coubertin responded promptly to Dragoumis and noted that he was "doubting the correctness of the resolution passed by his colleagues and expressing the sentiment that only a misunderstanding of the intentions of the International Olympic Committee" was responsible. Coubertin closed by asking that the Zappeion directors meet once more and reconsider their decision.[32] Coubertin did not receive his requested meeting, but instead Prime Minister Trikoupis paid him a personal visit. Trikoupis was friendly but essentially informed Coubertin that "you will be convinced that it is impossible."[33]

But Coubertin quickly decided that despite the financial and political situations, the citizens of Athens were wildly enthusiastic about the return of the Olympic Games. Not only did a few trips about the city assure him that the necessary sporting facilities were available to stage the Games, but everywhere he went he heard the wish expressed that the Olympics should be held. The strongest adherents of the Olympic Idea were the common people, the small shopkeepers, the taxi drivers, the everyday Athenians. According to Coubertin, while he was riding with Georgios Melas, son of the mayor of Athens and the Baron's new ally, the coachman suddenly climbed down and addressed Coubertin, "Mr. Georgie, I'm going to explain to you how your friend must deal with Trikoupis."[34]

But Coubertin was not content with the support of the common folk. He wanted it to be unanimous. He took the opportunity to address a meeting of the Parnassus Literary Society to strongly advocate the Games. His speech was well received; he ended it by noting, "We French have a proverb that says that the word 'impossible' is not in the French language. I have been told this morning that the word is Greek. I do not believe it."[35]

Convinced that he had the support of the public and the neutrality, at least, of Trikoupis, and feeling that, under such conditions, the directors of the Zappeion would be at his command, Coubertin boldly addressed a letter to the press announcing that the Games would be held in Athens and that an organizing committee would promptly be formed to take over their management.

Coubertin's courageous enthusiasm and his absolute refusal to let anything stand in the way of the success of his project swept everything before it. When he found that the directors of the Zappeion were still afraid to call a meeting for the organization of the Games, Coubertin called the meeting himself, and thanks to the support of Crown Prince Konstantinos, who accepted the presidency of the Organizing Committee, it proved successful. A tentative program including not only track and field athletics but also gymnastics, cycling, yachting, and fencing, was drawn up; and Coubertin left for France certain that his troubles were over.

But soon after he left Greece, the Organizing Committee began to fall apart. One of the four vice-presidents, Commandant Etienne Skouloudis, a close friend of Minister Trikoupis, called a meeting of the leaders of the Committee, to which the younger and more enthusiastic supporters of the Olympics were not invited. He convinced the group that Coubertin had underestimated expenses, intimated that the government would not support the lottery which had been proposed to raise money for the Games, and finally decided to submit the whole sad situation to the Crown Prince for his decision. At the same time, Trikoupis brought the question before the government, and it appeared that, after all, Coubertin's visit to Athens had borne little fruit.[36] Vikelas returned from Paris after his wife's funeral.

The credit for saving the 1896 Olympic Games for Athens belongs mostly to Vikelas and Greek Crown Prince Konstantinos. When the Committee, headed by Skouloudis, gave him their unfavorable report, the Prince met the members with a smile, accepted the report, thanked them, dismissed them, but noted that he would read the report at his leisure. His courageous action, or lack thereof, allowed the public and the press to make their sentiments known.

Based on Vikelas' advice and backed by strong popular approval, the Crown Prince reorganized and enlarged the committee, moving its headquarters into the Royal Palace. He also installed Timoleon Filimon, a former mayor of Athens, as its general secretary, and by his personal example united the Greek people in an enthusiastic movement to ensure the success of the Games.[37]

The enthusiastic Greeks poured thousands of contributions into a fund to finance the Olympic Games, eventually raising 330,000 drachmas. The Crown Prince appealed by letter to Georgios Averof, a wealthy Greek citizen who lived in Alexandria, asking him to pay for the restoration of the ancient Panathenaic Stadium, the cost of which was estimated at 580,000 drachmas. The letter was delivered to Averof personally by Secretary-General Timoleon Filimon. Averof agreed to pay for the restoration, which eventually cost 920,000 drachmas, stipulating that his money should be used to refinish the ancient Panathenaic Stadium at Athens in native marble. A set of postage stamps with Olympic themes was also produced and enthusiastically purchased by the Greek people, producing 400,000 drachmas for the Organizing Committee. Sales of tickets and commemorative medals raised 200,000 drachmas.

With the financial success of the Games now assured and enthusiasm in Greece running high, there was still no time for Coubertin to rest. The success of the Olympic Games depended on more than popular enthusiasm and adequate finances, as other factors would eventually contribute to their ultimate success.

There was first the many details of the organization. Most modern Greeks were not familiar with the ancient Olympic Games, and were much less familiar with the sports of the modern world, which would be essential to the success of any modern Olympic Games. Second, there was the question of foreign participation. The Greeks had few athletes, and without foreign athletes the Games would fail miserably. Since to this time the Games had existed only in the mind of Pierre de Coubertin, it was expected that he would have to deliver the athletes and solve the multitudinous problems.

Coubertin was overwhelmed by the thousands of details, such as the invitations, the design of the medals, the rules to be used, the prizes to be distributed, and many others. In addition to these questions there were also the problems of national jealousy, and the various sporting bodies also began to stake out their claims of dominance.[38]

Coubertin himself drew up the official invitations to the Games. The organizing committee was unable to settle on a design and on how to build a bicycle track, so Coubertin obtained the plans of the velodrome of Arcachon and sent them to Athens. But the committee instead copied the plans of the bicycle track at Copenhagen, which they had obtained from another source. No sooner had Coubertin had the invitations printed than the organizing committee wished to know exactly how many participants to expect despite the fact that the Games were still almost 1½ years off. There were only a few nations that even knew of them at that point.[39]

But Athens continued to prepare. The well-known Greek architect Anastasios Metaxas led the reconstruction of the Panathenaic Stadium. To preserve the antiquity but at the same time incorporate newer building methods, Metaxas consulted with archeologists from Germany and France. Reports differ, but the seating capacity was between 50,000 and 70,000. The cinder track was constructed with the help of Charles Perry, a groundskeeper from London. This constant work in the heart of the city stirred the interest of the Athenians about the forthcoming Olympic Games.

Meanwhile, the members of Coubertin's International Olympic Committee were spreading the word to their own nations and trying their best to interest their leading athletes in competing in the first Olympics. Sweden and Hungary, led by committee members Balck and Kemeny, probably displayed the most enthusiasm for the idea. In the United States, Professor Sloane organized a team of four college students from Princeton and six Boston athletes to represent the United States in track & field athletics. A French team was organized under the leadership of Raoul Fabens, but the French shooters refused to participate. The riflemen expressed surprise that "the Olympic Games should imagine that the French Shooting Federation would consent to become an 'annex of their Committee.'"[40]

In Great Britain the Games were still eyed rather coldly, the newspapers printing Coubertin's appeal for participation without enthusiasm and several of them suggesting that "Pan-Britannic" games be organized instead.[41] The London magazine *The Spectator* noted, "It is impossible to get honestly interested in the revival of the Olympic Games. We can see nothing classical about the celebration nor can we recognize in the presence of a number of Greek princes, American sightseers, or British sporting men anything particularly Greek."[42]

There was a strong German interest in the Olympics, and this was augmented by the nexus between the royal families of Germany and Greece. For some time it looked as though the Germans would organize a strong team to participate in Athens, but near the end of 1895, an official announcement was made that Germany would not participate. This affront was based upon a supposed interview in which Baron de Coubertin had been quoted as expressing pleasure that the Germans had not been at the Sorbonne Congress and that they would not be at Athens.[43]

Coubertin denied the statement, and was supported by Baron van Reiffenstein, Germany's unofficial Congress participant. A strong feeling against Coubertin and the Games swept across Germany, and because of the close relationship between Germany and Greece, it found a foothold among the Greeks. Henry described it well: "The German Olympic Committee under Dr. Willibald Gebhardt absolved Coubertin of any blame in the matter, and Germany finally did compete; but a few politicians and editors in Athens, now assured of the success of the Games and more and more convinced that the Games were theirs by right of inheritance, seized upon this pretext to ignore Coubertin despite the efforts of the Crown Prince to pay him the credit due him for his effort in reviving the historic contests."[44]

And so it came to pass that as the days for the first celebration of the Modern Olympic Games approached during the warm spring of 1896, Baron Pierre de Coubertin, by whose sole effort the Olympic Games had been revived, and upon whose shoulders the entire initiative of the organization of the first Games had fallen, found himself ignored by the very people to whom he had restored their inheritance. Further insult would come at the end of the first Olympic Games themselves.[45]

The Greek politicians could ignore him, but they could not kill either his enthusiasm for the Games or his interest in their success. He went to Athens early in the spring and kept in constant communication with the other members of the International Olympic Committee, and remained ready to help at all times. No better testimony to his enthusiasm can be found than a letter written by Coubertin from Athens on the eve of the Games:

Athens.
March 26, 1896

The Athenian spring is double this year. It warms not only the clear atmosphere but the soul of the populace. It pushes up sweet-smelling flowers between the stones of the Parthenon, and paints a happy smile on the fiery lips of the Palikares. The sun shines, and the Olympic Games are here. The fears and ironies of the year just past have disappeared. The skeptics have been eliminated; the Olympic Games have not a single enemy.

They have spread to the breezes the flags of France, Russia, America, Germany, Sweden, England ... The soft breezes of Attica joyously lift their folds, and the citizens in the street of Hermes rejoice at the spectacle. They know that the world is coming here, and they approve the preparations that have been made to receive her. Preparations are comprehensive. Everywhere people are shining up the marble, applying new plaster and fresh paint; they are paving, cleaning, decorating.

The road to the stadium is in full dress with its Arc de Triomphe and its Venetian matting. But this is not the favorite promenade. Interest is elsewhere, on the shores of the Ilissus, until now disdained. Every evening about five o'clock the citizens come here to cast an appraising eye upon the work being done at the stadium. As usual, the Ilissus is without water, but this passes unnoticed. A monumental bridge spans the celebrated stream and gives access to the great plain upon which they are restoring the ancient stadium.

The surroundings of the stadium produce an impression heightened by reflection. Here we have a tableau that the ancestral Greeks so often witnessed. It has sprung up before our eyes. We are not accustomed in these days to such constructions, and its lines are so unfamiliar as to surprise and disconcert us.

The silhouette of the Grecian temple has never been lost, its porticos and colonnades have known 20 renaissances. But the stadia disappeared with the athletes. People knew their architectural peculiarities but never restored them. A living stadium has not been seen for centuries. A few days now and this stadium will be alive with the animation given such structures by the crowds that fill them. We will see them again climbing the stairs, spreading out across the aisles, swarming in the passage-ways — a different crowd, doubtless, from that which last filled such a stadium, but animated nevertheless by similar sentiment, by the same interest in youth, by the same dreams of national greatness.

There is room for about 50,000 spectators. Portions of the seats are in wood, time having been lacking to cut and place all the marble. After the Games this work will be completed, thanks to the generous gift of M. Averof; bronze work, trophies, and columns will break up the severe monotony of its lines. The track is no longer dusty as of yore; a cinder track has replaced it, built by an expert brought from England for the purpose. Everyone believes the events will be strenuously disputed by the Greeks. For — here is an interesting fact — in this country where physical exercises have produced few experts, where fencing and gymnastic clubs recently organized have experienced considerable difficulty in recruiting members, it has been necessary only to mention the Olympic Games to create athletes. The young men have overnight become conscious of the native strength and suppleness of their race; their ardor has been so great and their training so serious that the visiting athletes will find in them improvised rivals of veteran caliber.

Already the Hungarians have arrived and they have been given an enthusiastic reception; speeches have been exchanged and music has been played. Today the Germans have come, and the Swedes and the Americans. The news that the Municipal Council of Paris has voted a fund for the French representatives came at the moment when the Organizing Committee was holding a meeting at the Prince's palace, and the Prince is delighted to know that the participation of France is finally assured.

Baron Pierre de Coubertin[46]

The 1896 Olympic Games

The festivities began on 5 April 1896 (24 March 1896*) with the unveiling of the marble statue of the primary benefactor, Georgios Averof, which had been erected in front of the Panhellenic Stadium. This was on an Easter Sunday, and the day was chosen by Coubertin for its significance. MacAloon has noted that Coubertin foresaw that in 1896 the Christian and Eastern Orthodox Easters would coincide, and thinking of the symbolism of the Resurrection, he scheduled the resurrected Olympic Games to open on Easter Monday. In addition, the first day of the Games, Monday, 6 April 1896, was the anniversary (25 March*) of Greek independence.[47]

That day saw the official opening of the Games of the First Olympiad of the Modern Era. After the arrival of King Georgios and Queen Olga of Greece, Crown Prince Konstantinos gave an inspired speech. King Georgios I then opened the Olympics with the following words, "I declare the opening of the first international Olympic Games in Athens. Long live the Nation. Long live the Greek people."

Next came the playing of the Olympic Hymn by nine bands and a chorus of 150. The music had been composed by Spyros Samaras, and the words came from a poem by the Greek national poet and novelist Kostis Palamas. This remains the official Olympic Hymn, although it was not

This was the date according to the Julian calendar, then in use in Greece and a few other parts of the world.

officially declared so until the 1958 IOC Session. The crowd demanded an encore because of the impression the hymn made.

The Games and the sporting events then began at 1530. The Games themselves were far from the caliber of sport one would expect today. Only 15 countries participated and many of the top athletes in the world did not compete, as the Games were not well advertised. As described above, Coubertin had difficulty getting interest in the Olympics among many of the nations of the world. Certainly, qualifying Olympic trials were conducted only in Greece, contrary to the wishes of the commission on the Olympics at the Sorbonne Congress.

There were many differences between the 1896 Olympic Games and the Olympics as they are known a century later. First, it should be noted that there was no such thing as a gold medal. The winners of the events received a diploma, a silver medal, and a crown of olive branches. The runners-up in each event received a diploma, a bronze medal and a crown of laurel. The medals had been designed by the French sculptor Jules Chaplain. Each athlete who competed also received a commemorative medal, which had been designed by the Greek artist Nikephoros Lytras. The diplomas had been designed by the famous Greek painter Nikolaos Gyzis. Separate medal ceremonies were not held. Instead, all of the prizes were given out by King Georgios at a special ceremony just prior to the closing ceremony on the last day of the Games.

Even the calendar was different in 1896. In today's terms, the Olympic Games lasted from 6 to 15 April. But at the time, Greece recognized the Julian Calendar, not the Gregorian Calendar used by much of the world then and now used universally. In Greek terms, the Games were held from 25 March to 3 April 1896, a 12-day difference.

There was also a major absence from the Olympics for the only time in the modern era — there were no women competitors. Coubertin did not approve of the idea of female sports and resisted female competition throughout his life. In 1896, women's sports had little organization and there was no impetus to include events for women on the program. They were officially excluded. Only in the marathon could there be said to have been a female presence. Two women unofficially ran the marathon course at around the time of the official race, but neither Melpomene nor Stamata Revithi competed officially.

The first event of the modern Olympics was the first heat of the 100 meters, won by Francis Lane, a student at Princeton. But the first championship decided was that of the triple jump, won by James Connolly, a Harvard student. He became the first known Olympic champion since Zopyros of Athens in boys' boxing and pankration at the 291st Olympic Games in A.D. 385.[48]

The 100 meter final was won by America's Thomas Burke, the only American competing who had been a national champion. He eventually won both the 100 and 400 meters in Athens. The Americans provided two other double champions in track & field athletics, as Robert Garrett won both the shot put and the discus throw, while Ellery Clark won the high jump and the long jump.

The top cyclist at the 1896 Olympics was the Frenchman Paul Masson. Masson was little known prior to the Olympics but in Athens he won three championships, triumphing in the one lap time trial, the 2,000 meter sprint, and the 10,000 meters on the track.

The top medal winner (in modern terms) of the 1896 Olympics was the German gymnast Hermann Weingärtner. The 32-year-old Weingärtner won three titles (horizontal bar and team championships on both the horizontal bar and parallel bars), was twice a runner-up (rings and pommelled horse) and also took one third place on the parallel bars. In modern terms, this was six medals won.

The athlete who won the most events in 1896 was also a German, Carl Schuhmann. The multifaceted Schuhmann won three events in gymnastics (horse vault and both team competitions on the horizontal bar and parallel bars) and also triumphed in Greco-Roman wrestling in a major upset. Schuhmann also competed in track & field athletics (in three events — long jump, triple jump, and shot put) and in weightlifting, where he finished tied for fourth in the barbell lifting.

In addition to Weingärtner, Schuhmann, and Masson, one other athlete won at least three events at the 1896 Olympics: another German, Alfred Flatow. Flatow was a gymnast who won the parallel bars and helped Germany win both gymnastics team events on the horizontal bar and parallel bars. His cousin, Gustav "Felix" Flatow, also competed in Athens in gymnastics for Germany, winning two titles in the team events. Both Flatows, of Jewish faith, would later lose their lives in Nazi concentration camps during World War II.

Only one Italian competed, although several entered and one other actually showed up in Athens hoping to compete. Carlo Airoldi was a distance runner who hoped to compete in the marathon race. Airoldi arrived in Athens by walking part of the way from Milan.[49] He was feted in Athens for this accomplishment and received by Prince Konstantinos at the Royal Palace. There, Airoldi admitted that he had received prize money for running and he was disqualified as a professional. An appeal by his club (the Società Pro-Italia in Milan) failed, and he was not allowed to compete after his titanic trek.

The Americans dominated the athletics events, winning all but the 800 meters, 1,500 meters, and marathon. The 800 meters and 1,500 meters were won by Edwin Flack, an Australian accountant for Price, Waterhouse who then lived and worked in England, representing the Amateur Athletic Association. He also attempted to run the marathon but did not finish.

The Olympic marathon race was suggested by Michael Bréal of France, a friend of Coubertin's who accompanied him to Athens in planning the 1896 Olympics. Bréal wrote Coubertin thusly, "If the Organizing Committee of the Athens Olympics would be willing to revive the famous run of the Marathon soldier as part of the program of the Games, I would be glad to offer a prize for this new Marathon race." The idea was immediately accepted.[50]

The marathon was based on the legend of Eucles or Pheidippides (alternately, Philippides), a Greek soldier who purportedly ran from the town of Marathon to Athens in 490 B.C. to announce the news of the Greek victory in the Battle of Marathon. Upon arriving in Athens, he supposedly proclaimed "Rejoice, we conquer!" and then fell dead. The legend is now felt to be apocryphal, but it was the reason for the creation of the race from Marathon to Athens, a distance of about 25 miles.[51]

In the marathon, there were several early leaders, notably Flack. But midway through the race, Spiridon Louis, a Greek water-carrier, took the lead and maintained it to the end. When he neared the stadium, messengers came into the ancient vestibule and cried out, "Hellas! Hellas!" (A Greek! A Greek!), sending the crowd into a frenzy. The Olympic pride based on millennia of tradition was then realized by the home crowd, which heretofore had been rather disappointed by the results of the Greek athletes. Louis won the race and became a hero, offered gifts and riches by many different Greek merchants. But he asked only for a cart to help him carry his water, and he returned to his small town of Amarousi.

The 1896 Olympic Games ended with two major festivities. On Sunday morning, 12 April (31 March), in the ballroom of the royal palace, the King gave a banquet for the athletes and many of the other dignitaries in attendance. He thanked all responsible for making a success of the First Modern Olympic Games, notably omitting the names of both Pierre de Coubertin and Demetrios Vikelas. At the end of his speech, he expressed his desire for all Olympic Games to remain in Greece: "Greece, the mother and the nursery of athletic contests in the Panhellenic antiquity, undertaking and carrying out these to-day with courage under the eyes of Europe and of the New World, can now, that the general success has been acknowledged, hope that the foreigners who honoured it will appoint our land as a peaceful meeting place of the nations, as a continuous and permanent field of the Olympic Games. With this wish, Gentlemen, I drink especially to all those who contributed to the success of this First Olympiad."[52]

The final ceremonies in 1896 were scheduled for Tuesday, 14 April (2 April), but it rained and washed out the festivities. The first closing ceremonies officially began at 1030 on Wednesday, 15 April 1896, when the royal family entered the Panathenaic Stadium. The Greek national anthem began the ceremony, followed by a "Pindaric" ode in ancient Greek which was recited by the British athlete and Oxford scholar George Stuart Robertson, who had composed it especially for this occasion.[53]

After Robertson's speech, the King proceded to award the prizes to the winning athletes in all events. Certain special awards were given for some of the events. The winners received their awards first, with Spiridon Louis being the last of the champions to receive his prizes. In addition to his silver medal, his diploma, and his crown of olive branches, Louis was given two special cups, one donated by Michel Bréal. The second-place finishers were then recognized.[54]

After the awards the prize-winning athletes marched around the stadium to the plaudits of the crowd. They were led by Spiridon Louis. The Olympic Hymn was then played for a final time, after which King Georgios closed the festivities with the statement, "I declare the First International Olympic Games terminated."[55]

The competitors in 1896 were unanimous in their approval of the first Olympic Games, and in particular, the American athletes agreed with King Georgios that Athens should be the permanent site.[56] The team wrote a letter to Crown Prince Konstantinos on 14 April 1896, which was published in *The New York Times* on 3 May, suggesting that all future Olympic Games be held in Athens. It read as follows:

Athens, April 14, 1896.
To His Royal Highness, Konstantinos, Crown Prince of Greece:

We, the American participants in the International Olympic Games at Athens, wish to express to you, and through you to the committee and the people of Greece, our heartfelt appreciation of the great kindness and warm hospitality of which we have been continually the recipients during our stay here.

We also desire to acknowledge our entire satisfaction with all the arrangements for the conduct of the Games. The existence of the Stadium as a structure so uniquely adapted to its purpose; the proved ability of Greece to competently administer the Games, and, above all, the fact that Greece is the original home of the Olympic Games; all these considerations force upon us the conviction that these Games should never be removed from their native soil.

John Graham
W. Welles Hoyt
Ellery H. Clark
James B. Connolly
Gardner B. Williams
Thomas P. Curtis
Thomas E. Burke
Arthur Blake
Robert Garrett, Jr.
Albert C. Tyler
Francis A. Lane
H. B. Jamison

We, the undersigned, citizens of the United States, who have been present at the Games, heartily concur in the foregoing.

> Eben Alexander
> Charles S. Fairchild
> Gifford Dyer
> Benj. Ide Wheeler
> George Dana Lloyd
> T. W. Heeremance
> Eugene P. Andrews
> Joseph Clark Hoppin
> Corwin Knapp Linson[57]

But it was not to be. The next Olympics would go to Paris as scheduled. They would be held alongside the Paris Exposition of 1900, and would play second fiddle to that World's Fair. An Interim Olympics was conducted in Athens in 1906, which is now no longer considered an Olympic Games by the IOC. As of 1996, no Olympic Games in the regular cycle had returned to Greece.

SUMMARY STATISTICS

1896 Olympic Games — Places Won by Countries

	1st	*2nd*	*3rd*	*Places*
Greece	10	16	19	45
United States	11	7	2	20
Germany	6	5	2	13
France	5	4	2	11
Great Britain and Ireland	2	3	2	7
Hungary	2	1	3	6
Denmark	1	2	3	6
Austria	2	1	2	5
Switzerland	1	2	–	3
Australia	2	–	–	2
Great Britain and Ireland/Germany	1	–	–	1
Egypt	–	1	–	1
Greece/Egypt	–	1	–	1
Great Britain and Ireland/Australia	–	–	1	1
Totals (43 events)†	43	43	36	122

†Two thirds in 100 meters (athletics — men); no third in 110 meter high hurdles (athletics — men); two seconds/no third in high jump (athletics — men); two thirds in pole vault (athletics — men); no third in 100 kilometer race cycling; no third in 12-hour race cycling; two thirds in foil fencing (men); no third in foil masters fencing (men); no second/third in horizontal bar, team (gymnastics — men); no third in parallel bars (gymnastics — men); no third in pommelled horse (gymnastics — men); no third in horizontal bar (gymnastics — men); no third in 100 meter freestyle (swimming — men); no third in 1,200 meter freestyle (swimming — men); and two thirds in tennis men's singles.

In 1896 men's doubles tennis, Germany and Great Britain and Ireland shared first place, Greece and Egypt shared second place, and Australia and Great Britain and Ireland shared third place.

Most Places Won (2 or more) [33]

	1st	2nd	3rd	Places
Herman Weingärtner (GER-GYM)	3	2	1	6 [1–1 with 6]
Carl Schuhmann (GER-GYM/WRE)	4	-	-	4
Alfred Flatow (GER-GYM)	3	1	-	4
Robert Garrett (USA-ATH)	2	1	1	4 [4–3 with 4]
Paul Masson (FRA-CYC)	3	-	-	3
Edwin H. Flack (AUS-ATH/TEN)	2	-	1	3
Louis Zutter (SUI-GYM)	1	2	-	3
Leon Flameng (FRA-CYC)	1	1	1	3
Ioannis Frangoudis (GRE-SHO)	1	1	1	3
A. Viggo Jensen (DEN-SHO/WLT)	1	1	1	3 [10]
Adolf Schmal (AUT-CYC)	1	-	2	3
Holger L. Nielsen (DEN-SHO/WLT)	-	1	2	3 [12–8 with 3]
Conrad Böcker (GER-GYM)	2	-	-	2
John M. P. Boland (GBR-TEN)	2	-	-	2
Thomas E. Burke (USA-ATH)	2	-	-	2
Ellery H. Clark (USA-ATH)	2	-	-	2
Gustav "Felix" Flatow (GER-GYM)	2	-	-	2
Alfred Hajos (HUN-SWI)	2	-	-	2
Georg Hilmar (GER-GYM)	2	-	-	2
Fritz Manteuffel (GER-GYM)	2	-	-	2 [20]
Karl Neukirch (GER-GYM)	2	-	-	2
Richard Röstel (GER-GYM)	2	-	-	2
Gustav Schuft (GER-GYM)	2	-	-	2
Launceston Elliot (GBR-WLT)	1	1	-	2
Georgios Orphanidis (GRE-SHO)	1	1	-	2
Sumner Paine (USA-SHO)	1	1	-	2
Ioannis Mitropoulos (GRE-GYM)	1	-	1	2
Dionysios Kasdaglis (GRE-TEN)	-	2	-	2
Stamatios Nikolopoulos (GRE-CYC)	-	2	-	2
James B. Connolly (USA-ATH)	-	1	1	2 [30]
Fritz Hofmann (GER-ATH/GYM)	-	1	1	2
Thomas Xenakis (GRE-GYM)	-	1	1	2
Sotirios Versis (GRE-ATH/WLT)	-	-	2	2 [33–21 with 2]

Most Championships Won (2 or more) [18]

	1st	2nd	3rd	Places
Carl Schuhmann (GER-GYM/WRE)	4	-	-	4 [1–1 with 4]
Hermann Weingärtner (GER-GYM)	3	2	1	6
Alfred Flatow (GER-GYM)	3	1	-	4

Paul Masson (FRA-CYC)	3	-	-	3 [4–3 with 3]
Robert Garrett (USA-ATH)	2	2	-	4
Edwin H. Flack (AUS-ATH/GYM)	2	-	1	3
Conrad Böcker (GER-GYM)	2	-	-	2
John M. P. Boland (GBR-TEN)	2	-	-	2
Thomas E. Burke (USA-ATH)	2	-	-	2
Ellery H. Clark (USA-ATH)	2	-	-	2 [10]
Edwin Flack (AUS-ATH)	2	-	-	2
Gustav "Felix" Flatow (GER-GYM)	2	-	-	2
Alfred Hajos (HUN-SWI)	2	-	-	2
Georg Hilmar (GER-GYM)	2	-	-	2
Fritz Manteuffel (GER-GYM)	2	-	-	2
Karl Neukirch (GER-GYM)	2	-	-	2
Richard Röstel (GER-GYM)	2	-	-	2
Gustav Schuft (GER-GYM)	2	-	-	2 [18–14 with 2]

Youngest Competitors, Men (10 athletes/15 performances)

Yrs-days

10-218* Dimitrios Loundras (GRE/GYM, Parallel bars [team]NB-3)
16-101 Ioannis Malokinis (GRE/SWI, 100 meters for sailors-1)
17-101 Alexandros Theofilakis (GRE/SHO, Free rifle [300 meters]-ac)
18-070 Alfréd Hajós (HUN/SWI, 100 meter freestyle-1)
18-070   Hajós (HUN/SWI, 1,200 meter freestyle-1)
18-097 Athanasios Skaltsogiannis (GRE/ATH, 110 meter hurdles-ac)
18-097   Skaltsogiannis (GRE/ATH, Long jump-ac)
18-100 Nikolaos Andriakopoulos (GRE/GYM, Rope climbing-1)
18-101 Dimitrios Petrokokkinos (GRE/TEN, Doubles-2)
18-101   Petrokokkinos (GRE/TEN, Singles-=8)
18-358 Gardner Williams (USA/SWI, 100 meter freestyle-ac)
18-358   Williams (USA/SWI, 1,200 meter freestyle-ac)
19-095 Ioannis Persakis (GRE/ATH, Triple jump-3)
19-097 Dimitrios Golemis (GRE/ATH, 1,500 meters-ac)
19-099   Golemis (GRE/ATH, 800 meters-3)

Youngest Top Three, Men (10 athletes/13 performances)

Yrs-days

10-218 Dimitrios Loundras (GRE/GYM, Parallel bars [team]-3)
16-101 Ioannis Malokinis (GRE/SWI, 100 meters for sailors-1)
18-070 Alfréd Hajós (HUN/SWI, 100 meter freestyle-1)
18-070   Hajós (HUN/SWI, 1,200 meter freestyle-1)
18-100 Nikolaos Andriakopoulos (GRE/GYM, Rope climbing-1)
18-101 Dimitrios Petrokokkinos (GRE/TEN, Doubles-2)
19-095 Ioannis Persakis (GRE/ATH, Triple jump-3)

For cases in which exact birth dates are unknown, estimated ages are given in italics; years (and days) are counted using 1 January for "youngest" entries and 31 December for "oldest."

19-097   Miltiadis Gouskos (GRE/ATH, Shot put-2)
19-097   Léon Flameng (FRA/CYC, 100 km.-1)
19-098   Pantelis Karasevdas (GRE/SHO, Military rifle [200 meters]-1)
19-099   Dimitrios Golemis (GRE/ATH, 800 meter-3)
19-100   Flameng (FRA/CYC, 10 km.-2)
19-100   Flameng (FRA/CYC, 2,000 meters-3)

Youngest Champions, Men (10 athletes/12 performances)

16-101   Ioannis Malokinis (GRE/SWI, 100 meters for sailors-1)
18-070   Alfréd Hajós (HUN/SWI, 100 meter freestyle-1)
18-070   Hajós (HUN/SWI, 1,200 meter freestyle-1)
18-100   Nikolaos Andriakopoulos (GRE/GYM, Rope climbing-1)
19-097   Léon Flameng (FRA/CYC, 100 km.-1)
19-097   Miltiadis Gouskos (GRE/ATH, Shot put-2)
19-098   Pantelis Karasevdas (GRE/SHO, Military rifle [200 meters]-1)
19-297   Gustav Schuft (GER/GYM, Horizontal bar [teams]-1)
19-297   Schuft (GER/GYM, Parallel bars [teams]-1)
19-349   Ioannis Georgiadis (GRE/FEN, Sabre-1)
20-013   Friedrich Adolph "Fritz" Traun (GER/TEN, Doubles-1)
20-061   Eugene-Henri Gravelotte (FRA/FEN, Foil-1)

Oldest Competitors, Men (10 athletes/38 performances)

40-010   Charles Waldstein (USA/SHO, Military rifle [200 meters]-ac)
39-352   Sidney Merlin (GBR/SHO, Free rifle [300 meters]-ac)
39-351   Merlin (GBR/SHO, Pistol [25 meters]-dnf)
39-350   Merlin (GBR/SHO, Military pistol [25 meters]-dnf)
39-349   Merlin (GBR/SHO, Military rifle [200 meters]-10)
36-103   August Goedrich (GER/CYC, Road race-2)
36-102   Georgios Orfanidis (GRE/SHO, Free rifle [300 meters]-1)
36-101   Orfanidis (GRE/SHO, Pistol [25 meters]-2)
36-101   Orfanidis (GRE/SHO, Free pistol [30 meters]-5)
36-100   Orfanidis (GRE/SHO, Military pistol [25 meters]-ac)
36-099   Orfanidis (GRE/SHO, Military rifle [200 meters]-5)
34-053   Eugen Schmidt (DEN/ATH, 100 meters-ac)
34-052   Schmidt (DEN/SHO, Military rifle [200 meters]-=12)
34-102   Anastasios Metaxas (GRE/SHO, Free rifle [300 meters]-4)
34-099   Metaxas (GRE/SHO, Military rifle [200 meters]-4)
31-226   Hermann Weingärtner (GER/GYM, Parallel bars-ac)
31-225   Weingärtner (GER/GYM, Horizontal bar-1)
31-225   Weingärtner (GER/GYM, Horizontal bar [teams]-1)
31-225   Weingärtner (GER/GYM, Parallel bars [teams]-1)
31-225   Weingärtner (GER/GYM, Pommelled horse-2)
31-225   Weingärtner (GER/GYM, Rings-2)
31-225   Weingärtner (GER/GYM, Horse vault-3)
31-158   Karl Neukirch (GER/GYM, Parallel bars-ac)
31-157   Neukirch (GER/GYM, Parallel bars [teams]-1)

31-157	Neukirch (GER/GYM, Horizontal bar [teams]-1)
31-157	Neukirch (GER/GYM, Horizontal bar-ac)
31-157	Neukirch (GER/GYM, Horse vault-ac)
31-157	Neukirch (GER/GYM, Pommelled horse-ac)
30-130	Louis Zutter (SUI/GYM, Parallel bars-2)
30-129	Zutter (SUI/GYM, Horse vault-2)
30-129	Zutter (SUI/GYM, Pommelled horse-1)
30-129	Zutter (SUI/GYM, Horizontal bar-ac)
29-115	Holger Louis Nielsen (DEN/SHO, Free pistol [30 meters]-2)
29-114	Nielsen (DEN/SHO, Pistol [25 meters]-3)
29-114	Nielsen (DEN/SHO, Military pistol [25 meters]-5)
29-114	Nielsen (DEN/SHO, Military rifle [200 meters]-dnf)
29-114	Nielsen (DEN/ATH, Discus throw-ac)
29-113	Nielsen (DEN/FEN, Sabre-3)

Oldest Top Three, Men (10 athletes/30 performances)

36-103	August Goedrich (GER/CYC, Road race-2)
36-102	Georgios Orfanidis (GRE/SHO, Free rifle [300 meters]-1)
36-101	Orfanidis (GRE/SHO, Pistol [25 meters]-2)
31-225	Hermann Weingärtner (GER/GYM, Horizontal bar-1)
31-225	Weingärtner (GER/GYM, Horizontal bar [teams]-1)
31-225	Weingärtner (GER/GYM, Parallel bars [teams]-1)
31-225	Weingärtner (GER/GYM, Pommelled horse-2)
31-225	Weingärtner (GER/GYM, Rings-2)
31-157	Karl Neukirch (GER/GYM, Parallel bars [teams]-1)
31-157	Neukirch (GER/GYM, Horizontal bar [teams]-1)
30-130	Louis Zutter (SUI/GYM, Parallel bars-2)
30-129	Zutter (SUI/GYM, Horse vault-2)
30-129	Zutter (SUI/GYM, Pommelled horse-1)
29-115	Holger Louis Nielsen (DEN/SHO, Free pistol [30 meters]-2)
29-114	Nielsen (DEN/SHO, Pistol [25 meters]-3)
29-113	Nielsen (DEN/FEN, Sabre-3)
27-333	Sumner Paine (USA/SHO, Free pistol [30 meters]-1)
27-332	Paine (USA/SHO, Military pistol [25 meters]-2)
27-164	James Brendan Bennet Connolly (USA/ATH, High jump-=2)
27-161	Connolly (USA/ATH, Long jump-3)
27-160	Connolly (USA/ATH, Triple jump-1)
27-099	Tilemakhos Karakalos (GRE/FEN, Sabre-2)
26-335	Carl Schuhmann (GER/WRE, Unlimited class-1)
26-333	Schuhmann (GER/GYM, Horizontal bar [teams]-1)
26-333	Schuhmann (GER/GYM, Horse vault-1)
26-333	Schuhmann (GER/GYM, Parallel bars [teams]-1)
26-190	Alfred Flatow (GER/GYM, Parallel bars-1)
26-189	Flatow (GER/GYM, Horizontal bar [teams]-1)
26-189	Flatow (GER/GYM, Parallel bars [teams]-1)
26-189	Flatow (GER/GYM, Horizontal bar-2)

Oldest Champions, Men (10 athletes/18 performances)

36-102 Georgios Orfanidis (GRE/SHO, Free rifle [300 meters]-1)
31-225 Hermann Weingärtner (GER/GYM, Horizontal bar-1)
31-225   Weingärtner (GER/GYM, Horizontal bar [teams]-1)
31-225   Weingärtner (GER/GYM, Parallel bars [teams]-1)
31-157 Karl Neukirch (GER/GYM, Horizontal bar [teams]-1)
31-157   Neukirch (GER/GYM, Parallel bars [teams]-1)
30-129 Louis Zutter (SUI/GYM, Pommelled horse-1)
27-333 Sumner Paine (USA/SHO, Free pistol [30 meters]-1)
27-160 James Brendan Bennet Connolly (USA/ATH, Triple jump-1)
26-335 Carl Schuhmann (GER/WRE, Unlimited class-1)
26-333   Schuhmann (GER/GYM, Horizontal bar [teams]-1)
26-333   Schuhmann (GER/GYM, Horse vault-1)
26-333   Schuhmann (GER/GYM, Parallel bars [teams]-1)
26-190 Alfred Flatow (GER/GYM, Parallel bars-1)
26-189   Flatow (GER/GYM, Horizontal bar [teams]-1)
26-189   Flatow (GER/GYM, Parallel bars [teams]-1)
26-003 John Bryant Paine (USA/SHO, Military pistol [25 meters]-1)
25-216 Thomas Pelham Curtis (USA/ATH, 110 meter hurdles-1)

Total Known Competitors

	Ath	Cyc	Fen	Gym	Sho	Swi	Ten	Wlt	Wre	Subtotal	Totals
AUS	1	-	-	-	-	-	1	-	-	2	1
AUT	-	1	1	-	-	2	-	-	-	4	3
CYP	1	-	-	-	-	-	-	-	-	1	1
DEN	3	-	1	1	3	-	-	1	-	9	3
EGY	-	-	-	-	-	-	1	-	-	1	1
FRA	6	2	4	1	1	-	1	-	-	15	13
GBR	5	2	-	1	2	-	2	1	1	14	10
GER	5	5	-	11	-	-	1	1	1	24	19
GRE	27	8	9	9	28	9	6	3	2	101	98
HUN	3	-	-	2	-	1	1	1	1	9	7
ITA	-	-	-	-	1	-	-	-	-	1	1
SMY	1	1	-	-	-	-	-	-	-	2	2
SUI	-	-	-	2	1	-	-	-	-	3	3
SWE	1	-	-	1	-	-	-	-	-	2	1
USA	10	-	-	-	3	1	-	-	-	14	14
Total	63	19	15	28	39	13	13	7	5	202	177
Nations	11	6	4	8	7	4	7	5	4	**56**	**15**

Total Estimated Competitors

The above numbers for known competitors are the same for all nations and all sports with the exception of Greece. Certain Greek athletes in gymnastics, shooting, and swimming definitely competed, but no evidence can be found as to their exact identity. It is also possible that one or two Greek swimmers may have yet to be identified, but that is less certain.

	Ath	*Cyc*	*Fen*	*Gym*	*Sho*	*Swi*	*Ten*	*Wlt*	*Wre*	**Subtotal**	**Totals**
GRE	27	8	9	*52*	*50*	*15*	6	3	2	172	166
Total	63	19	15	71	61	19	13	7	5	273	245

Known Competitors by Nation

	Subtotal	*2-sport*	*3-sport*	*4-sport*	*Total*
Australia	2	1	-	-	1
Austria	4	1	-	-	3
Cyprus	1	-	-	-	1
Denmark	9	1	1	1	3
Egypt	1	-	-	-	1
France	15	2	-	-	13
Germany	24	2	-	1	19
Great Britain & Ireland	14	1	-	1	10
Greece	101	3	-	-	98
Hungary	9	-	1	-	7
Italy	1	-	-	-	1
Smyrna	2	-	-	-	2
Switzerland	3	-	-	-	3
Sweden	2	1	-	-	1
United States	14	-	-	-	14
Totals	202	12	2	3	177
Nations	15	8	2	3	15

Competitors, Nations, and Events by Sports

	Known Athletes	*Estimated Athletes*	*Nations*	*Events*
Athletics (Track & Field)	63	63	11	12
Cycling	19	19	6	6
Fencing	15	15	4	3
Gymnastics	28	*71*	8	8
Shooting	39	*61*	7	5
Swimming	13	*19*	4	4
Tennis (Lawn)	13	13	7	2
Weightlifting	7	7	5	2
Wrestling	5	5	4	1
Subtotals	202	273	56	43
Multisport Athletes	17	28	—	—
Totals	177	245	15	—

Athletes Competing in Two or More Sports in 1896 [17]

Four Sports [3]—*Denmark:* Jensen, Viggo. Athletics/Gymnastics/Shooting/Weightlifting. *Germany:* Schuhmann, Carl. Athletics/Gymnastics/Weightlifting/Wrestling. *Great Britain:* Elliot, Launceston. Athletics/Gymnastics/Weightlifting/Wrestling.

Three Sports [2]—*Denmark:* Nielsen, Holger. Athletics/Fencing/Shooting. *Hungary:* Topavicza, Momcsilló. Tennis/Weightlifting/Wrestling.

Two Sports [12]—*Australia:* Flack, Edwin Harold. Athletics/Tennis. *Austria:* Schmal, Adolf. Cycling/Fencing. *Denmark:* Schmidt, Eugen. Athletics/Shooting. *France:* Grisel, Alphonse. Athletics/Gymnastics. Lermusiaux, Albin. Athletics/Shooting. *Germany:* Hofmann, Fritz. Athletics/Gymnastics. Traun, Friedrich Adolf "Fritz." Athletics/Tennis. *Great Britain:* Robertson, George Stuart. Athletics/Tennis. *Greece:* Papasideris, Georgios. Athletics/Weightlifting. Petmezas, Aristovoulos. Gymnastics/Shooting. Versis, Sotirios. Athletics/Weightlifting. *Sweden:* Sjöberg, Henrik. Athletics/Gymnastics.

NOTES

1. Three other nations had athletes entered in events at the 1896 Olympics, but these athletes never competed. The noncompeting nations were Belgium, Chile, and Russia. In addition, both Bulgaria and Serbia are often considered to have been represented at the 1896 Olympics. Charles Champaud was a Swiss national who competed in gymnastics in 1896, but was living and studying in Sofia, Bulgaria, at the time of the Olympics. He is often listed incorrectly as Bulgarian. Momcsilló Topavicza competed in tennis (lawn), weightlifting, and wrestling in 1896. He was from what is the current province of Vojvodina within the republic of Serbia in modern-day Yugoslavia. But in 1896 this was a part of the Austro-Hungarian Empire, and considered a part of Hungary.

2. The last three constituted a special committee for handling the funds for the renovation of the stadium at the indication of the generous donor Georgios Averof.

3. Kokkidis replaced the originally elected Mr. Markos N. Dragoumis, who went abroad.

4. Ian Buchanan and Bill Mallon, *Historical Dictionary of the Olympic Movement* (Lanham, Md.: Scarecrow, 1996) p. xxiv.

5. Coubertin, *Mémoires Olympiques* (Lausanne: Bureau International de Pédagogie Sportive, 1931).

6. *Ibid.*, p. 11.

7. Richard D. Mandell, *The First Modern Olympics* (Berkeley: University of California Press, 1976), pp. 83–84.

8. John J. MacAloon, *This Great Symbol: Pierre de Coubertin and the Origins of the Modern Olympic Games* (Chicago: University of Chicago Press, 1981), pp. 164–166.

9. *Ibid.*, p. 167.

10. Wolf Lyberg, *The History of the IOC Sessions. I. 1894–1930* (Lausanne: International Olympic Committee, Oct. 1994), p. 7.

11. David C. Young, *The Olympic Myth of Greek Amateur Athletes* (Chicago: Ares, 1984), p. 61.

12. IOC, *Bulletin du Comité International des Jeux Olympiques* (Paris: IOC, July 1894), p. 4.

13. *Tidning för Idrott*, 26 April 1894.

14. MacAloon, *op. cit.*, pp. 166-167.

15. The correct French name was the Union des Sociétés Françaises de Sports Athlétiques (USFSA).

16. Coubertin, *Mémoires Olympiques*.

17. Bill Henry, *An Approved History of the Olympic Games* (New York: G. P. Putnam's Sons, 1948), p. 32.

18. Lyberg, *op. cit.*, pp. 9–10.

19. MacAloon, *op. cit.*, p. 171.

20. MacAloon, *op. cit.*, pp. 171–172, quoting from the *Times* of London, 18 June 1894.

21. IOC, *loc. cit.*

22. IOC, *loc. cit.*

23. *Ibid.*, p. 10.

24. Joanna Davenport, "Athens 1896: The Games of the 1st Olympiad," in *Historical Dictionary of the Modern Olympic Movement*, ed. John E. Findling and Kimberly D. Pelle (Westport, Conn.: Greenwood Press, 1996), p. 4.

25. Mandell, *op. cit.*, p. 91, referenced to Coubertin, *L'Idée olympique*, pp. 5–7.

26. Coubertin, *Une Campagne de vingt-et-un ans* (Paris: 1908).

27. Henry, *op. cit.*, p. 37.

28. *Ibid.*

29. *Ibid.*, pp. 38–39.

30. *Ibid.*, p. 39.

31. *Ibid.*, pp. 39–40.

32. Coubertin, *Une Campagne de vingt-et-un ans.*

33. *Ibid.*, p. 40.

34. MacAloon, *op. cit.*, p. 185, referencing Coubertin, *Une Campagne de vingt-et-un ans*, p. 114; and *Mémoires olympiques*, p. 26.

35. Henry, *op. cit.*, pp. 40–41; and MacAloon, *op. cit.*, pp. 189–190; referencing Coubertin, *Une Campagne de vingt-et-un ans*, pp. 114–115.

36. Henry, *op. cit.*, p. 41.

37. Henry, *op. cit.*, pp. 41–42.

38. *Ibid.*, pp. 42–43.

39. *Ibid.*, p. 43.

40. *Ibid.*

41. *Ibid.*, pp. 43–44.

42. Michael Sheridan, *Good Reasons: 100 Years of Olympic Marathon Races* (n.p.: 1996), p. 11.

43. Henry, *loc. cit.*

44. Henry, *loc. cit.*

45. *Ibid.*

46. Henry, *op. cit.*, pp. 44–46.

47. MacAloon, *op. cit.*, p. 209.

48. Recently discovered evidence of later Olympic champions than the usually listed Varasdates of Armenia in A.D. 369 comes from U. Sinn, "Neue Erkenntnisse zu den letzten Olympischen Spielen in der Antike — ein Neufund aus Olympia," *Antike Welt* 26, 2 (1995): 155.

49. Airoldi walked from Milan to Ragusa (present day Dubrovnik), then took a ship from there to Corfu, and then boarded another ship to Patras. He walked from Patras to Athens, arriving in Athens in the afternoon of 31 March. From *La Bicicletta*, 9 April 1896.

50. David E. Martin and Roger W. H. Gynn, *The Marathon Footrace*, pp. 5–6.

51. *Ibid.*, pp. 3–4.

52. The Baron de Coubertin; Philemon, Timoleon; Lambros, Spiridon P.; and Politis, Nikolaos G., editors, *The Olympic Games 776 B.C.—1896 A.D.; With the Approval and Support of the Central Council of the International Olympic Games in Athens, under the Presidency of H.R.H. the Crown Prince Constantine* (Athens: Charles Beck, 1896), p. 151.

53. *Ibid.*, pp. 153–155.

54. *Ibid.*

55. *Ibid.*

56. See also the article by Robertson reproduced herein (pages 54–63), which strongly supported keeping the Olympics in Greece in perpetuity.

57. *The New York Times*, 3 May 1896.

Summary Articles

The Olympian Games at Athens
Charles Waldstein

REJOICE! *We have conquered!* The two Greek words shouted by one panting runner were taken up by a hundred thousand voices, and rang through the Stadium, across the Ilissus to the distant Pentelicus, to the Hymettos on the right, and on the left the rocks of the Acropolis caught up the sound and sent it back. But the shout lost itself in one cavern of the rock, where it lingered, and seemed held as by the familiarity of some vague and distant association. The shouting multitude in and about the Stadium were not aware of what was going on in the grotto of Pan, under the rock of the Acropolis. For the old god Pan, who had been sleeping here for two thousand years, awoke and smiled. He remembered how, 2276 years ago, he had gladdened the heart of the runner Pheidippides when he raced back from Sparta in despair at not obtaining Lakonian help to meet the Persian foe threatening Athens before Marathon; how he, the great god Pan, had promised him and the Athenians success against their barbarian enemies. But it was not Pheidippides who, after the victory of Marathon, as Browning puts it,

> flung down his shield,
> Ran like fire once more; and the space 'twixt the fennel-field
> And Athens was stubble again, a field which fire runs through,
> Till he broke, "Rejoice, we conquer!" Like wine through clay,
> Joy in his blood bursting his heart, he died — the bliss!

The Marathon runner who died with the blessed words on his lips, sinking down in the market-place of Athens, according to the account of Lucian, was a certain Philippides.

It is impossible to describe the enthusiasm within the Stadium — nay, in the whole city of Athens — over the result of this the most important contest in the Games during these ten days. The Stadium packed with over 50,000 people; the walls around it, the hills about, covered with a human crowd that from the distance looked like bees clustering over a comb; and this mass of humanity rising in one great shout of joy with the advent — the one runner who was the first to cross the line within the Stadium, caught in the arms of the Crown-Prince, who led him before the King, embraced and kissed by those who could get near him; all this and much more sent a thrill through every heart which few could have experienced before with the same intensity. It might almost have been Philippides of old bringing to the anxious inhabitants of Athens the news of their glorious victory, the salvation of their county and home.

We can well understand how the Greeks themselves should, from all these associations, have viewed this race as especially their own; and we must admire them the more for the fairness and generosity with which they received the news (while the pole-jumping, in which the American, Hoyt, proved victorious, was going on in the Stadium) that Flack, the Australian, and then that Blake, the Boston man, were leading after 20 kilometers. But when, finally three of their own men came in as the leaders, we can equally sympathize in their unbounded joy. While, with strong protests on his part, the victor was being rubbed down in the dressing-rooms behind the Stadium, presents were showered upon him. One person sent a gold watch, another a gold cigarette-case; I am told that he has had a small farm given him, daughters offered in marriage — in fact, all that a hero can wish for. I hope this will not counteract one of the chief aims of these games, namely, the preservation of strict amateur principles in not giving valuable prizes.

Both Flack, the Austalian, and Blake of Boston say that they were fairly outrun by these Greek peasants, who have not been trained systematically over a prepared course. It is one thing to run long distances on a course, another to keep up pace up and down hill over a rough road. The distance from Marathon to Athens is forty kilometers, about twenty-five miles. I saw the victor, Spiros Loues. He is a peasant's son from Amaroussi, a village in Attica, not far from Athens. He is about twenty-four years of age, slightly over medium height, slim and strong, with fine features, clear bright gray eyes, and dark hair. He is as yet quite simple and unspoilt, and we must hope that his success will not turn his head. He remains the true Greek peasant — a hardy, clear-headed, honest, and kind tiller of the soil — than which no better type of man exists in the world. It was a delight to see him in his clean fustanella, his blue embroidered waistcoat jacket with the long sleeves, his red Greek cap and tassel, his embroidered gaiters and red pointed *zarucchia*, or shoes, walking with his old peasant father, cheered by the enthusiastic crowd as he passed through the streets of Athens.

I have dwelt so long on this Marathon race because it is a type of the joyful like which these Games have brought into the place. Only it cannot illustrate the generous joy and enthusiasm which moved the Greeks and all the visitors at each victory, to whatever nation it might have fallen. Still, I venture to say that the greatest glee was shown at each successive victory that fell to our nation, the youngest of all, that carried off the palm and gained by far the greater number of prizes, namely, the Boston and Princeton boys. T.E. Burke's running, Curtis's hurdle-racing, Clark's jumping, Connolly in the triple jump (hop, skip and jump), Garrett's putting the weight and throwing the diskos, Hoyt's pole-jumping, the brothers Paine's pistol-shooting — each of these carried off a first prize. But whenever their own man was beaten and the stars and stripes were hoised at the end of the Stadium to indicate the nationality of the winner, the Greeks raised a shout of applause. This they did for the other nations as well — the English (Flack, the Australian), in the 1500 meters race; Elliott (lifting the weights with one hand); the Frenchmen (at bicycling); the Germans (at gymnastics and wrestling); the Dane (at lifting weights with two hands); the Hungarians (at swimming); their own men (gymnastics on rings and two prizes in rifle-shooting); but with none was the cheer as hearty as with the Americans. There can be no doubt that "our boys" were the most popular with the mass of the people and with the officials. Prince George of Greece (the powerful naval officer who saved the life of his cousin the Czar of Russia, in Japan felling the would-be assassin with one blow of a light cane) who acted as chief umpire throughout, said to me: "We all love the American athletes. They behaved so well, and are such good fellows. They taught our people a lesson with their true interest in sport itself. They would sit down and discuss sport with them without any idea that they were rivals."

This first celebration of the Olympic Games has thus been a stupendous success; and Mr.

Bikelas, the president of the International Committee, Baron de Coubertin, the originator of the idea; the Crown-Prince of Greece, who proved himself the most capable and energetic organizer of all the work here; his brothers, Prince George and Prince Nicholas (the latter making all arrangements for the magnificent shooting-stands); the secretaries, Messrs. Philemon, Manos, Streit, Melas and Metaxas—all are to be heartily congratulated. Several American friends expressed the same sentiment when they said that only once in their lives had they been impressed as powerfully as when they sat in the Stadium on a full day, namely, at some scenes in the Chicago Exposition.

But all this would not have been possible had it not been for the local receptacle for all this human energy and enthusiasm.

The Stadium

Pausanias, the ancient traveller, who visited Athens in the time of the Antonines, states that the Stadium was built by Herodes Atticus, and the greater part of the marble from the quarries of the Pentelicon was used in its construction.

But Pausanias is wrong in maintaining that Herodes built the Stadium. We know from Plutarch that it existed in the time of the orator Lycurgus, and an inscription of his tells us that in 330 B.C. Eudemos gave 1000 yoke of oxen towards its building. What Herodes did was to clothe it all in resplendent marble; and the mass of marble required to cover all the seats of this huge structure might well have exhausted one vein of the quarries of Mount Pentelicus, which, however, supplies its beautiful stone to the modern community at the present moment, and is used for the restoration of the Stadium now. Herodes is reported to have formed the project of this splendid gift to Athens while he was witnessing the Panathenaic games in the Stadium. He promised the spectators that when they assembled for the next Panathenaic festival they should find it covered with marble. He kept his promise. And the ancients owed much to this wealthy friend of Hadrian and teacher of Marcus Aurelius.

After about 1760 years another Herodes Atticus has arisen. Mr. Averoff, a wealthy Greek living at Alexandria, has generously given the funds with which the Stadium is to be restored in order to be used in the new "Panathenaic" games, which now bring together all nations which are the inheritors of ancient Hellenic and Athenian life, the truly civilized nations of Europe and America. He has already contributed over 500,000 francs, and he is determined to complete the marble and stone seats throughout the whole Stadium; at least all below the zone or passage which divides the tiers horizontally. At present a lower row of marble seats runs round the whole Stadium, while at the crescent, or semicircular portion, the throne-like seats below and several upper rows are in marble, the rest being temporarily erected in wood.

An idea of the size of this structure, in the shape of an elongated horseshoe, can be formed when one realizes that the length of the inner portion of the Stadium itself, round which the seats rise is 236 meters. The usual length of the stadium was 600 Greek feet, and this became the standard measure of distance for the ancients—about one-eighth of a mile.

It is a mistake to believe that chariot or horse races took place in the Stadium. It was reserved for the foot-race, the oldest of Greek games. This consisted of the single race or *stadion*; the *diaulos*—down the course, turning the post, and back again; the *dolichos*, the long-distance race of 24 stadia; and the *hoplitodromos*, in which they ran in armor. It is also probable that some of the other contests, such as wrestling (*pygme*), boxing (*pale*), the *pancration* (a combination of wrestling and boxing), and perhaps even throwing the discus and the spear took place here.

Under the able direction of the Greek architect, Mr. Metaxas, this edifice (identified as early as the seventeenth century, and partly excavated in 1863) has now been restored. All the indications of antique remains have been most carefully followed, so that now the interior, the seats, the underground passage leading out of the Stadium to the dressing-room of the athletes, are exactly as they were two thousand years ago.

In principle, I have always been opposed to *restorations* of ancient monuments. But this is the one exception in which I consider such a complete restoration called for, instructive and adequate in every way. A temple like the Parthenon, or any building in which beauty of conception and execution, truly artistic qualities of composition and of detail, are essential, and are the very soul of the monument, it would be sacrilege and folly to attempt to restore. But here the artistic quality is one of purity of line in the whole structure, of proportion in its construction, and this has been reproduced literally. An interesting point was made clear, hitherto unknown — *i.e.*, a gentle curve in the rows of seats converging on either side of the centre, and thus not uniformly parallel to the inner Stadium.

The really impressive and instructive feature of the Stadium is the magnitude and spaciousness of its dimensions, and its capacity of holding 50,000 people witnessing the efforts of their athletic youths. Besides this number of seated Athenians, the *helots*, or slaves, were allowed to stand about the upper portion above the seats. As now many thousands of the poor population filled this space, so was it crowded in antiquity. The Acropolis, the museums and the monuments scattered over the country and abroad, bring home to us the refinement of taste and the height of Athenian culture. This Stadium, especially when filled with such a vast population, brings us face to face with the grandeur and power of the ancient community of Athens. It shows us the bulk and magnitude of their life, which before one hardly realized. It has often happened to me to hear travellers coming from Egypt remark upon the smallness of scale of all they met here, their eyes having been accustomed to the huge proportions of the monuments of the Pharaoh's building with slaves; though they were entranced by the beauty, grace, and refinement of the work they found in Athens. The Stadium now will convey to the visitor some impression of magnitude, not in a monument erected by slaves for the glorification of one ruler, but in a structure to house a free and powerful community, uniting in the peaceful delight at physical strength and skill.

The immediate aim, the encouragement of athletics, has been fully attained. But in a still more gratifying manner has the further and higher purpose, the spread of international good feeling and fellowship, been carried out. Rarely, if ever, have so many people of all civilized nations been brought together for a common purpose, and never have they shown themselves to such advantage.

Here the Greek committee, and especially the King of Greece and the royal family, deserve especial gratitude from all. Throughout they have acted as a powerful link between all the nationalities. At a grand luncheon, in the large hall of the royal palace, to which all the winners and foreign representatives were invited, the King, in a graceful speech in French and then in Greek, thanked all the foreigners for coming and contributing to the great success of this noble enterprise. He ended by saying, "Not good-by, but *au revoir*." Then he and his sons mingled among the guests, talking and jesting with all, and making them all feel that they were really at home in his country.

The games opened in the presence of all the royalties, the King and Queen in the centre; the Crown-Prince advanced before them in the middle of the sphendoné, his two brothers beside him with the committee, and made his opening speech, to which the King answered. Upon this followed, sung by a large chorus with double orchestra, the splendid hymn composed by the Greek Samara (the composer of the operas *Flora, Mirabilis*, and *Le Martyr*) — a most impressive opening. The Olympic Games ended by the conferring of the simple bay wreath to each victor, led up before the King, in the Stadium, in the presence of thousands of admiring people of all nations, as two thousand years ago the victor stepped before the high-priest of Zeus and received the bay wreath before the great temple at Olympia.

The Field, May 1896

THE OLYMPIC GAMES OF 1896
Pierre de Coubertin

The Olympic games which recently took place at Athens were modern in character, not alone because of their programs, which substituted bicycle for chariot races, and fencing for the brutalities of pugilism, but because in their origin and regulations they were international and universal, and consequently adapted to the conditions in which athletics have developed at the present day. The ancient games had an exclusively Hellenic character; they were always held in the same place, and Greek blood was a necessary condition of admission to them. It is true that strangers were in time tolerated; but their presence at Olympia was rather a tribute paid to the superiority of Greek civilization than a right exercised in the name of racial equality. With the modern games it is quite otherwise. Their creation is the work of "barbarians." It is due to the delegates of the athletic associations of all countries assembled in congress at Paris in 1894. It was there agreed that every country should celebrate the Olympic games in turn. The first placed belonged by right to Greece; it was accorded by unanimous vote; and in order to emphasize the permanence of the institution, its wide bearings and its essentially cosmopolitan character, an international committee was appointed, the members of which were to represent the various nations, European and American with whom athletics are held in honor. The presidency of this committee falls to the country in which the next games are to be held. A Greek, M. Bikelas, has presided for the last two years. A Frenchman now presides, and will continue to do so until 1900, since the next games are to take place at Paris during the Exposition. Where will those of 1904 take place? Perhaps at New York, perhaps at Berlin, or at Stockholm. The question is soon to be decided.

It was in virtue of these resolutions passed during the Paris Congress that the recent festivals were organized. Their successful issue is largely owing to the active and energetic cooperation of the Greek crown prince Constantine. When they realized all that was expected of them, the Athenians lost courage. They felt that the city's resources were not equal to the demands that would be made upon them; nor would the government (M. Tricoupis being then prime minister) consent to increase facilities. M. Tricoupis did not believe in the success of the games. He argued that the Athenians knew nothing about athletics; that they had neither the adequate grounds for the contests, nor athletes of their own to bring into line; and that, moreoever, the financial situation of Greece forbade her inviting the world to an event preparations for which would entail such large expenditures. There was reason in the objections; but on the one hand, the prime minister greatly exaggerated the importance of the expenditures, and on the other, it was not necesary that the government should bear the burden of them directly. Modern Athens, which recalls in so many ways the Athens of ancient days, has inherited from her the privilege of being beautified and enriched by her children. The public treasury was not always very well filled in those times any more than in the present, but wealthy citizens who had made fortunes at a distance liked to crown their commerical career by some act of liberality to the mother-country. They endowed the land with superb edifices of general utility-theaters, gymnasia, temples. The modern city is likewise full of monuments which she owes to such generosity. It was easy to obtain from private individuals what the state could not give. The Olympic games had burned with so bright a luster in the past of the Greeks that they could not but have their revival at heart. And furthermore, the moral benefits would compensate largely for all pecuniary sacrifice.

This the crown prince apprehended at once, and it decided him to lend his authority to the organizing of the first Olympic games. He appointed a commission, with headquarters in his own palace; made M. Philemon, ex-mayor of Athens and a man of much zeal and enthusiasm, secretary-general; and appealed to the nation to subscribe the necessary funds. Subscriptions began to come in from Greece, but particularly from London, Marseilles, and Constantinople, where there are wealthy and influential Greek colonies. The chief gift came from Alexandria. It was this gift which made it possible to restore the Stadion to its condition in the time of Atticus Herodes. The intention had been from the first to hold the contests in this justly celebrated spot. No one, however, had dreamed that it might be possible to restore to their former splendor the marble seats which, it is said, could accommodate forty thousand persons. The great inclosure would have been utilized, and provisional wooden seats placed on the grassy slopes which surround it. Thanks to the generosity of M. Averoff, Greece is now the richer by a monument unique of its kind, and its visitors have seen a spectacle which they can never forget.

Two years ago the Stadion resembled a deep gash, made by some fabled giant, in the side of the hill which rises abruptly by the Ilissus, and opposite Lycabettus and the Acropolis, in a retired, picturesque quarter of Athens. All that was visible of it then were the two high earth embankments which faced each other on opposite sides of the long, narrow race-course. They met at the end in an imposing hemicycle. Grass grew between the cobblestones. For centuries the spectators of ancient days had sat on the ground on these embankments. Then, one day, an army of workmen, taking possession of the Stadion, had covered it with stone and marble. The first covering served as a quarry during the Turkish domination; not a trace of it was left. With its innumerable rows of seats, and the flights of steps which divide it into sections and lead to the upper tiers, the Stadion no longer has the look of being cut out of the hill. It is the hill which seems to have been placed there by the hand of man to support this enormous pile of masonry. One detail only is modern. One does not notice it at first. The dusty track is now a cinder-path, prepared according to the latest rules of modern athletics by an expert brought over from London for the purpose. In the center a sort of esplanade has been erected for the gymnastic exhibitions. At the end, on each side of the turning, antiquity is represented by two large boundary-stones, forming two human figures, and excavated while the foundations were being dug. These were the only finds; they add but little to archaeological data. Work on the Stadion is far from being completed, eighteen months having been quite insufficient for the undertaking. Where marble could not be placed, painted wood was hastily made to do duty. That clever architect, M. Metaxas cherishes the hope, however, of seeing all the antique decorations restored — statues, columns, bronze quadrigæ, and, at the entrance, majestic proplyæa.

When this shall be done, Athens will in truth possess the temple of athletic sports. Yet it is doubtful whether such a sanctuary be the one best suited to worship of human vigor and beauty in these modern days. The Anglo-Saxons, to whom we owe the revival of athletics, frame their contests delightfully in grass and verdure. Nothing could differ more from the Athenian Stadion than Travers Island, the summer home of the New York Athletic Club, where the championship games are decided. In this green inclosure, where nature is left to have her way, the spectators sit under the trees on the sloping declivities, a few feet away from the Sound, which murmurs against the rocks. One finds something of the same idea at Paris, and at San Francisco, under those Californian skies which so recall the skies of Greece, at the foot of those mountains which have the pure outlines and the iridescent reflections of Hymettus. If the ancient amphitheater was more grandiose and more solemn, the modern picture is more *in-time* and pleasing. The music floating under the trees makes a softer accompaniment to the exercises; the spectators move about at friendly ease, whereas the ancients, packed together in rigid lines on their marble benches sat broiling in the sun or chilled in the shade.

The Stadion is not the only enduring token that will remain to Athens of her inauguration of the new Olympiads: she has also a velodrome and a shooting-stand. The former is in the plain of the modern Phalerum, along the railway which connects Athens with the Piraeus. It is copied after the model of that at Copenhagen, where the crown prince of Greece and his brothers had an opportunity of appreciating its advantages during a visit to the King of Denmark, their grandfather. The bicyclists, it is true, have complained that the track is not long enough, and that the turnings are too abrupt; but when were bicyclists ever content? The tennis courts are in the center of the velodrome. The shooting-stand makes a goodly appearance, with its manor-like medieval crenelations. The contestants are comfortably situated under monumental arches. Then there are large pavilions for the rowers, built of wood, but prettily decorated, with boat-houses and dressing-rooms.

WHILE the Hellenic Committee thus labored over the scenic requirements, the international committee and the national committees were occupied in recruiting competitors. The matter was not as easy as one might think. Not only had indifference and distrust to be overcome, but the revival of the Olympic games had aroused a certain hostility. Although the Paris Congress had been careful to decree that every form of physical exercise practised in the world should have its place on the program, the gymnasts took offense. They considered that they had not been given sufficient prominence. The greater part of the gymnastic associations of Germany, France and Belgium are animated by a rigorously exclusive spirit; they are not inclined to tolerate the presence of those forms of athletics which they themselves do not practise; what they disdainfully designate as "English sports" have become, because of their popularity, especially odious to them. These associations were not satisfied with declining the invitation sent them to repair to Athens. The Belgian federation wrote to the other federations, suggesting a concerted stand against the work of the Paris Congress. These incidents confirmed the opinions of the pessimists who had been foretelling the failure of the fêtes, or their probable postponement. Athens is far away, the journey is expensive, and the Easter vacations are short. The contestants were not willing to undertake the voyage unless they could be sure that the occasion would be worth the effort. The different associations were not willing to send representatives unless they could be informed of the amount of interest which the contests would create. An unfortunate occurrence took place almost at the last moment. The German press, commenting on an article which had appeared in a Paris newspaper, declared that it was an exclusively Franco-Greek affair; that attempts were being made to shut out other nations; and furthermore, that the German associations had been intentionally kept aloof from the Paris Congress of 1894. The assertion was acknowledged to be incorrect, and was powerless to check the efforts of the German committee under Dr. Gebhardt. M. Kemeny in Hungary, Major Balck in Sweden, General de Boutowski in Russia, Professor W. M. Sloane in the United States, Lord Ampthill in England, Dr. Jiri Guth in Bohemia, were, meantime, doing their best to awaken interest in the event, and to reassure the doubting. They did not always succeed. Many people took a sarcastic view, and the newspapers indulged in much pleasantry on the subject of the Olympic games.

EASTER MONDAY, April 6, the streets of Athens wore a look of extraordinary animation. All the public buildings were draped in bunting; multicolored streamers floated in the wind; green wreaths decked the house-fronts. Everywhere were the two letters "O.A.", the Greek letters of the Olympic games, and the two dates, B.C. 776, A.D. 1896, indicating their ancient past and their present renascence. At two o'clock in the afternoon the crowd began to throng the Stadion and to take possession of the seats. It was a joyous and motley concourse. The skirts and braided jackets of the *palikars* contrasted with the somber and ugly European habiliments. The women used large paper fans to shield them from the sun, parasols which would have obstructed the view, being prohibited. The king and queen drove up a little before three o'clock, followed by Princess Marie, their daughter, and her fiancé, Grand Duke George of Russia. They were received by the crown prince and his brothers, by M. Delyannis, president of the Council of Ministers, and by the members of the Hellenic Committee and the international committee. Flowers were presented to the queen and princess, and the cortège made its way into the hemicycle to the strains of the Greek national hymn and the cheers of the crowd. Within, the court ladies and functionaries, the diplomatic corps, and the deputies awaited the sovereigns, for whom two marble arm-chairs were in readiness. The crown prince, taking his stand in the arena, facing the king, then made a short speech, in which he touched upon the origin of the enterprise, and the obstacles surmounted in bringing it to fruition. Addressing the king, he asked him to proclaim the Olympic games, and the king, rising, declared them opened. It was a thrilling moment. Fifteen hundred and two years before, the Emperor Theodosius had addressed the Olympic games, thinking, no doubt, that in abolishing this hated survival of paganism he was furthering the cause of progress; and here was a Christian monarch, amid the applause of an assemblage composed almost exclusively of Christians, announcing the formal annulment of the imperial decree; while a few feet away stood the Archbishop of Athens, and Pere Didon, the celebrated Dominican preacher, who, in his Easter sermon in the Catholic cathedral the day before, had paid an eloquent tribute to the pagan Greece. When the king had resumed his seat, the Olympic ode, written for the occasion by the Greek composer Samara, was sung by a chorus of one hundred and fifty voices. Once before music had been associated with the revival of the Olympic games. The first session of the Paris Congress had been held June 16, 1894, in the great amphitheater of the Sorbonne, decorated by Puvis de Chavannes; and after the address of the president of the congress, Baron de Coubertin, the large audience had listened to that fragment of the music of antiquity, the hymn to Apollo, discovered in the ruins of Delphi. But this time the connection between art and athletics was more direct. The games began with the sounding of the last chords of the Olympic ode. That first day established the success of the games beyond a doubt. The ensuing days confirmed the fact in spite of the bad weather. The royal family was assiduous in its attendance. In the shooting contest, the queen fired the first shot with a flower-wreathed rifle. The fencing-matches were held in the marble rotunda of the Exposition Palace, given by the Messrs. Zappas, and known as the Zappeion. Then the crowd made its way back to the Stadion for the foot-races, weight-putting, discus-throwing, high and long jumps, pole-vaulting, and gymnastic exhibitions. A Princeton student, Robert Garrett, scored highest in throwing the discus. His victory was unexpected. He had asked me the day before if I did not think that it would be ridiculous should he enter for an event for which he had trained so little. The stars and stripes seemed destined to carry off the laurels. When they ran up the "victor's mast", the sailors of the San Francisco, who stood in a group at the top of the Stadion, waved their caps, and the members of the Boston Athletic Association below broke out frantically, "B.A.A.! rah! rah! rah!" These cries greatly amused the Greeks. They applauded the triumph of the Americans, between whom and themselves there is a warm feeling of good-will.

The Greeks are novices in the matter of athletic sports, and had not looked for much success for their country. One event only seemed likely to be theirs from its very nature — the long-distance run from Marathon, a prize for which has been newly founded by M. Michel Bréal, a member of the French Institute, in commemoration of that soldier of antiquity who ran all the way to Athens to tell his fellow-citizens of the happy issue of the battle. The distance from Marathon to Athens is 42 kilometers. The road is rough and stony. The Greeks had trained for this run for a year past. Even in the remote districts of Thessaly young peasants prepared to enter as contestants. In three cases it is said that the enthusiasm and the inexperience of these young fellows cost them their lives, so exaggerated were their preparatory efforts. As the great day approached, women offered up prayers and votive tapers in the churches, that the victor might be a Greek!

The wish was fulfilled. A young peasant named Loues, from the village of Marousi, was the winner in two hours and fifty-five minutes. He reached the goal fresh and in fine form. He was followed by two other Greeks. The excellent Australian sprinter Flack, and the Frenchman Lermusiaux, who had been in the lead the first 35 kilometers, had fallen out of the way. When Loues came into the Stadion, the crowd, which numbered sixty thousand persons, rose to its feet like one man, swayed by extraordinary excitement. The King of Servia, who was present, will probably not forget the sight he saw that day. A flight of white pigeons was let loose, women waved fans and handkerchiefs, and some of the spectators who were nearest to Loues left their seats, and tried to reach him and carry him in triumph. He would have been suffocated if the crown prince and Prince George had not bodily led him away. A lady who stood next to me unfastened her watch, a gold one set with pearls, and sent it to him; an innkeeper presented him with an order good for three hundred and sixty-five free meals; and a wealthy citizen had to be dissuaded from signing a check for ten thousand francs to his credit. Loues, himself, however, when he was told of this generous offer refused it. The sense of honor, which is very strong in the Greek peasant, thus saved the non-professional spirit from a very great danger.

Needless to say that the various contests were held under amateur regulations. An exception was made for the fencing-matches, since in several countries professors of military fencing hold the rank of officers. For them a special contest was arranged. To all other branches of the athletic sports only amateurs were admitted. It is impossible to conceive the Olympic games with money prizes. But these rules, which seem simple enough, are a good deal complicated in their practical application by the fact that definitions of what constitutes an amateur differ from one country to another, sometimes even from one club to another. Several definitions are current in England; the Italians and the Dutch admit one which appears too rigid at one point, too loose at another. How to conciliate these divergent or contradictory utterances? The Paris Congress made an attempt in that direction, but its decisions are not accepted everywhere as law, nor is its definition of amateurship everywhere adopted as the best. The rules and regulations, properly so called, are not any more uniform. This and that are forbidden in one country, authorized in another. All that one can do, until there shall be an Olympic code formulated in accordance with the ideas and the usages of the majority of athletes, is to choose among the codes now existing. It was decided, therefore, that the foot-races should be under the rules of the Union Française des Sports Athlétiques; jumping, putting the shot, etc., under those of the Amateur Athletic Association of England; the bicycle-races under those of the International Cyclists' Association, etc. This had appeared to us the best way out of the difficulty; but we should have had many disputes if the judges (to whom had been given the Greek name of ephors) had not been headed by Prince George, who acted as final referee. His presence gave weight and authority to the decisions of the ephors, among whom there were, naturally, representatives of different countries. The prince took his duties seriously, and fulfilled them conscientiously. He was always on the track, personally supervising every detail, an easily recognizable figure, owing to his height and athletic build. It will be remembered that Prince George, while traveling in Japan with his cousin, the czarevitch (now Emperor Nicholas II) felled with his fist the ruffian who had tried to assassinate the latter. During the weight-lifting in the Stadion, Prince George lifted with ease an enormous dumb-bell, and tossed it out of the way. The audience broke into applause, as if it would have liked to make him the victor in the event.

Every night while the games were in progress the streets of Athens were illuminated. There were torch-light processions, bands played the different national hymns, and the students of the university got up ovations under the windows of the foreign athletic crews, and harangued them in the noble tongue of Demosthenes. Perhaps this tongue was somewhat abused. That Americans might not be compelled to understand French, nor Hungarians forced to speak German, the daily programs of the games, and even invitations to luncheon, were written in Greek. On receipt of these cards, covered wtih mysterious formulae, where even the date was not clear (the Greek calendar is twelve days behind ours), every man carried them to his hotel porter for elucidation.

Many banquets were given. The mayor of Athens gave one at Cephissia, a little shaded village at the foot of the Pentelicus. M. Bikelas, the retiring president of the international committee, gave another at Phalerum. The king himself entertained all the competitors, and the members of the committees, three hundred guests in all, at luncheon in the ball-room of the palace. The outside of this edifice, which was built by King Otho, is heavy and graceless; but the center of the interior is occupied by a suite of large rooms with very high ceilings opening one into another through colonnades. The decorations are simple and imposing. The tables were set in the largest of these rooms. At the table of honor sat the king, the princes, and the ministers, and here were also the members of the committees. The competitors were seated at the other tables according to their nationality. The king, at dessert, thanked and congratulated his guests, first in French, afterward in Greek. The Americans cried "Hurrah!", the Germans , "*Hoch!*", the Hungarians, "*Eljen!*", the Greeks, "*Zito!*", the French, "*Vive le Roi!*" After the repast the king and his son chatted long and amicably with the athletes. It was a really charming scene, the republican simplicity of which was a matter of wonderment particularly to the Austrians and the Russians, little used as they are to the spectacle of monarchy thus meeting democracy on an equal footing.

Then there were nocturnal festivities on the Acropolis, where the Parthenon was illuminated with colored lights, and at the Piraeus, where the vessels were hung with Japanese lanterns. Unluckily, the weather changed, and the sea was so high on the day appointed for the boat-races, which were to have taken place in the roadstead of Phalerum, that the project was abandoned. The distribution of prizes was likewise postponed for twenty-four hours. It came off with much solemnity, on the morning of April 15, in the Stadion. The sun shone again, and sparkled on the officers' uniforms. When the roll of the victors was called, it became evident, after all, that the international character of the institution was well guarded by the results of the contests. America had won nine prizes for athletic sports alone (flat races for 100 and 400 meters; 110-meter hurdle-race; high jump; broad jump; pole-vault; hop, step, and jump; putting the shot; throwing the discus), and two prizes for shooting (revolver, 25 and 30 meters); but France had the prizes for foil-fencing and for four bicycle-races; England scored highest in the one-handed weightlifting contest, and in single lawn-tennis; Greece won the run from Marathon, two gymnastic contests (rings, climbing the smooth rope), three prizes for shooting (carbine, 200 and 300 meters; pistol 25 meters), a prize for fencing with sabers, and a bicycle-race; Germany won in wrestling, in gymnastics (parallel bars, fixed bar, horse-leaping), and in double lawn-tennis; Australia, the 800-meter and 1500-meter foot-races on the flat; Hungary, swimming-matches of 100 and 200 meters; Austria, the 500-meter swimming-match and the 12-hour bicycle race; Switzerland, a gymnastic prize; Denmark, the two-handed weight-lifting contest.

The prizes were an olive-branch from the very spot, at Olympia, where stood the ancient Altis, a diploma drawn by a Greek artist, and a silver medal chiseled by the celebrated French engraver Chaplain. On one side of the medal is the Acropolis, with the Parthenon and the Propylæa; on the other a colossal head of the Olympian Zeus, after the type created by Phidias. The head of the god is blurred, as if by distance and the lapse of centuries, while in the foreground, in clear relief, is the Victory which Zeus holds on his hand. It is a striking and original conception. After the distribution of the prizes, the athletes formed for the traditional procession around the Stadion. Loues, the victor of Marathon, came first, bearing the Greek flag; then the Americans, the Hungarians, the French, the Germans. The ceremony, moreover, was made more memorable by a charming incident. One of the contestants, Mr. Robertson, an Oxford student, recited an ode which he had composed, in ancient Greek and in the Pindaric mode, in honor of the games. Music had opened them, and Poetry was present at their close; and thus was the bond once more renewed which in the past united the Muses with feats of physical strength, the mind with the well-trained body. The king announced that the first Olympiad was at an end, and left the Stadion, the band playing the Greek national hymn, and the crowd cheering. A few days later Athens was emptied of its guests. Torn wreaths littered the public squares; the banners which had floated merrily in the streets disappeared; the sun and the wind held sole possession of the marble sidewalks of Stadion street.

It is interesting to ask oneself what are likely to be the results of the Olympic games of 1896, as regards both Greece and the rest of the world. In the case of Greece, the games will be found to have had a double effect, one athletic, the other political. It is a well-known fact that the Greeks had lost completely, during their centuries of oppression, the taste for physical sports. There wre good walkers among the mountaineers, and good swimmers in the scattered villages along the coast. It was a matter of pride with the young *palikar* to wrestle and to dance well, but that was because bravery and a gallant bearing were admired by those about him. Greek dances are far from athletic, and the wrestling-matches of peasants have none of the characteristics of true sports. The men of the towns had come to know no diversion beyond reading the newspapers, and violently discussing politics about the tables of the cafes. The Greek race, however, is free from the natural indolence of the Oriental, and it was manifest that the athletic habit would, if the opportunity offered, easily take root again among its men. Indeed, several gymnastic associations had been formed in the recent years at Athens and Patras, and a rowing-club at Piraeus, and the public was showing a growing interest in their feats. It was therefore a favorable moment to speak the words, "Olympic games." No sooner had it been made clear that Athens was to aid in the revival of the Olympiads than a perfect fever of muscular activity broke out all over the kingdom. And this was nothing to what followed the games. I have seen, in little villages far from the capital, small boys, scarcely out of long clothes, throwing bit stones, or jumping improvised hurdles, and two urchins never met in the streets of Athens without running races. Nothing could exceed the enthusiasm with which the victors in the contests were received, on their return to their native towns, by their fellow-citizens. They were met by the mayor and municipal authorities, and cheered by a crowd bearing branches of wild olive and laurel. In ancient times the victor entered the city through a breach made expressly in its walls. The Greek cities are no longer walled in, but one may say that athletics have made a breach in the heart of the nation. When one realizes the influence that the practice of physical exercises may have on the future of a country, and on the force of a whole race, one is tempted to wonder whether Greece is not likely to date a new era from the year 1896. It would be curious indeed if athletics were to become one of the factors in the Eastern question! Who can tell whether, by bringing a notable increase of vigor to the inhabitants of the country, it may not hasten the solution of this thorny problem? These are hypotheses, and circumstances make light of such calculations at long range. But a local and immediate consequence of the games may already be found in the internal politics of Greece. I have spoken of the active part taken by the crown prince and his brothers, Prince George and Prince Nicholas, in the labors of the organizing committee. It was the first time that the heir apparent had had an opportunity of thus coming into contact with his future subjects. They knew him to be patriotic and high-minded, but they did not know his other admirable and solid qualities. Prince Constantine inherits his fine blue eyes and fair coloring from his Danish ancestors, and his frank, open manner, his self-poise, and his mental lucidity come from the same source; but Greece has given him enthusiasm and ardor, and this happy combination of prudence and high spirit makes him especially adapted to govern the Hellenes. The authority, mingled with the perfect liberality, with which he managed the committee, his exactitude in detail, and more particularly his quiet perseverance when those about him were inclined to hesitate and to lose courage, make it clear that his reign will be one of fruitful labor, which can only strengthen and enrich his country. The Greek people have now a better idea of the worth of their future sovereign: they have seen him at work, and have gained respect for and confidence in him.

So much for Greece. On the world at large the Olympic games have, of course, exerted no influence as yet; but I am profoundly convinced that they will do so. May I be permitted to say that this was my reason for founding them? Modern athletics need to be *unified* and *purified*. Those who have followed the renaissance of physical sports in this century know that discord reigns supreme from one end of them to the other. Every country has its own rules; it is not possible even to come to an agreement as to who is an amateur, and who is not. All over the world there is one perpetual dispute, which is further fed by innumerable weekly, and even daily newspapers. In this deplorable state of things professionalism tends to grow apace. Men give up their whole existence to one particular sport, grow rich by practising it, and thus deprive it of all nobility, and destroy the just equilibrium of man by making the muscles preponderate over the mind. It is my belief that no education, particularly in democratic times, can be good and complete without the aid of athletics; but athletics, in order to play their proper educational role, must be based on perfect disinterestedness and the sentiment of honor.

If we are to guard them against these threatening evils, we must put an end to the quarrels of amateurs, that they may be united among themselves, and willing to measure their skill in frequent international encounters. But what country is to impose its rules and its habits on the others? The Swedes will not yield to the Germans, nor the French to the English. Nothing better than the international Olympic games could therefore be devised. Each country will take its turn in organizing them. When they come to meet every four years in these contests, further ennobled by the memories of the past, athletes all over the world will learn to know one another better, to make mutual concessions, and to seek no other reward in the competition than the honor of the victory. One may be filled with desire to see the colors of one's club or college triumph in a national meeting; but how much stronger is the feeling when the colors of one's country are at stake! I am well assured that the victors in the Stadion at Athens wished for no other recompense when they heard the people cheer the flag of their country in honor of their achievement.

It was with these thoughts in mind that I sought to revive the Olympic games. I have succeeded after many efforts. Should the institution prosper,—as I am persuaded, all civilized nations aiding, that it will,—it may be a potent, if indirect, factor in securing universal peace. Wars break out because nations misunderstand each other. We shall not have peace until the prejudices which now separate the different races shall have been outlived. To attain this end, what better means than to bring the youth of all countries periodically together for amicable trials of muscular strength and agility? The Olympic games, with the ancients, controlled athletics and promoted peace. It is not visionary to look to them for similar benefactions in the future.

The Century Magazine 53, 31 (November 1896) 39–53

THE OLYMPIC GAMES
Miss Maynard Butler

"O King!" said the Crown Prince Konstantine, in his address the opening day of the Festival in Athens, "the International Convention, held in Paris, decided that the Olympic Games should first be celebrated in the land in which they originated and in which they reached such excellence"—therein is contained the history of the Premiers Jeux Olympiques Internationaux. To bring together the strong, the active, the skilled men of all nations, upon the common ground of physical perfection, and to have the first of the friendly contests take place in the chief city of the country from which the ideal of that perfection was derived, was the aim of Coubertin and Bikelas. Through labor and discouragement, led by their President, the Crown Prince Konstantine, the Committee has reached its goal, and may congratulate itself upon a great success.

Well might the London "Times," in a leader some time before the Olympic Festival, say: "We are sorry that in this revival England, and especially Oxford and Cambridge, will not be well represented. For most of the contests we could send competitors whom we could trust, and in some of them, as in cricket and boating, we might fairly expect to hold our own against the world. Possibly on the next occasion, in 1900, when the Games are held at Paris, we shall make a better show, but it will poorly compensate us for having missed the first chance. Olympic games at Paris will have a local color of their own, but it will not be that of Olympic games in Greece, and, as Bacon says, the first precedent, if good, is seldom attained by imitation."

The quiet of Holy Week, preceding the seventy-fifth anniversary of the expulsion of the Turk from Greece, intensified the joy natural to the national celebration. The streets of the city on Good Friday night were densely crowded with the processions of the different parishes, and, unless one had come within doors before nine o'clock, it was impossible to walk from square to square. Squads of boys and men preceded the four, sometimes six and eight, priests who held extended above their heads a rectangular V-shaped cloth of silk, upon which the figure of the Saviour, done in embossed work, lay. Each priest carried a large altar-taper, and the men, women, and little children who followed, the candles. The figure thus carried, typifying the bier of the Lord, and the funeral marches played by the bands, with the hymns and cries of "Kyrie eleison! Kyrie eleison!" in a weird, half-chanting tone, presented an extraordinary scene. As every such bier passed, the people on the pavements crossed themselves in the waving manner evidently customary here, unlike the fashion of the Roman Catholics, and rather grand than otherwise. Portions of regiments with reversed arms (as for funerals), schools and choirs passed in endless numbers, and not until two o'clock was Athens quiet. As one looked over the balcony of the Hotel Angleterre, a diplomat pointed out her Majesty Queen Olga, clad in black, walking incognito and in the very closest crush of the untidy but quietly devout throng, leaning upon the arm of her relative, the Grand Duke Georgius of Russia, betrothed of the Princess Marie. The perfect simplicity and evident unconsciousness of the act quite won one's heart.

Saturday the church bells were tolling, at intervals, all day, and the shops were closed. But the streets seemed to grow fuller and fuller. Easter is, in the Greek Church, rather more than in the Roman, a time of especial demonstrations of joy, and the week ushered in by it this year, having the gayeties of the Independence Day and the opening of the Stadion added to it, was exceptionally full of excitement. At twelve o'clock Saturday night the fast of the forty days—no mere form in this country—was over, and in every true Athenian house a meal was prepared upon the return from the services. Sunday morning dawned bright and clear, but, with a rapidity not equaled even by the changes of the New England coast, clouds had gathered by ten o'clock, and it became evident that the ceremony of the unveiling of the statue of Avéroff would have to take place in the rain. But it was nevertheless an interesting event, the effect of which was singularly heightened by the fact that the man whom the Athenian sculptor Brutos had molded is still living, at the age of eighty-two, and had intended to be present. His great age, and the strain of emotion unavoidable upon such an occasion, however, induced him to follow the advice of his physicians and remain in Alexandria. The address of Mons. Philemon, General Secretary of the Olympian Games and a former Mayor of Athens, reviewed the benefactions of the patriotic banker, and formally presented the statue to Athens. It was received by the Crown Prince in a few dignified words, in which he laid stress upon the latest gift of Averoff— the restoration of the Stadion. Monday morning was beautiful, and the Te Deum in the metropolis, in commemoration of the deliverance from the Turkish invaders, drew great masses of people about the doors and the streets leading to the church. The fine voices of ten men and boys rang out from the choir, without accompaniment, as the royal family entered, the body of the church being filled with a mass of officers, guards, ladies, and servants, men and small children of every class, all standing — Greek churches affording no seats. The chanting of the Chief Priest in this, as in the three other Greek services I heard, was not pleasant, the tone adopted being thick and rasping in quality and the pitch, though well maintained, being too high for musical effect. The responses of the choir were in every case absolutely pure in quality, and the shading of the voices well managed.

And now excitement in the town reached an intense point: in two hours and a half the long-talked of moment would arrive, the magnificent Stadion be opened and the Games begin. In the chief hotels and cafés people scrambled for places, and in a large number of private houses breakfasts were being given and parties arranged to go to the great horseshoe-shaped inclosure.

Only the carriages of the Ministers, Committee, and the officers of state are admitted over the line drawn by the police, and the occupants even of these are obliged to alight before the gate is reached. M. Mataxas, the architect chosen by Averoff to make the restoration, is, as is fitting, also a Greek by birth. He has spent infinite care and thought and research upon his work, and the result is superb. The sweep of the semicircle, the tiers upon tiers of seats, the double-faced statues, found while the work was going on, the marble chairs for the King and Queen, in the ancient shape, the hills rising up either side, and now covered with people — make a picture beyond the fancy of the foreigner. Seats are found with little difficulty, those provided for foreign correspondents and the honorary members of the Committee being generously chosen from among the best. The Royal Family enter, the "Olympiode Ymnoe" begins, the composer Samaras directing; the Crown Prince formally presents the Stadion to the King, and requests him to declare it opened. The King replies: "I proclaim the opening of the First International Olympic Games in Athens. Long live the nation! Long live the Greek people!"— and the Games begin. Across the field, in answer to the Herald's trumpet, come two Hungarians, a Chilian, a Frenchman, a German, an Englishman and an American, to run the 100-meters race. Lane, of the United States, must have felt a sense of responsibility as he took his place, and if, silent sympathy is conveyed in the air, he must also have been impelled by the hopes of his countrymen, who believed in him — and not in vain, for it is the American who arrives first! Cheer upon cheer resounds, in which the Greeks join heartily, for our nation is popular here, thanks to its genial representative at the Court. The starter's shot is fired for the second heat; again it is an American, Curtis, of the Boston Athletic Association, who outdistances a Greek, an Englishman, two Frenchmen, a Dane, and a Hungarian. The third heat, and Burke, of the same Association wins over a Swede, two Greeks and three Germans. His time is 11¼ seconds; Lane's 12⅕. Curtis's 12⅕. The first event is over, and the victory in each heat belongs to the United States. The time is posted and the flag unfurled, and Americans examine their list of the day's sports eagerly. The hop, skip and jump, contested by two Frenchmen, four Germans, one Greek and by Connolly, of the Boston Athletic Association, is won by Connolly, who makes a distance of 13 meters and 71 centimeters, leaving behind all his fellow-competitors in amazement, and filling the hearts of his compatriots with joy. He leaves the field amidst a storm of applause, and a little son of an American professor residing in Athens, is unable to repress his delight, and hurrahs in his young voice again and again. In the 800-meter run, next announced, a most beautiful stride is exhibited by the Australian Flack, who wins in 2 minutes 10 seconds in the first heat, and Lermusiaux, of the Paris Racing Club, called a famous runner in France, takes the second in 2 minutes 16⅗ seconds. No Americans appear in this event. Then comes the throwing of the disk, in which

Grisel, of France; Paraskevopoulos and Versis, of Greece; Robertson, of England, the well-known thrower of the hammer; Jensen, of Denmark, Sjöberg, of Sweden, and Garrett of the United States are entered. As Garrett arrived in Athens only the night before, and the two Greeks are popular heroes in this national sport, Americans tremble for their country. But unnecessarily. The accustomed cunning of the skillful shot-putter does not forsake him. His second throw rectifies the swerve of his first, and with his last he leaps past the marks of the Greeks and is the winner. Frantic though the enthusiasm of the Princeton and Boston athletes is, proud as are the old and young Harvard men who rush down to the "cave" to greet Garrett, every foreigner feels with the Greeks, who cannot but be keenly disappointed. There is, for a moment, an uncomfortable silence, and then, with their accustomed politeness and never-failing kindliness, they join in the cheers. Let every nation represented at this first international contest in 1896 remember this lesson in courtesy taught them by the Greeks.

"I couldn't have congratulated my opponent if he had beaten me on my own ground, as a Greek fellow down in the cave did me," said an American athlete a few days afterward — "and it was a mighty fine thing to do." It was indeed.

Jamison, of Princeton, and Burke again, add to the list of victories and complete the events of the day. Great excitement prevails in the streets all the evening, and timid attempts at an imitation of the college rah-rah-rah are made by the Athenian youths. Tuesday, Wednesday and Thursday morning are occupied by shooting and fencing contests, the former being opened by the Queen, who fired the first shot. Tuesday afternoon at the Stadion included a hurdle race, run in two heats, won respectively by Grantley Goulding, of England, and Curtis, of the United States, the deciding heat for the prize to be run on Friday. Clark, of the Boston Athletic Association, won the long jump in a distance of 6 meters 35 centimeters, his Greek fellow-competitors showing great possibilities, which all athletes agree will make them formidable in 1900. Putting the shot was Garrett's second victory, his distance being 11 meters 22 centimeters; Gouskos, a superb Greek thrower being second. The double-hand dumbbell lifting was won by Jensen, the Dane, who put up 111½ kilograms; and the single-hand by Eliott, of London, who put up 71 kilograms.

Then came the first and only American loss, their man Blake, the well-known long distance runner, being second to Flack the Australian, who did the 1,500-meter race in 4 minutes 33 second. Flack's rhythmic swing of arms and feet was a pleasant sight, and his stride the American athletes say, is like Kilpatrick's, the New York winner.

The day closed with America the victor in four out of seven events. On Wednesday morning the contest with foils was won by Gravelotte, a Frenchman, and in the afternoon, at the Velodrome, at Phaleron, a Frenchman also came in first in the bicycle race. The ride, a distance of 100 kilometers, was done in 3 hours 8 minutes 19 seconds, by Flameng, who was pluckily followed by two Greeks, one of whom, Kolettis, persisted to the end, though his bicycle broke twice during the course.

Thursday was occupied with swimming matches, in which many fine exhibitions were made, especially by the Greek sailors and the Hungarian; by exhibitions on parallel bars, with rings, etc, at the Stadion, and by a concert in the evening. On Friday, the day of the Marathon race, the crowds from all the provinces increased, and the struggle for food in the hotels and cafés became so uncomfortable that for an hour the doors of the most popular ones near the palace were locked, that those already within might be served. The final course in the hurdle-jumping, the first of the events in the afternoon, was won by Curtis, of Boston, over Goulding, of England; leaping with a pole by Tyler of Princeton, over Hoyt, of Boston — the other competitors, Greeks and Germans, retiring before them; the wrestling by Schumann of Germany. The runners from Marathon were to leave that place, twenty-four and three quarter miles away, at exactly two o'clock, and by half-past four the strain of curiosity as to the man first on the road was raised to an unbearable pitch by the rushing of an orderly along the path to tell the King who was first. "Is it a Greek?" the crowd began to shout, and a representative of the chief Athens morning paper left his seat, determined to find out. He returned in about five minutes, his brown eyes dancing, and said, "A Greek, a Greek!" and then arose a tremendous sound. Not even the runner of old who fell dead at the feet of the King was awaited with keener interest; and as he came up to the gates, a brown-faced, white and blue clad figure, making the countryman's sign of greeting to his Princes, the whole sixty thousand people within and the forty thousand with-out the gates joined in a loud cry. Either side of him as he approached the seat of the King, ran the handsome Princes and as he made his obeisance each flung an arm about him. Greece had indeed won, and every stranger rejoiced with her. There will not be soon a scene like that again. An officer of the war-ship San Francisco, familiar with many lands and who has seen many strange sights, was heard to say that he knew nothing comparable with it. Long may the spontaneous, courteous country live, and long the noble, generous, manly family at its head! May its politi-cal life be unified, its resources be developed, its incomparable art treasures be preserved! May it come more closely into touch with the nations of western Europe and American, yet retain untouched its own peculiar character!

And now, what have American athletes learned from this first International Olympic con-test? Much. They return undoubtedly the first among the twelve nations represented. They have done their work well and have received the unaffected admiration of their fellow-competitors. They have been charmingly entertained by the Athenians, and more than graciously received by the head of the Committee, the Crown Prince Konstantine, and Prince George, whose unflagging attention to their duties might serve as a model of faithfulness. And from this success, attention, and graciousness they will, as observing Americans, learn two things: one, that as athletes they must look to their laurels in long-distance running; and the other, as men, that they must remember in 1900 and 1904 the pattern of generosity in defeat set them by the Athenians in 1896.

The prizes, diplomas, olive branches, and special vases, cups, etc. were distributed to-day by the King. An ode, in ancient Greek, upon the Olympic Revival was read by Robertson, of Oxford, and several wreaths of laurel were presented by Germans, Hungarians, and Danes to the Crown Prince as President of the International Committee. This evening a soirée is held in the Hotel Grand Bretagne, in honor of the athletes and foreign correspondents — and the great festival of joy will be over. [Athens, April 15.]

Outlook 53 (30 May 1896): 993–995

HIGH HURDLES AND WHITE GLOVES
Thomas P. Curtis

The way our U.S. team was selected for those first modern Olympic games held at Athens in 1896 would seem extraordinary to an athlete of 1932. In effect we selected ourselves. When an invitation was received in this country, asking the United States to send representatives to Greece, the powers of the Boston Athletic Association went into a huddle and decided that the B.A.A. had a pretty good track team which had met with reasonable success at home and that the Association could afford to send a group of seven athletes and a coach to the first Olympiad. Princeton University also decided to send over a small team, and as the amateur standing of all was satisfactory, that was all there was to it. Naïve? Yes, but so was the whole idea, which had blossomed in the brain of Baron Pierre de Coubertin. So were the competitors and so were the spectators. So were most of the governments which sent representatives to Athens, and so were many of the incidents, which seem just as funny today as they did at the time, perhaps even more so, in view of modern developments.

We sailed by the southern route to Naples, passing the Azores, and we kept in condition as well as we could by exercising on the afterdeck. At Gibraltar the British officers invited us to use their field for practice, and we managed to get rid of our sea legs to a certain extent. But when we arrived at Athens on the day preceding the opening of the games — after crossing Italy by train, spending twenty-fours hours on the boat from Brindisi to Patras, and then crossing Greece by train — we were not exactly in what today's Olympic coaches would call the pink.

Nor did our reception at Athens, kind and hospitable as it was, help. We were met with a procession, with bands blaring before and behind, and were marched on foot for what seemed miles to the Hôtel de Ville. Here speech after speech was made in Greek, presumably very flattering to us, but of course entirely unintelligible. We were given large bumpers of the white-resin wine of Greece and told by our advisors it would be a gross breach of etiquette if we did not drain these off in response to the various toasts. As soon as this ceremony was over, we were again placed at the head of a procession and marched to our hotel. I could not help feeling that so much marching, combined with several noggins of resinous wine, would tell on us in the contests the following day.

My doubts were deepened on meeting the proprietor of our hotel. He asked me in what events I was going to compete, and when I named particularly the high hurdles, he burst into roars of laughter. It was some time before he could speak, but when he had calmed down enough, he apologized and explained that it had seemed to him inexpressibly droll that a man should travel 5000 miles to take part in an event which he had no possible chance to win. Only that afternoon, the Greek hurdler in practice had hung up an absolutely unbeatable record.

With a good deal of anxiety, I asked him what this record was. He glanced about guiltily, led me to a corner of the room, and whispering in my ear like a stage conspirator, said that the record was not supposed to be made public but that he had it on unimpeachable authority that the Greek hero had run the hurdles in the amazing time of nineteen and four-fifths seconds!

Again he was overcome with mirth but recovered to say that I should not be too discouraged, perhaps I might win second place. As I had never heard of anyone running the high hurdles, 110 meters, in such amazingly slow time, I decided that I should not take the mental hazard of the Great Greek Threat too seriously.

One of the British hurdlers, however, was more disturbing. He had quite a number of medals hung on his waistcoat and these he insisted on showing me. "You see this medal," he would say. "That was for the time I won the championship of South Africa. This one here was from the All-England games" — and so on. He was perfectly certain that he would win the Olympic event, but he, too, consoled me with the possibility of my taking second place. I never met a more confident athlete.

The next day the games opened in a superb stadium, gift of a wealthy and patriotic Greek, built of Pentelic marble and seating seventy-five thousand spectators. Around and above it, on three sides, rose bare hills, which provided free space for the local deadheads — a sort of Athenian Coogan's Bluff. In building the stadium, the Greeks had unearthed four statues which had marked the turns in the ancient Athenian games held on the same site, and these were now installed at the four turns of the new cinder track for the first Olympic revival. The track, by the way, was well intended and well built, but it was soft, which accounted in part for the slow times recorded. After the opening ceremonies before the King and Queen, the taking of the Olympic oath, and the lighting of the Olympic torch, we proceeded to business.

The first event was a trial heat in the 100-meter dash. Entered in the heat with me were a German, a Frenchman, an Englishman, and two Greeks. As we stood on our marks, I was next to the Frenchman, a short stocky man. He, at that moment, was busily engaged in pulling on a pair of white kid gloves, and have some difficulty in doing so before the staring pistol. Excited as I was, I had to ask him why he wanted the gloves. "Ah-ha!" he answered, "zat is because I run before ze Keeng!"

Later, after the heat was run, I asked him in what other events he was entered. He was in only two, "ze *cent metre* and ze marathon," to me a curious combination. He went on to explain his method of training. "One day I run a lettle way, vairy queek. Ze next day, I run a long way, vairy slow."

I remember the last day of the games. The marathon had been run. All the other runners who had finished had completed the race. The King and Queen had left, and the stadium was about to be closed for the night. And then, all alone, the little Frenchman came jogging into the stadium, running "vairy slow," and passed in front of the empty thrones of the Royal Box, wearing his little white kid gloves, even though "ze Keeng" was not there to see them.

When it came to high hurdles, I learned how the Greek Threat had managed to spend nineteen and four-fifths seconds in covering the distance. It was entirely a matter of technique. His method was to treat each hurdle as a high jump, trotting up to it, leaping and landing on both feet. At that, given the method, his time was really remarkable. In the finals, I met the confident Britisher who was, in fact, a better hurdler than I. However, he was not so fast on the ground, and I beat him in the stretch, whereupon he stopped neither to linger nor to say farewell, but went from the stadium to the station and took the first train out of Athens.

Apropos of the Greek Threat it is only fair to add that Greece, as a nation, knew very little about modern track and field sports. They had imported an English trainer named Perry shortly before the games. In the sprints, the middle, and the long distance runs, he could give them useful hints on form and condition, but the pole vault and the hurdles and high jump were too difficult for satisfactory results from any such athletic "cramming." The Greek hopes — aside from those of my hotel proprietor — centered on two events, the discus and the marathon run. For the first they had the classic example of the *Discobolus* to study and analyze, and for the second they had the equally classic precedent of Pheidippides, who had run over almost identically the same course to death and immortal glory.

In the discus they were doomed to disappointment by a performance which illustrates as well as anything else the naïveté of the contests. We had on our team a Princeton representative, Robert Garrett, a very powerful, long-armed athlete who had never seen a discus, let alone thrown one, but who decided to enter the event just for the sport of it. When the moment came, the Greek champion assumed the attitude of the *Discobolus*, which incidentally is a very trying and complicated attitude, and proceeded to make three perfect throws in the classic manner.

Garrett, with no knowledge of form or of how to skim the awkward discus, caused infinite merriment by running up to the mark and completely flubbing his first two attempts. On his third attempt, aided by his great strength, great length of arm, and an enormous amount of good luck, he succeeded in "sailing" the discus to a new record, beating the champion by almost a foot. This was a tragedy for Greece, but high comedy for us.

I think it was on the third or fourth day of the games that the Americanization of Europe began. Our team sat in a box not far from that of the King and whenever the circumstances seemed to call for it, such as a win for the United States or a particularly good performance, we gave the regular B.A.A. cheer, which consisted of "B.A.A. — Rah! Rah! Rah!" three times, followed by the name of the individual performer who had evoked it. This cheer never failed to astonish and amuse the spectators. They had never heard organized cheering in their lives. During one of the intervals between events we were much surprised to see one of King George's aides-de-camp, an enormous man some six feet six tall, walk solemnly down the track, stop in front of us, salute and say: "His Majeste, ze King, requests zat you, for heem, weel make once more, zat fonnee sound." We shouted "B.A.A. -Rah! Rah! Rah!" three times and then ended up with a mighty "Zito Hellas!" whereupon the King rose and snapped into a salute and everyone applauded vigorously.

King George was much intrigued by this barbarian custom. When we breakfasted with him the day after the completion of the games, he asked us to cheer in the middle of breakfast. If we had only known then about the movies and Hollywood and Henry Ford and mass production, we might have considered ourselves the advance agents of Americanization and committed suicide.

When we left Athens, more than a hundred undergraduates of the University were at the station and gave us an organized cheer in Greek — such as never was heard before on sea or land. It was a pity that a group of Elis were not there to respond with the Frog Chorus -"Brek-ek-kek, co-ax, co-ax"— but probably the Greeks would not have understood it, Greek though it claims to be.

On the whole, our team did very well. William Hoyt won the pole vault, Ellery Clarke the high jump and broad jump, Tom Burke the 100 meters and 400 meters. I won the high hurdles, and Arthur Blake was second in, I think, the 1500 meters. Our finest performances were by the two sons of General Paine of Boston, Sumner and John, who won the revolver and pistol contests against the pick of the military and civilian shots of Europe. These were really outstanding achievements.

For the aquatic events we had on our team a very fast short-distance swimmer, who had won many races in warm American swimming pools. He journeyed to the Piraeus on the day of the first swimming competition blissfully ignorant that even the Mediterranean is bitterly cold in the month of April.

He had traveled 5000 miles for this event, and as he posed with the others on the edge of the float, waiting for the gun, his spirit thrilled with patriotism and determination. At the crack of the pistol, the contestants dived headfirst into the icy water. In a split second, his head reappeared, "Jesu Christo! I'm freezing!"; with that shriek of astonished frenzy he lashed back to the float. For him the Olympics were over.

The Greek people, from high to low, treated us with great courtesy and friendliness. Sometimes their kindness was embarrassing. If we had won an event, our return to our quarters would be attended by admiring followers shouting "*Niké!*" — "Victory!" Shopkeepers would herd us into their shops and invite us to help ourselves to their wares gratis. One merchant successfully insisted on each of us taking three free neckties. Gazing on their color and design, I saw a new meaning in the phrase, *timeo Danaos, et dona ferentes*. But the whole thing was so simple, so naïve, that in spite of our amusement, we were touched and pleased.

On the last day of the games, Greece came into her own. Loues, a Greek donkey boy, led all the other contestants home in a great marathon. As he came into the stretch, a hundred and twenty-five thousand people went into delirium. Thousands of white pigeons, which had been hidden in boxes under the seats, were released in all parts of the stadium. The handclapping was tremendous. Every reward which the ancient cities heaped on an Olympic victor, and a lot of new ones, were showered on the conqueror, and the games ended on this happy and thrilling note.

We stayed on in Athens for about ten days of entertainment and merrymaking. I recall especially a great reception at Mme. Schliemann's and also a picnic in the Vale of Daphne, which the Crown Prince, later King Constantine, and his brother, Prince George attended. Their Royal Highnesses were extremely interested in learning how American baseball was played. We explained to them the functions of the pitcher, catcher, infielders, and outfielders and the theory of running bases.

Nothing would do, however, except a demonstration, and as the picnic yielded little in the way of paraphernalia, we were obliged to demonstrate with a walking stick and an orange. We appointed Prince George pitcher and the Crown Prince catcher, and, for my sins, I was named batter. At the first orange pitched, I struck not wisely but too well, and the stick cut the orange in halves, both of which the Crown Prince caught in the bosom of his best court uniform. He was a good sport and joined in the somewhat subdued laughter, but I think the Americanization of Greece ended right there.

The Sportsman 12, 1 (July 1932): 60–61

THE NEW OLYMPIAN GAMES
Rufus Richardson

It seemed a hazardous experiment to institute a series of international athletic contests under the name of Olympic Games. The sun of Homer, to be sure, still smiles upon Greece, and the vale of Olympia is still beautiful. But no magician's wand and no millionaire's money can ever charm back into material existence the setting in which the Olympic Games took place. It is only in thought that we can build again the imposing temples and porches, set up the thousands of statues, make the groves live again, bring back the artists, musicians, poets, philosophers, and historians, who came both to gaze and to contribute to the charm of the occasion. Never again will athletes move in such an athletic atmosphere, winning eternal glory in a few brief moments. The full moon of the summer evening with Pindar's music and wreaths upon the victor's brow belong to the days that are no more, to the childhood of the world free and joyous. We are those "upon whom the ends of the world are come."

Another race hath been and other palms are won.

For most of us life is serious, if not sad.

But although no athletic contest will ever have the splendor of Olympia, the experiment of international contests was not really hazardous. The athletic *habit* may be in a measure lost, as has been shown especially in Greece, but the athletic instinct never dies. Let a man try how far he can jump or throw a weight almost anywhere, in any civilized county, and for aught I know also among savages, and the unoccupied bystanders feel as irresistible impulse to join in an impromptu athletic contest. The desire to outleap, outrun, and outwrestle is just as strong now as it was when old Homer recorded: "A man has no greater glory as long as he lives than what he does with his hands and his feet." Clergymen and professors over fifty years old have been caught in summer-time in the North Woods, or elsewhere showing more pride in a long jump than in their learning or their standing.

Back of Olympia, against which the philosoper Xenophanes protested, and back of the modern "athletic craze" so feared by some of the serious friends of the colleges, lies the athletic instinct, which has caused history thus to repeat itself. The International Committee was safe in appealing to this instinct, and the first contest at Athens has been a brilliant success.

If it did not have the old setting at Olympia, which was the growth of ages, all that could be done to replace this was provided. The restored Panathenaic Stadion; innumerable bands of music; concerts; illuminations at Athens and Peiraeus; torchlight processions and fireworks; the presence of the royal family of Greece in the Stadion, accompanied by the King of Servia, the Grand Duke George of Russia, whose engagement to Princess Marie, the daughter of the King of Greece, was announced on the day before the opening of the games, and the widow of the late Crown Prince Rudolf of Austria with her two daughters; and more than all, a maximum attendance of sixty thousand people, gave something to replace Olympia, and almost persuaded one that the old times had come around again when there was nothing more serious to do than to outrun, outleap and outwrestle.

There were some intellectual accompaniments of the occasions. The "Antigone" of Sophokles was presented twice at Athens and once at the Peiræus, in the original text, with music for the choruses by Mr. Sakellarides, a Greek well versed in Byzantine music, who also with his fine voice and boundless enthusiasm officiated as chorus-leader. The newspapers, which for the most part represented a rival faction in music, had for some time made merriment at the idea of Sakellarides vying as a composer with Mendelssohn. For the first hour of the first presentation the theatre was in a hubbub, but Sophokles, who is always effective, silenced it. The music, which was somewhat uniform, achieved a triumph, in that some of the opposing faction confessed that it was not so bad as they had expected, which is a good deal for a musical partisan to say. The greatest wrong done to Sophokles was that the actors of the two leading roles, Kleon and Antigone, put little soul into their parts, which made the play a disappointment to one who had seen "Antigone" presented at Vassar College in 1893. A fine opportunity was lost.

The dead also were not forgotten. A procession of native and foreign scholars marched past the Academy to Kolonos, and with appropriate ceremonies placed wreaths upon the somewht neglected monuments of Karl Gottfried Müller and Charles Lenormont.

But the kernel of everything was the events of the Stadion. Here for a week everything centred. The wiles of the diplomats ceased. There was no call for "poring over miserable books." Bodily excellence, especially the power to gather all one's forces together for one supreme effort, came to the front. Almost anyone who had gifts of strength or skill had an opportunity to display them and to win generous applause. Young men full of the *gaudium certaminis* were the heroes of the hour.

An ancient Greek, had he come to life again, would have missed some of the events of his old games. The pancration, with its brutalities, was happily lacking. Even boxing was omitted. He might have asked with some reason why the pentathlon was not retained as a test of general athletic excellence. He would hardly have acquiesced in the substitution of the boat-races at Phaleron for the ancient chariot-races, and would doubtless have thought the pistol and rifle shooting a poor substitute for throwing the javelin. Probably he would have approved of the swimming matches, and looked curiously at the fencing. But of all the additions to his old list of games he would have found lawn-tennis and bicycling the most removed from ancient athletics. Considering, however, not the shades of ancient Greeks but the modern world, ought not the patrons of the contest to have persuaded Englishmen and Americans to add to the sports games of football and baseball?

It was a happy thought of the committee to bring the first contest to Greece, the mother of athletics. The visiting contestants were forced into contact with history, and their visit to Greece was an education. The Greek athletes, on the other hand, have received an impulse and a suggestion of higher standards than they had hitherto thought possible. In four years from now they will be among the foremost contestants for athletic honors. The effect will be good on both sides.

Of course it must be conceded that the success achieved at Athens might have been even more brilliant at Paris or New York, but who knows? Two circumstances were adverse to Athens: First, it is a small city of only 130,000 inhabitants, and some of its best citizens felt that a wrong was being done to it in thrusting upon it the burden of an honor to which it was inadequate, and that foreigners would simply come to "see the nakedness of the land." But in spite of the shortness of the time allowed for preparation, Athens responded nobly to the call, and put the doubters to shame. It was, however, chiefly George Averoff who, by furnishing the money to restore the old Panathenaic Stadion, contributed to this success. The visitors are unanimous in their praise of the adequate and warm hospitality afforded them by the Athenian people.

The other difficulty was the season of the year, and this difficulty proved in a measure irremediable. The time was prescribed within somewhat narrow limits. Summer was excluded on account of heat, and winter on account of certain bad weather. October was a possibility but, some time in the spring was the natural time of Greece to be the place. Perhaps a mistake was made in choosing a date a few weeks earlier than necessary. But even the first part of May would hardly have obviated the difficulty, which excluded, for example, the New York Athletic Club, *viz.*, that it was impossible for the members to get into good form for track athletics, and take the field in a country so distant as Greece so early in the year. The same feeling was expressed by the Germans, who did come. This consideration, to say nothing of some incipient national jealousies, lessened somewhat the number of contestants from several countries. England notably was not well represented.

For America the time was particulary unfavorable, as it practically excluded college athletes, for whom a visit to Greece was greatly to be desired as an educational stimulus. It was almost impossible for students, especially seniors approaching graduation, to secure leave of absence at this time of the year. Princeton alone of the colleges, perhaps largely through the influence of Professor Sloane, who has been interested in the enterprise from its inception, sent a direct representation of four men: Robert Garrett, Jr., Captain, H. B. Jamison, F. A. Lane, and A. C. Tyler. The Boston Athletic Association sent a delegation composed of Arthur Blake, T. E. Burke, E. H. Clarke, T. P. Curtis, and W. W. Hoyt. J. B. Connolly, of the Suffolk Athletic Club, accompanied them. Blake, Clarke, Hoyt and Connolly were members of the Harvard University, which was thus indirectly represented. In the same way Burke represented Boston University, and Curtis represented the Massachusetts Institute of Technology and Columbia College. Thus the athletes who represented America in the Stadion were all college men, making for America a fair and genuine representation. Greece will not soon forget this frank response from so remote a land. In spite of the poor representation of England and the total defection of Italy, Russia and Turkey, the games took on a fairly international character.

There was also a danger that in the first part of April there might be bad weather. In the first days of May there was certainty of good weather. Still, even in April one might count the danger as slight. But this year the worst that could be expected actually happened. The multitude present at the unveiling of the statue of Averoff at the entrance to the Stadion, on Sunday, the day before the opening of the games, was drenched by a heavy, persistent rain. Clouds also hung heavy and dark over the Stadion all the afternoon of Monday, in spite of which, however, the games went on without interruption. Wednesday was the coldest day since February, and is likely to have caused much illness in connection with the bicycle races and the lawn-tennis tournament, since a cutting north wind swept over the plain of Phaleron where those contests were held. On Thursday, April 9th, the spite of the elements appeared most conspicously. Pentelicus was covered with snow nearly down to its base, an event probably unparalleled in the weather record for this time of the year. On the following Monday the boat-races at Phaleron were postponed, and ultimately given up, on account of a steady gale from the south, and the crew of the San Francisco lost their chance in the races, as they had to leave the Peiræus the next morning. The distribution of the prizes, which was to take place on the following day, was prevented by a rain like that of Easter. The crowd dispersed after an hour of fruitless waiting under umbrellas. All this more than justified the forbodings of the King, who remarked, when he heard of the time proposed for the games, that we often had bad weather about Independence day; and sent the visitors away with the false impression that Greece did not have much advantage over more northern countries in its spring weather.

For Greece the time was in one way conspicuously, brilliantly opportune. Sunday, April 5th, was the Greek Easter, which on this year concided with the European Easter. This was as usual celebrated with pomp and noise like our Fourth of July, the law prohibiting the sale of large torpedoes being in abeyance on that day. The next day, the opening day of the games was the anniversary of Greek Independence, when all the army is wont to appear in fine array. This made a congeries of holidays almost bewildering to one wishing to be quite sure that he was celebrating, and gave to the period of Easter a character befitting the name given it by the Greeks, "Lambri," the brilliant. Easter itself was made the proagon to the games by the unveiling of the statue of Averoff.

The attendance in the Stadion, in spite of cold weather, ran up to 35,000 on the first day. It was somewhat less on subsequent days until Friday, the last great day, when the Stadion was filled to its utmost capacity, i.e., with 50,000 people. But outside and above the enclosing wall of the Stadion, especially on the west side, where the hill runs up much higher than this wall, were congregated from seven to ten thousand more, poor people, a sea of down-turned faces, reminding one of those old Athenians who, not getting into the theatre, contented themselves with "the view from the poplar." Many more stood outside the entrance to the Stadion, just across the Ilissos, on ground even lower than the floor of the Stadion, where they could see nothing of what was going on inside, but could only catch something of the spirit of the occasion from proximity. On Friday probably nearly one hundred thousand people were massed in and about the Stadion, besides which the whole road to Marathon was lined with spectators.

Entrance to the Stadion was, according to our ideas, cheap enough, being two drachmas for the lower half and one for the upper. The drachma, which at par is a franc, owing to the depreciated currency of poor Greece, has now a value of only about 12 cents. It is significant of the *res augusta domi* in Greece that the newspapers made an appeal to the committee during the games to reduce the price of admission by one-half, on the ground that heads of families could not afford to pay such prices. The reduction, it was claimed, would fill the Stadion, and the committee was reminded that the object of the games was not to make money, but to have a joyous festival for all. Yawning chasms of seats were indeed repellant. There was absolute safety if every seat was filled. Nothing could give way and cause a panic, inasmuch as the seats of Peiræus stone, wood and marble were but a lining of the solid hillside beneath. But no reduction was made, and when the interest was strong enough the Stadion was filled without it.

The forty thousand or more people who were present at the opening were enough to stir that deep feeling caused by the presence of a multitude, the feeling which made Xerxes weep at the Hellespont. When King George entered with his family, and walked the length of the Stadion, accompanied all the way by the acclamations of this mass, he is said to have declared his emotion to have been so great that he could with difficulty compose himself for the great historic act of reopening the Olympic Games after they had remained in abeyance for fifteen centuries.

The audience, like the athletes, was cosmopolitan. All the tongues of Europe were heard. But all the foreigners together amounted to only a few thousands. At least nineteen-twentieths of the mass were Greeks. For the reason that the greater part of the events of the Stadion were won by foreigners the enthusiasm, which on such occasions is more important than mere numbers or even sharpness of competition, was during much of the time somewhat lacking. The applause was generous, but not wild.

While at Olympia a mass of fellow townsmen watched each contestant with the keenest interest, in the Athenian Stadion, even if the crowd had been tolerably evenly apportioned according to the nationalities of the contestants, it is doubtful whether the intensity of feeling between Frenchman and German, or Englishman and Greek, could have equalled that which was evoked at Olympia between Dorian and Ionian. Indeed the closer the tie and the more intimate the acquaintance the sharper often was the rivalry. A Mantinean could more easily endure defeat at the hands of an Athenian or a Locrian than at the hands of a neighbor from Tegea who might cross his path any day.

In the games at Athens the generous national rivalry was acknowledged by the displaying, after each event, of the flag of the victor's country on a pole erected at the entrance to the Stadion. Our own country became conspicuous at the outset. On Monday, in the first contest of the games, Lane, of Princeton, won the first heat in the 100 meter race. This seemed almost glory enough for one day; but Burke and Curtis proceeded to win the other two heats also. Next came the triple jump, which was won by Connolly, and the first flag that was run up was ours. After the intervention of another event, in which no American was entered, came the throwing of the discus, in which Garrett beat the Greeks at what was regarded as their own game, and again the American flag went up. Next came the 400 meter race, in which both heats were taken by Americans — Jamison and Burke. In the five contests of the day, then, the Americans had won the only two that were decided, and in two of the others they had won all the heats. It is no wonder that the victories of the Americans became the talk of the town. The Hungarians, who alone of all the athletes wore a distinctive mark on the street — straw hats with uniform bands — had scored the first point in the favor of the populace by stepping forward and depositing a wreath at the foot of the Averoff statue at the unveiling. And they remained popular all through the festival. But now they were relegated to the second place. The American athletes were the heroes of the hour. They were lionized and followed by enthusiastic crowds wherever they went at evening. One paper accounted for their prowess by the consideration that in their composite blood "they joined to the inherited athletic training of the Anglo-Saxon the wild impetuosity of the red-skin." Even the Australian, who, on the second day won the 1,500 meter race, was set down as one of us. An educated Greek, whose notions of geography being derived from school days were probably a little vague, said to me, "Australian, why it is the same." Being busy in watching another American victory I had no time to set him right.

This second day went much like the first. Curtis began by winning one of the two heats in the hurdle race, Hoyt coming in second. Then the long jump narrowed down to three Americans, who finished in the order, Clark, Garrett, Connolly. Then in the final heat in the 400 meter race resulted in Burke first, Jamison second. Then, after a close contest, Garrett succeeded in putting the shot farther than his Greek competitor, the favorite of the Stadion, whom the crowd called Hermes, from his fine form and motions.

The Americans were also evidently great favorites with the audience, partly perhaps because they lived so far away as to take the place occupied in Homer by "the blameless Æthiopian," almost beyond the sphere of their jealousies and antipathies. An old priest who sat two seats in front of me kept turning and asking, with smiles, "Is that one of yours?" adding, after an affirmative answer, "Yours are doing well." The danger now was that if the few American spectators made too much demonstration this good-will might be turned to envy.

Three times again this second day the American flag went up, and not until the fifth event, the lifting of heavy weights, did another flag reach the masthead during these two days; then the Danish flag was displayed for the victory in lifting with two hands, and the British flag for the victory with one hand. In the sixth and last event of the second day, the 1,500 meter race, for the first time an American was beaten by a man of another nation, Blake coming in second, while the first place was taken by Flack, an Australian, but that was "the same thing."

It was almost a relief when Wednesday was given up to contests outside the Stadion, and when on Thursday the Germans came out strong on their favorite "Turn" exercise, their squad excelling the Greeks in the accomplishment of more difficult exercises even when the Greeks squads kept better form. The Germans also showed some brilliant individual practice. On this day the Greeks also succeeded in getting their flag to the masthead.

But the gymnastic exercises did not fill the Stadion as the running matches had done, and the individual contest in vaulting the wooden horse, with twenty contestants, and the horizontal bar contest, with about the same number, nearly emptied it. The victories of this day depended on the judgment of a committee, and however fair the award might be, it was, after all, a matter of opinion, and the spectators seeing that the award resulted sometimes from discussion and compromise, kept their own opinion, which was sometimes at variance with that which found expression at the masthead.

The real athletic contest is that which is decided by measurements and time-keeping beyond the possibility of dispute, affording results which the spectators can see for themselves. Such is pre-eminently the run. This, in the present games, as always and everywhere, evoked the keenest interest. It is explicable that for over fifty years at Olympia the games consisted simply of running matches, and that they were always regarded as the central events. It is no wonder that the great apostle, a Hebrew of the Hebrews, was so impressed by this feature of the Greek games that he is constantly alluding to it, saying, "So run," "Ye did run well," "I press toward the mark." In the Athenian Stadion the "cloud of witnesses" also was brought vividly to mind.

With this reassembling in the Stadion on Friday came a heightening of the good will between the Greeks and the Americans, caused by the American athletes displaying little Greek flags besides their own and the distinctive marks of orange and black for Princeton and the unicorn's head for the Boston Athletic Association. There came also a repetition of the same story of American victories. The first event was the final heat in the 100 meter race, which was won by Burke, with Hoffmann, German second. Then the competition in the high jump narrowed down, like the long jump of Tuesday, to three Americans — Clark, Garrett and Connolly, and was finally won by Clark. Then followed the final heat of the hurdle race, won by Curtis in an exciting contest, the Englishman, Goulding, being neck and neck with him at the last hurdle. Then came the pole vault, which was immeasurably drawn out by the bar being lifted inch by inch for Greek competitors, long before the Americans, Hoyt and Tyler, had felt called upon to take off their "sweaters" and really compete. These two finally settled the contest at a height about a foot and a half above that at which the other contestants had struggled. When Hoyt had won, the King requested him to try a still higher notch, 3.30 meters, which he accomplished to the King's evident satisfaction. But even this was below Hoyt's own previous record. It is worthy of note that in the whole course of games no world record was broken.

Three times already before this the American flag, and no other, had gone up on this day. A detachment of the crew of the San Francisco, who had not, like the other Americans, got tired of cheering on former days, roared lustily everytime the flag was displayed. But with the pole-vaulting America rested its case; and even before its flag went up for this fourth time the great event of this great day came in, preventing envy, and stopping for a time the talk of American invincibility.

The Greeks had waited long for their turn. On Tuesday they thought that in putting the shot their man had won, whereas he had not reached by several inches a mark attained by Garrett in one of his earlier trials. For the first time one then felt the real heaving of the heart of the multitude. Misled by the applause and sharing the general impression, the man intrusted with the posting of the record put up the number of the Greek as the winner. The revulsion of feeling which came with the speedy correction of the error was all the more painful. It was not until a quarter past five on Thursday that the Greek flag was up, when the judges decided that Metropoulos had surpassed the others in the gymnastic exercise with the rings. Then the difference was made manifest between generous applause hitherto bestowed on foreigners and real delight in victory, all the more intense for the long delay and the disappointment. Then it was that if the seats had not rested upon solid earth they might have come down. The young victor after being carried about on the shoulders of the crowd went to the dressing-room, kissed by his father and brother as he passed them. At last the Greeks had an Olympionikes, although it was only in a minor feat of gymnastics. But greater things were yet to come.

The run from Marathon was felt by all the Greeks to be the principal event of the games. National pride would have been deeply touched at losing it. Some of those who had practised this run in anticipation would have been almost, if not quite, content to reach the goal, and like the ancient runner on the day of the great battle, shout out with their remaining breath, *chairete nikomen*, and die.

For this run there were eighteen entries, twelve of them Greeks. Germany, France, Hungary, the United States, and Australia were also represented. Stories were circulated regarding the prowess of the Australian and the American, who had come in first and second in the 1,500 meter race. A mile run, to be sure, was a different thing from coursing that long road from Marathon. Still the Greeks were anxious. The men started from Marathon at two o'clock on Friday, to run into the Stadion to a string stretched out at the Sphenodone, a distance of forty kilometers, or about twenty-five miles. The one hundred thousand people waiting for them in and about the Stadion could know nothing of the stages of the contest, how three foreigners, the dreaded Australian and the dreaded American, and even before them, the Frenchman, took the lead and held it up to a point within a few miles of Athens; how they one by one then felt the awful strain of the agony, and at last succumbed easily to anyone who seemed to have retained more strength than they; and how others, fiercely laboring, came one by one into the first places — stages afterward so graphically told by those who watched them.

Shortly after half-past four a cannonshot, the signal that the leading runner was approaching electrified the mass. The pole vaulting could not go on. After awhile a man wearing the Greek colors, light blue and white, was seen struggling towards the Stadion amid the yells of myriads of throats, "Elleen! Elleen!" (A Greek! A Greek!), and as he made his way through the Stadion the crowd went mad for joy. The stalwart Crown Prince, the president of the games, and the still more stalwart Prince George, the referee, led or rather almost carried, this victor before the royal seat in the Sphenodone, and the usually quiet king himself had meanwhile nearly ripped off the visor of his naval uniform cap in waving it wildly in the air. Pity it would have been had a foreigner won this race. None felt this more keenly than the foreign athletes themselves. All who were present will remember this commotion of the crowd in the Stadion in that moment of victory as one of the greatest scenes of their lives. In the gentle light of the sun of Attica, as it inclines toward the horizon, a light not known elsewhere in the world, the magnificent gift of Averoff, the new Stadion — and yet the old — receives its real dedication. Athletics were crowned in it as never before in modern times. Here was an inspiration for a painter.

The one coveted honor of the games was fairly won by the Greeks, and held almost beyond the reach of envy. Shortly after the winner's arrival came two other Greeks, and then an Hungarian. The next five in order were also Greeks. It was a Greek victory with a vengeance.

The winner, who accomplished the run in the remarkably short time of two hours, fifty-eight minutes and fifty seconds, is Spyridon Loues, a well-to-do farmer, twenty-four years old, from Marousi, a village on the road from Athens to Kephissia, and near to the latter place. He was one of the latest entries for the race. Just before going out to Marathon on Friday he is said to have taken the sacrament from the priest of his native village, saying that he wished to invoke the aid of heaven in his great struggle.

It is difficult to ascertain just what Loues has been doing since the race. A cycle of myths is already growing up about him. It is not uninteresting to be present at this genesis of myths in which the newspapers play a considerable part. It was reported of Loues that he declined all gifts offered him, and declared that all he wished was the royal clemency for his brother, who was in prison. But since he has asserted in print that he has no brother in prison, and since others have asserted for him that he has no brother at all, that myth is for the present disposed of as far as Athens is concerned; but who can stop a fiction that is gone out into all the earth? The same may be said of another story published in the papers here in regard to Garrett, to the effect that after his victory in putting the shot he send home to Princeton this telegram, "Guskos conquered Europe, but I conquered the world." A newspaper man subsequently confessed that this telegram was a fiction of his, but he took great pride in it; for he said it was what Garrett ought to have sent. It was also reported in the papers that the American athletes just before running and jumping bowed their heads and "said American prayers."

But to return to Loues, what seems to be known about him is that while everybody in Athens wanted to get hold of him and give him something — watches, suits of clothes, freedom of barber shops and cafés for life, in short, to spoil him — he hurried away to his native village to share his happiness with his most intimate friends. On Sunday, dressed in fustanella, he took breakfast at the royal palace with the other athletes and members of the committee in charge of the games and bore himself with becoming modesty, but with composure, even in the presence of the King. As he went out he was met at the door by his father, who, as they drove slowly through the streets, enjoyed his son's glory so visibly that one hoped it might be as continuous as that of one of the old Olympic victors, and that he might remain also as modest as before the victory. If he does fulfil the latter wish his victory in this will be even greater than that already won. Of course he has not been able to prevent cafés from being named after him, but has refused an offer of 25,000 drachmas from one man and 100 drachmas a month for life from another, partly, at least, from a desire to keep his amateur standing as an athlete, and perhaps run again from Marathon in 1900.

The thorough and unquestioned amateur spirit of the whole contest is most conspicuously shown in this case of Loues; but besides this a charge made in one of the papers that a German, Schumann, who won the wrestling match, was a professional, was thoroughly sifted and disproved. The entire absence of betting also is another pleasant feature in which the games differed from many other athletic contests of the modern world. Athletics moved on a high plane, and were carried on with a dignity that ought not soon to be forgotten.

The amateur spirit of the occasion was emphasized again at the final scene, the distribution of the prizes. Although the bestowal of a prize can never equal in interest the winning of it, still an enormous crowd had gathered in the Stadion on Wednesday morning after the disappointment of Tuesday. It was the gala day of the festival, with no anxious straining of mind or muscle, but pervaded by general gladness. The prizes looked very simple, the committee having decided to award no prizes of value. But there lay one prize which an Olympian might well covet, branches of wild olive, fresh from Olympia, to be given to each victor along with his medal and diploma. Those who had won two contests received two branches. When the king had given to each victor his prizes with fitting words and smiles, the crowd appropriated the remainder of the pile of branches. Every twig and every leaf was treasured up as a souvenir of the occasion.

The Crown Prince had offered a silver cup to the victor with the discus. The king for a moment gave place to the Crown Princess, the sister of the Emperor of Germany, who presented this beautiful cup to Garrett. Loues also must needs have something more than the "corruptible crown." He received the magnificant silver cup given by the Frenchman Breal, as well as an ancient vase portraying a race, which he afterwards, with rare good sense, presented to the museum. The appearance of Loues was again the signal for the crowd to turn frantic with joy. Greek flags appeared everywhere, from the big one at the masthead to the little ones carried up into the air by numerous doves. Flags and flowers literally filled the air.

As the participants and patrons of the games reflect over the events of the ten days their unanimous feeling is well expressed in the phraseology employed by one of their number. "I am an optimist," said he, "and I always expected a success but I never expected such a success." Greece has not only won the Marathon run, but it has gained a standing among the nations of the world, whose delegates will never forget their reception here. It is a small and poor kingdom, but like ancient Hellas, great in qualities of soul.

During and since the games events have in one way taken an unexpected turn. So elated were the Greeks with the happy way in which everything was going that they early began to think of having the next meet also at Athens. The thought perhaps did not originate with them. It was reported at first as a suggestion of England, coming as an expression of the Prince of Wales. Nobody seems to have thought of the incongruity of England, which was hardly represented in the present contest, being the proposer; but the proposal was eagerly caught up. King George was only voicing the sentiment of which the air was full, when, at the breakfast given to the athletes at the palace, he expressed the hope that, "in view of the success of the games the strangers who have honored Greece with their presence, and who have been so cordially received, will fix upon our country as a European meeting-place of the nations, as the continuous and abiding field of the Olympic Games." This utterance was seconded a few days later by the following memorial, drawn up and signed by all the American athletes:

To His Royal Highness, Constantine, Crown Prince of Greece.

We, the American participants in the International Olympic Games of Athens, wish to express to you, and through you to the Committee and to the people of Greece, our heartfelt appreciation of the great kindness and warm hospitality of which we have been continually the recipients during our stay here.

We also desire to acknowledge our entire satisfaction with all the arrangements for the conduct of the games.

The existence of the Stadion as a structure so uniquely adapted to its purpose; the proved ability of Greece to competently administer the games; and above all, the fact that Greece is the original home of the Olympic Games; all these considerations force upon us the conviction that these games should never be removed from their native soil.

This memorial, signed also by many resident Americans, had all the more significance from the fact that America had already been designated by the International Athletic Committee as the place for the games in 1904.

But this movement was especially unwelcome to the French, who had counted upon having the games as an ornament to their great exhibition at Paris in 1900. Baron Coubertin, the member of the International Committee for France, and perhaps more than any other one man the originator of the whole project of the revival of the Olympic Games, was too good a diplomatist to give up this great advantage without an effort. In a semi-official conference with the Crown Prince he proposed what he wished to have regarded as a compliance with the general desire: that Athens should have its quadrennial games, and that foreign athletes should be invited to take part in them; but that these games should be called the "Athenaia," as a more suitable name, and that they should take place in 1898, 1902 and so on. That the International Games already projected should be held according to the programme orignially drawn up by the committee: in Paris, in 1900; in America, in 1904; Stockholm 1908; London or Berlin being suggested as the next place, all the great capitals to have their turns sooner or later.

It did not require much perspicacity on the part of the Greeks to see that this was only a seeming compliance, and that the "Athenaia" would be overshadowed by the games at the great capitals which would bear the name "Olympic Games." With them it was *"Aut Cæsar, aut nullus."*

While Coubertin falls back on an international agreement, the Greeks plead that not only is a neutral country the natural gathering-place, but that contrary policy is confronted by a danger threatening to shipwreck the games so successfully launched, viz., that if the games are held in Paris in 1900, Germany will never tolerate waiting twelve years longer for her turn, will perhaps even take umbrage at France being preferred for the first place.

From all this it seems clear that the Olympic Games, wherever they are to be held — and this rests with the International Committee — have become the prize in an international contest, and that it is extremely doubtful whether America secures that prize in 1904.

Scribner's Magazine 20, 3 (September 1896): 267–286

THE OLYMPIC GAMES BY A COMPETITOR AND PRIZE WINNER

G. S. Robertson

To those who followed closely the preliminaries to the revival of the Olympic Meeting, it appeared certain that the games would be a disastrous failure. This was not the case, though the nature of the success obtained can scarcely have corresponded with the expectations of the promoters.

These games differed from other athletic meetings in one most important feature — they did not stand or fall with the excellence of their athletics. Their promoters obviously expected that prodigious athletic results would be obtained, they expected to see the best athletes of the world perform the toilsome journey to Athens to win the olive branch of victory. It was apparently forgotten that few athletes are classical scholars, and that still fewer have either the time or the money to make so long a voyage. Then, too, what we may call the international perspective of the committee was at fault. They seemed to suppose that the participation of all nations was of equal importance to the success of the games. They did not consider, or, if they did, they gave no indication of having done so, that every nation except England and America is still in an absolutely prehistoric condition with regard to athletic sports. Unless England and America took a large share in the Olympic meeting, it was bound to be an athletic failure. In this matter the committee pursued the suicidal policy of devoting the greater share of their attention to Continental athletes. The original programme and book of rules was printed in French. Later on there appeared an edition in German. This, however, was disowned as unofficial by a member of the committee to the present writer, though as a matter of fact it had been sent to the Cambridge Athletic Club as an official document. It differed in some not unimportant particulars from the French edition. But the really notable point is, that no edition of the rules was ever issued in English till very shortly before the games, when a private firm produced one. This, when we consider the importance of English and American athletes to the success of the enterprise, is really an extraordinary fact. It seems as though in the committee's eyes true internationality in athletics was equivalent to international mediocrity.

Of all Anglo-Saxon athletes those at present in residence at Oxford and Cambridge were the most likely to be able to take part in the meeting. The Easter Vacation was exactly suited for a visit to Athens, and the English University man would, of all men, require the least pressure to induce him to pay a visit to Greece. What was done to persuade Oxford and Cambridge men to compete in the Olympic Games? Practically nothing. Two Englishmen represented England on the international committee, but neither of them had any present connection with the Universities. An obscure notice, indeed, was posted up in Oxford and a paragraph inserted in an unimportant Oxford journal, but it was not till March, so far as can be ascertained, that any direct appeal was made to the Presidents of the University Athletic Clubs. Even then the inducements and persuasion directed to them were of the mildest nature. It is, therefore, unjust to blame English athletes in general and University athletes in particular for not having taken part in greater numbers in these games. When an athletic meeting is scarcely advertised at all, and when an invitation to competitors from a certain district is markedly omitted, it is only fair that they should conclude, firstly, that the meeting is unimportant, and secondly that their presence at it is not desired. Of the method in which the committee dealt with the athletes of America, we are not in a position to speak. The manner in which American athletics are organized, and the system by which athletic teams form part of great social clubs enabled a fully equipped team of American athletes to visit Athens. The Boston Athletic Club furnished the greater portion of the team, and there were also two or three excellent athletes from Princeton College. We may venture to say, however, that the effort which this American team made to come to Athens, was not due to any overwhelming persuasion on the part of the international committee, but to the natural enterprise of the American people and to the peculiarly perfect method in which athletics are organized in the United States.

English athletes, seemingly, waited to be invited to go to Athens and consequently, never went. Those, who did go, did not go as representatives of any club, but, for the most part as private pleasure-seekers. They won the 800 and 1,500 meter races, the single-handed weightlifting, the single and double lawn tennis, a victory in *mousiké*, and a second place in several events. Their total number was six, of whom one was resident in Athens. The bulk of the competitors was, therefore, Greek and Continental, and it may be safely asserted that their performances were not of the highest class. In fact, wherever an Anglo-Saxon appeared as a competitor, he defeated his foreign opponents in practically every case. The French, who, we fear, were largely responsible for the mismanagement of the international arrangements, sent several athletes, who were lamentably unsuccessful. In the 800 meters race Lermusiaux, the only even passable runner among them, contrived to win a heat in very poor time, but none of their other runners did anything. Their successes were confined to bicycling and fencing, the latter a form of sport in which they have long excelled, the former a kind of exercise, by many scarcely admitted to the domain of sport, in which they are rapidly conquering a kingdom. The French, in fact, have not progressed so fast in the cultivation of athletics as other Continental nations, who have adopted the practice of them. The reason is somewhat hard to discover, but is probably to be found in a certain inpatience and lack of necessary physique.

The Germans wisely confined themselves for the most part to those gymnastic exercises in which they are so extraordinarily proficient. Three of their party competed in other forms of sport; of these Hofmann of Giessen was a good second in the 100 meters, while Schumann, a little, elderly man, seemd to compete in every event. On the strength of this we have seen him termed "the best all-round athlete at the games," but, in reality, he would have served his reputation better, had he refrained from exhibiting himself in many of the events in which he competed. His victory in the wrestling, however, was gained by sheer pluck and presence of mind, and his gymnastic performances were excellent.

Here we may notice incidentally another fault in the organization of the meeting. This arose from a incorrect idea of the relative importance of '*different branches of athletics.' It may be replied that, if any event is once admitted into the programme of the games, it should be treated as on an equality with all other events. We do not agree with this view. The climax was perhaps reached in connection with the vaulting horse. There were two olive branches, medals and diplomas granted for this exercise, one for leaping the horse, the other for maneuvering upon a horse with pommels. The exercises performed in the first of these divisions seemed to the athletic and ungymnastic eye to be puerile, and those in the second division little less so. One would at least have expected to see some fine running vaulting from a springboard, as in the English gymnasiums. Yet the winners received the same olive branch as the winner of the 100 meters; even the seconds in these absurd gyrations gained the same laurel branch as the second in the Hurdles. They were proclaimed Olympian victors, they returned to their native Germany and Switzerland with a halo of glory, while the second in the 1,500 meters, for instance, a fine runner though quite untrained, had to recross the Atlantic bearing with him the consciousness of merit alone. Of course there can be no graduation of prizes for single events; a winner is a winner, however unimportant be the feat which he has accomplished. But we would suggest that at the next meeting several of these gymnastic and other events should be combined, and a prize awarded for an aggregate of marks. An Olympic wreath is far too precious a thing to be squandered on good form on hopping over a horse or swarming up a rope.

The Germans displayed magnificent style in their squad exercises in the horizontal and parallel bars. In the former case they won without contest; indeed opposition would have been hopeless. In the latter set of exercises, they were opposed by two Greek teams, which performed what may be described as kindergarten evolutions, in perfect time. It seemed to us that any ordinary body of men could have done as well with two days' practice. The Germans, on the other hand, performed difficult exercises in beautiful style, but naturally with a few mistakes. They were at once awarded the prize. The Greek public then, perhaps on this one occasion only, forgot its good manners, and displayed its ignorance of gymnastics, by greeting the decision with yells of "*adika.*"

The Hungarians were the only nation, except the Americans, which attempted to send an all-round team. They certainly possess the art of self-advertisement to a very high degree. They and their blue and white ribbons seemed to be ubiquitous; if one did not meet them driving in a cab with the Hungarian flag at mast-head, one found them blocking the traffic in a compact line stretched across the Rue de Stade. In company with the Philharmonic Society of Coreyra they laid a solemn wreath at the foot of M. Averoff's statue on the Sunday before the games. Unfortunately their athletic performances did not justify their conspicuousness, scarcely indeed their visit. They won one or two second places in the heats, and one of them finished fourth in the Marathon Race, but, as a matter of fact, their only good performer was a swimmer, who seemed to be really first-class. Wonderful tales had been told of their high jumper, but he did not appear. It is noticeable, by the way, that the German high jumper stood at attention for half a minute after each jump, apparently supposing that it was more important to appear to be undisturbed after a jump than to clear a respectable height.

We have not yet described the doings of the English athletes. Mr. Flack, an Australian member of the London Athletic Club, carried off the 800 and 1,500 meter races without any difficulty. He runs with the most perfect ease, and with a stride of superlative length; indeed the Greek journals described his lower limbs as "superhuman." Mr. Goulding, of Gloucester, was undoubtedly a better hurdler than the American who beat him. His defeat was due partly to the fact that the race was run upon cinders, in the American style, to which he was unaccustomed, and partly to a mistake at the start, which lost him at least two yards. He was only beaten by a foot. Mr. Elliott won the single-handed weight-lifting without trouble, but in the double-handed lift he was defeated by an extraordinarily good performer, Jensen, of Denmark. Mr. Gmelin, of Oxford, entered at the last moment for the 400 meters, and gained second place. In the bicycle race from Marathon we were represented by a servant of the British Embassy at Athens. It seems that he would have won had not he collided with a fellow-servant who was accompanying him. A Greek then proved the victor. We are sorry to have to record that it was previously attempted to exclude these two Englishmen from amateur games at Athens on the ground that they were servants, though no one could cast the slightest slur upon their amateurism. This was the more discreditable in the light of their success when they were finally admitted. Mr. Boland, of Christ Church,

Oxford, who happened to be in Athens as a visitor, purchased all requisites on the spot, and was victorious in the single, and, in company with a German, in the double lawn-tennis.

The record of the doings of the American team is practically an account of victory unrelieved by defeat. They were, as they should have been, invincible. Not only did they win almost every event for which they entered, but they also succeeded in gaining second, and sometimes both second and third places in addition. Mr. Garrett, of Princeton, won the Disc and the Weight; Mr. Burke, of Boston, the 100 and 400 meters; Mr. Clark, of Harvard, the high and long jumps. Mr. Hoyt, of Harvard, the pole-jump, Mr. Curtis, of Boston, the Hurdles, and Mr. Connolly, of Suffolk, the triple jump. In the pole-jump and 1,500 meters they gained second place, and in the high and long jumps both second and third places. It must be remembered that the team was formed solely to compete in track and field athletics, though one member entered for the swimming, in which he was not successful. Two Americans at large, the brothers Paine, accomplished striking performances in the revolver shooting, winning two events with scores of 442 in each as against scores of only 205 and 285 made by a Greek and a Dane.

The other foreign countries sent few athletes of note. A Swiss, resident in Greece, was victorious on the vaulting horse with pommels, an Austrian won the 500 meters swimming race, and a Dane the two-handed lifting of weights. The only Italian competitor, who walked from Milan to Athens, in order, as he supposed, to get himself into proper training, was disqualified on his arrival.

It now remains for us to discuss the most interesting point of all — the form shown by the Greeks themselves. It seems to be an undoubted fact that, except for throwing a primitive discus, a primitive hop, step and jump, and a modicum of lawn-tennis, athletics were absolutely unknown to the Greeks till two years ago. Then the nation was seized with a remarkable fit of athleticism. A number of clubs were started, and athletics have been pursued with unabated vigour ever since. At the present moment one sees athletics being practised almost at every street corner. Sometimes one discovers infants putting a rude weight, some six times too heavy for them; at other times one finds every man and boy in a quarter of the town long-jumping, with a policeman and a soldier to keep the course clear. And there seems to be every likelihood that the enthusiasm will continue. The result so far has been that the Greeks have obtained a very notable degree of success, considering the shortness of their training. This is the more remarkable if we consider the disadvantages against which they have had to contend. Their physical gifts do not favour athletics, their disposition is on the whole opposed to active exercise, and their climate renders violent exertion difficult. The great danger is lest they may be led to suppose that they are already a great athletic nation, and do not any longer need elaborate training. It might be thought that their defeats in the Stadium would have persuaded them that they are not yet far advanced in athletic skill, but popular enthusiasm is never logical. Their journalists tend to encourage any nascent feeling of conceit which they may possess. They would not admit for a moment that a Greek over middle height is an exception, that Greeks are usually short and slightly corpulent in figure, and that they perhaps require more training than most nations to induce in them an athletic habit. In fact it is a commonplace for them to compare a well-built Greek to the Hermes of Praxiteles. No modern Greek could possibly resemble Praxiteles' Hermes in the least.

We must give Greece full credit for what she has already accomplished in athletics, but it would be fatal to forget to qualify our admission by remembering that her progress is only great in comparison to the shortness of the time which it has occupied. To deal with their performances in detail — they won undoubted victories in the rings and rope-climbing, in which their champions easily distanced their rivals, and in the weight putting Gouskos made a very good appearance. It was interesting to see how his style improved during the competition, owing to his careful imitation of his American rival. The latter only won by an inch, but was putting two or three feet below his proper form. This was due to the size of the square, which had sides of two meters, and therefore corresponded with no known rules. The blunder was the more remarkable as this event purported to be held under English rules.

In the Disc-throwing the Greeks were beaten, contrary to all expectation, by Mr. Garrett, of Princeton. It is true that he only won by a few inches, but it is not true that he was not the best disc-thrower in the contest. The Greeks had practised with the disc for a considerable time, and indeed it is an ancestral sport of theirs. The American, whether he had practised with anything resembling a disc before or not, undoubtedly had never seen a disc like that with which he threw till the morning of the contest. What, then, is the explanation? Simply this—the best of the Greek throwers was not really good at all. 95 feet is an absurdly short distance to throw a flat missile of under four and a half pounds. Had English or American athletes practised the sport, the records would have been nearer 130 feet than 95 feet. The American won simply because he was accustomed to the throwing of weights, and knew how to bring his strength and weight to bear on the missile. The Greek had brought the knack of throwing to greater perfection, but one could see that he did not know how to apply any large portion of his strength to the throw.

We now come to the great glory of the Greeks—the victory in the Marathon Race. This event was reckoned the chief feature of the meeting, and in many ways it deserved its position. It possessed greater historical interest than any other of the competitions, and was, no doubt, also the greatest criterion of endurance. The race was won by a Greek, who had hitherto no reputation. The second was a Greek, who had already won one of the trial races. It certainly seemed to the impartial spectator that the winner was nothing of a runner. He arrived in the Stadium with a stride of a foot or so, but apparently not much exhausted. The second man arrived in excellent style, seven minutes behind him. We can only explain the fact by supposing that the winner succeeded by monumental perseverance at a moderate speed, though, strangely enough, his time for the distance was really first-rate. It must be remembered, however, in comparing his time with the track-record, that a road course is very favourable to fast times—the remarkable performances recorded in the Eton Mile are sufficient proof of this. Now we do not wish to minimise the Greek victory, but only seek to regard it fairly. A statement was made in a daily journal not long since, by one who writes in true Greek style under the initials "J.G.," that "the well-trained English and American athletes had been defeated by the Greeks who had had no real training." This is an absurd misrepresentation. Does "J.G." really suppose that the English system of training cannot render a man capable of finishing in a race of twenty-five miles along a road, but that that feat is reserved for the heaven-gifted and nature-nursed Greek athlete? As a matter of fact, the Englishman arrived in Athens ten days, the American five days before the race. Neither of them did anything which could possibly be termed regular training during their stay, neither of them had seen the course till they drove to Marathon the night before the race, and certainly neither of them had ever run over it. Their lack of training was shown in the fact that the Englishman ran in splendid form till six kilometers from home, when he broke down entirely; the American had given up a little earlier. The Greeks, on the other hand, had practised over the course for months, and had all been engaged in trial-races over the distance. Every cross-country runner must know the inestimable value of such experience. Let, then, the Greeks have every credit for their diligence in training, and the excellent form which they showed, but let them not be led by irresponsible journalists to claim a measure of credit which is not due to them. The honour they have gained by the progress made in so short a time is great enough to enable them to dispense with false claims to distinction.

Our criticism of the athletic performances from a national standpoint has already shown in part that they did not reach a very high standard. The 800 meters race, for instance, equivalent to five and a half yards less than half a mile, was only accomplished in two minutes eleven seconds. The 1,500 meters, one hundred and twenty and a half yards less than a mile, occupied four minutes thirty-three and one-fifth seconds. We should have expected a half-mile in an international meeting to have been run at least well within the two minutes, and 800 meters, therefore in four-fifths of a second or so less. 1,500 meters ought not to have occupied more than four minutes eight seconds. The 400 meters (437 yards) occupied fifty-four and one-fifth seconds — a moderately good time would have been fifty-one seconds. But in the times made in the longer races, two considerations have to be taken into account, one of which applies also to the shorter races. In the first place, the track was not in a satisfactory condition. The English ground-man, who was responsible for it, naturally found it difficult to obtain the necessary materials in Athens, and, as a result, the track was not laid down sufficiently long before the meeting to enable it to be brought to proper perfection. Even after it was completed difficulties still had to be faced, especially the insufficiency of the water supply. At the time of the games, therefore, the track seemed to be over-hard underneath, while it was loose and treacherous on the surface. The ground man is not to be blamed at all for this; his energy and devotion did all that was possible to do for the success of the meeting. In the second place, the shape of the track rendered fast times impossible. In ancient times, when the two limbs of the track were practically parallel, and the runners had to turn round a sharp corner at either end, fast running must have been even more difficult. Even in the present Stadium, where the track has been laid out in a more gradual ellipse, we calculated that the runners lost two seconds in every round, owing to the turns, in the two longest races, and three seconds in the 400 meter race. Thus we must make an allowance of four seconds in the 800 meters, and eight seconds in the fifteen hundred. The three seconds in the 400 meters is not at all an excessive allowance. The runners literally seemed to come to a standstill as compared with their previous pace, when they arrived at the bends. The record of twelve seconds for 100 meters (109.3 yards) was only average. Mr. Burke, who has competed against us with great success in America, could do much better under more favorable conditions. A fortnight's travelling does not produce a good state of training. The 110 meters (120⅓ yards) Hurdle Race took considerably longer than one would have expected, judging from the excellence of the competitors; the result may have been due in some measure to "the unusual arrangements of the hurdles."

The results obtained in the disc-throwing and weight-putting we have already criticized sufficiently. The jumping was the most satisfactory portion of the athletics. The triple jump is not customary in England, but to the unaccustomed eye Mr. Connolly's performance seemed as good as it could be. For the pole-jump America had sent over two of her best performers, and the height cleared, 10 ft. 9¾ in., does not compare unfavourably with the record of 11 ft. 5 in. for this style of vaulting (without climbing). Mr. Clark, of Harvard, peformed splendidly both in the high and long jumps; in the former he cleared 5 ft. 11¼ in., 6 inches more than his opponents, in the latter 20 ft. 9¾ in. The latter performance is not remarkably good on the face of it, but Mr. Clark in reality jumped a great deal further. Unfortunately the committee were under an extraordinary delusion, which is not unknown in England, as to the manner in which a long jump should be judged. They attempted to decide after each jump, whether the competitor's toe had projected over the take-off board, and consequently disqualified Mr. Clark's best jumps. Everyone ought to know that the only criterion of a competitor having passed the board is failure in his jump. No one who passes the board can make a good jump. Even if it were possible, which it is not, to judge whether half an inch or his toe projects beyond the board, it stands to reason that he has taken fairly off the board, if his jump succeeds; and therefore it should be allowed. The results of this absurd judging was that the American competitors were forced for safety to jump from six inches or even a foot behind the line.

We may now turn from the athletic results of the games to the organization, and first to the organization of the athletics themselves. It was only to be expected from the inexperience of the committee that mistakes would be made. Mistakes were made, but they were not very serious. The greatest uncertainty was always allowed to prevail as to the events which would take place on any particular day, and as to the order in which they would take place. Competitors, had, as a rule, to rely upon the slippery authority of the Greek newspapers. Again, the committee had a firm belief in the inspired character of its own programmes. It desired them to be regarded as absolutely unalterable, and, when any impossible arrangement which they had made was pointed out to them, they required unlimited persuasion before they could be induced to alter it. For instance, the 800 and 1,500 meter races were to have been run in the heats (the former was actually so run, though there were only nine competitors), and the finals of both were fixed for the same day as the final of the Marathon Race. An Englishman was engaged in all three races, won two of them, and made a bold bid for victory in the third. It is needless to say that, had the committee been allowed to persevere, he would probably only have been able to run in one.

Much time was wasted in the drawing of places for heats and other purposes. The competitors were expected to attend at the general office for an unlimited period over and over again. Time is of little value in Greece. There was considerable delay between the various competitions in the Stadium, and in the course of the competitions themselves. This was due, to some extent, to the distance of the dressing-rooms from the arena, fully 200 yards, and to the lack of accommodation for competitors in the arena itself. The high and pole-jumps commenced at ridiculously low heights, and became inexpressibly tedious. The latter, indeed, lasted no less than an hour and three-quarters.

All these were, after all, minor blemishes, which were inseparable from the holding of a colossal meeting like the Olympic games in a hitherto unathletic country. Some of the confusion arose from the co-existence of two committees, the Greek organizing committee and the international athletic committee. The former had general superintendence before and during the games, the latter was confined to judging the contests. It was inevitable that the two committees should clash now and then and interfere with one another's arrangements, but such collisions were infrequent. The English and American competitors owe a great debt to Messrs. Finnis and Wheeler, their representatives on the committee, for the admirable way in which they protected their interests when it was necessary.

But we are anxious to admit that the Greek organizers dealt with foreign athletes throughout in the most sportsmanlike way. Exceptions were very few, though in one instance we cannot but maintain that the right course was not pursued. A trial race had been held to select the Greeks who should compete in the race from Marathon. The race was run and the team selected. Entries for the Olympic Games closed, for Greeks, a fortnight before their commencement. A few days only before the games the Greek authorities seem to have become alarmed at the prospect of foreign competition in the Marathon Race, and especially at the fame of Mr. Flack, and, like Nicias before the last sea-fight at Syracuse, thought that perhaps they had not yet done all that was possible. They held another trial race, selected a second team, which included the ultimate winner, and made a post-entry of it. We fail to see how this proceeding can possibly be justified. Such an action as this, however, was quite exceptional; as a rule, the treatment of foreign competitors by the Greek committee and the Greek people was extraordinarily liberal.

While the organization of the actual athletics was, with the above-mentioned exceptions, wonderful under the circumstances, the organization of the meeting generally seemed to us to be very nearly perfect, and in connection, with the organization as a whole, we should not omit to mention the untiring efforts of the three eldest Princes, whose absolute devotion — for we can call it nothing less — was of supreme importance to the general result. The Stadium holds something over sixty thousand spectators and on two occasions it was full to the uttermost corner. Yet we never observed any confusion or disagreeable incidents of any kind. There is no doubt that the Greeks are a patient people and allow themselves to be organized. The committee were fortunate in not having to deal with a north-country football crowd. The Stadium was divided into blocks and tickets were obtainable for a particular block. Within that block no definite seats were reserved, and consequently to obtain a good seat in one's block it was necessary to arrive in the Stadium at a very early hour. But, inasmuch as the Athenian public, like the visitors at Bayreuth, lived for nothing but the games so long as they lasted, this expenditure of time was no great disadvantage. Perhaps, however, it may be permissible to suggest that on the next occasion the tickets for a particular day should be on sale a little earlier, and also that it would bring the games more into touch with ancient custom if the upper portion of the seats at least were not charged for.

The behaviour of the crowd under very trying circumstances was most exemplary. The Greeks suffered one disappointment after another. Yet even when they lost the Disc, they showed no vigorous signs of disapproval. This may have been partly due to their temperament, which is not in the least emotional, but must also be attributed to a great extent to gentlemanly feeling. A still greater trial of their patience came when the Greek's number was hoisted by accident as winner in putting the weight, soon to be replaced by that of the American.

But as the public seemed disinclined for vigorous expressions of disapproval, so it also was incapable of expressing very great enthusiasm. Much has been written in the papers about the tremendous scene at the conclusion of the race from Marathon. The *coup d'oeil* indeed was surpassingly fine, but the outward expression of emotion really amounted to very little. It seemed to us that the five thousand people who were present at the conclusion of the Oxford and Yale sports in 1894, displayed, proportionately, much more outward enthusiasm than the one hundred and twenty thousand people who witnessed the termination of the Marathon race in 1896. Yet the whole scene can never be effaced from one's memory.

It was expected in Athens that swarms of foreign visitors would grace the games with their presence. The committee appointed Messrs. Cook their agents for foreign parts, and apparently thought that this alone was sufficient to ensure an enormous concourse of foreigners. This turned out to be a very unfortunate mode of procedure. The price at which the agents advertised rooms in Athens was so preposterous, that many persons, who intended to visit Athens at the season of the games, abstained from going. We can vouch to having found several parties in Italy, who were intentionally delaying their visit to Athens till after the termination of the games. The audience, then, in the Stadium was almost exclusively composed of Greeks. The newspapers, both in Greece and England, continued even after the end of the meeting, to estimate the number of foreigners present at twenty thousand. As a matter of fact, there can be no doubt that one thousand would be a large estimate. Foreigners may have won the greater part of the events, the sports may have been veritably international, but the body of spectators was not international at all. If "Olympic" in the modern sense means "international," this audience was not an Olympic audience. The fact cannot be denied, the reason is not far to seek. The organization which failed to attract foreign competitors also failed to attract foreign spectators. The so-called agents of the committee only provided information if applied to, and even then the intelligence given was very meagre. If one wrote to the central committee one was liable to be told that all information could be obtained by subscribing a considerable sum to the journal of the committee. Apparently the committee did not think it its duty or its advantage to supply information without immediate reward. The lack of foreign attendance at these games was peculiarly unfortunate because it may prevent their success from becoming duly spread abroad, and so may stand in the way of a favourable issue on the next occasion.

We have called the games successful, but it may be thought that our comments hitherto point rather to failure than to success. What then was the peculiar triumph of these games? The triumph which was inseparably connected with them, the triumph of sentiment, of association of distinction of unique splendour.

The Stadium was till very recently a scene of desolation. It became the property of the King; he, assigned by German advice, commenced the task of revealing its ancient glories. Much had been done towards restoring its original features, when the notion of an international athletic assembly was first suggested. An international committee was formed in Paris, mainly under the patronage of Frenchmen, and the international games were decided upon. It was then that M. Bikelas, the leader of modern Greek literature, suggested Greece as the scene of the first meeting. Olympia was out of the question as the place of contest, and all eyes were turned upon the Stadium at Athens. It was found that the configuration of the ground permitted the restoration of the edifice to something of its ancient magnificence with no very great expenditure. At this moment patriotism, as it has so often done in the history of modern Greece, came to the assistance of the nation. M. Averoff, of Alexandria, professed his readiness to bear the cost of the restoration, and even, like a second Herodes Atticus, to restore the whole building in Pentelic marble. The genius of M. Metaxas, the architect, carried the work to a temporary termination. The Stadium is not yet completed in marble; that task is already being performed and will be ended by the next Olympiad; but the whole stands even now in all essentials the same as in the third century of our era. Twice was the vast arena filled to the uttermost with its sixty thousand eager watchers, twice the expectant throng completely hid M. Averoff's marble and its wooden substitute from the eye. On one side of this vast area rises a peaked hill, gently sloping at the angle of the seats; on this was packed an even denser mass, numbering perhaps some twenty thousand. All round the upper rim of the Stadium another crowd was closely pressed, resting at the extreme ends of the line, where the Stadium projected from its guardian hills, upon a narrow ledge backed by a sheer fall of forty feet or more. Before the broad entrance, on the level road without, was another crowd, eager as the others, but entirely shut out from any view of the contests; it extended for fifty yards in either direction from the barrier and may be estimated also at twenty thousand.

On every day of the meeting the crowd present was enormous, but the two central moments were the conclusion of the Marathon Race and the presentation of the prizes. Then every available inch of space was occupied. The onlooker could think of nothing but that he had before him a serried throng of humanity, greater than any that had been marshalled before man's sight hitherto. The competitor, as he hurried through the gloom of the ancient tunnel, the Crypte, which led from his quarters on the hill behind to the arena, if he possessed a particle of imagination, felt himself now to be a Phayllus or a Phidippides, about to accomplish feats to excite the amazement, and arouse the suspicions, of all future times, now a martyr of the early Christian ages, whom a lion or bear awaited where the gloom gave way to the sunlight. The spectator, on the one side, gazed towards the temple of Zeus Olympius and the Museum Hill, and further to the north, where the Acropolis shut off the Sacred Way, on the other side he looked towards Marathon and upon so much of Lycabettus as the committee's great panorama of lath and plaster permitted him. Behind all rose crimson-tinted Hymettus, and, beyond it, purple Pentelicus smiled upon its offspring. Over all was the friendly sun and the "delicate" air. Such was the scene, unsurpassed and unsurpassable. Who, who was present there, does not wish that he may once again be permitted to behold it? After the ode had been recited and the olive-branches presented, everyone's first desire must have been for a repetition of the whole. The feeling of absolute entrancement with the beauty of the sight, the rapture of sensations, and the joy of recollection, which overmastered all who shared in this spectacle, found vent in ardent wishes that the Olympian games should be reserved to dignify Athens and to be glorified by her glory. No one, while under the glamour of the moment, could have ventured to oppose this suggested reservation, and even now, when the splendour has somewhat faded from the mind, it is difficult to criticize this impulsive proposal. Yet it has great practical difficulties to face. In the first place, it would have to meet French opposition of the most forcible kind. The French regard themselves as the nursing-fathers of the first Olympic games. They consider the permission granted to Greece to hold the first meeting at Athens as a special favour, which is bound up inseparably with the stipulation that the next Olympic Games shall be held in Paris in 1900. It seems likely that Greek enthusiasm, aided by considerations of sentiment and propriety, might under ordinary circumstances carry the day against French contentions. The Greeks would be supported by the whole body of scholars and lovers of antiquity and by most educated athletes. Unfortunately the French have a most powerful ally to support their claims — their great Exhibition. Even supposing that the Greek arguments prevailed, we cannot doubt that Paris would hold a rival international meeting. In that case we much fear that Paris and modern display, within a moderate distance of Central Europe, would prevail against Athens and the soberness of antiquity in the remoter East. The opposition between the claims of utility and of taste and sentiment in this matter seems to be irreconcilable: on the one side we have the probability of a truly representative international meeting, conducted on purely modern lines, in a modern arena unconnected with the memories and glories of the age which has provided models of grace and strength for all time, on the other we find the possibility of non-representative competitions, held in a spot which, with every beauty of form and position, is connected undyingly with all the magnifence of that golden age of athletics, whose ideals it should be the object of these international gatherings to promote. The opposition is so sharp that it would be fair to describe it by asserting that these games, if held at Athens, would be Olympic but, we fear, not international; if held elsewhere than at Athens, international but not Olympic.

Fortnightly Review 354 (1 June 1896): 944–957

Athletics (Track & Field)

Track & field was the most watched sport at the 1896 Olympic Games, as it has been in almost all celebrations of the Modern Olympics. The track & field events were held in the ancient Panathenaic Stadium in Athens. It was beautiful for the spectators but difficult for the runners. The track was short, at only about 330 meters in circumference, with long straight-aways and very short, sharp turns. It also consisted of very soft, loose cinders and made running difficult. In addition, the 1896 Olympic Organizing Committee chose to have the runners run in a clockwise direction, opposite to the norm for current running events, although in 1896 some English track races (though not all) were run in this manner.

The Athens Organizing Committee elected to use the rules of the Union des Sociétés Françaises de Sports Athlétiques (USFSA) for the running events and the Amateur Athletic Association of England for the throwing and jumping events. The running events were contested in metric distances, which had not been contested before by an international field, thus many records could have been expected had the track been more conducive to record-setting performances. The weather for the most part was quite good during the Olympics, with mostly sunny days and no rain. On 6–7 April, however, it was quite chilly, and actually snowed in the mountains outside of Athens.

The field for the first Olympic track & field events was a disappointment. None of the great British runners of the time were present, and the American team, although they swept most of the events, included only one American national champion. This did not dampen the enthusiasm of the fans, who filled the stadium every day.

The eleven nations which competed at Athens were as follows, with number of competitors in parentheses: Australia (1), Cyprus (1), Denmark (3), France (6), Great Britain (5), Germany (5), Greece (27), Hungary (3), Smyrna (1), Sweden (1), and the United States (10). Only Greece and the United States had 10 or more competitors, with 63 athletes competing in track & field athletics at Athens.

Seven of these eleven nations had competitors win medals, with only Cyprus, Denmark, Smyrna and Sweden failing to medal. The United States was the dominant nation, winning 16 of the 37 medals, and 9 of the 12 events — the others going to Greece (the marathon) and Australia (the 800 and 1,500 meters).

There was much which could be criticized concerning the first Olympic track & field competition — the poor condition of the track, the sharp turns, the subsequent lack of world records, the small turnout, and the lack of many top international comeptitors. But, more importantly, there was much to be commended. Though there were only 63 competitors, they did represent 11 nations, by far the largest representation of countries at any international athletics meeting ever held. The quality of the competition was only fair, but the sportsmanship of some of the outclassed competitors set a standard which may not yet have been surpassed. Most importantly, the 1896 Olympic track & field meeting served as an index, setting the stage for international competition in this most wide-spread of all sports.

Site:	Panathenaic Stadium	
Dates:	6–7, 9–10 April (25–26, 28–29 March)	
Events:	12	
Competitors:	63 (63 Men)	
Nations:	11	

	Competitors	1st	2nd	3rd	Places
Australia	1	2	-	-	2
Cyprus	1	-	-	-	-
Denmark	3	-	-	-	-
France	6	-	1	1	2
Germany	5	-	1	-	1
Great Britain	5	-	1	1	2
Greece	27	1	3	6	10
Hungary	3	-	1	2	3
Smyrna	1	-	-	-	-
Sweden	1	-	-	-	-
United States	10	9	6	2	17
Totals	63	12	13	12	37
Nations	11	3	6	5	7

100 Meters

A: 15¹*; E: 27; C: 9; D: 6, 10 April (25, 29 March)

The first event of the Modern Olympic Games was the first heat of the 100 meter dash, held on 6 April. Five runners toed the mark, with Francis "Frank" Lane of the United States, and Princeton University, winning the first Modern Olympic "event." Lane was trailed by Hungary's Alajos Szokolyi and Britain's Charles Gmelin. In heat two, Thomas Curtis (USA) defeated Greece's Alexandros Khalkokondilis. Thomas Burke of the United States won heat three quite easily, defeating Germany's Fritz Hofmann. Thus began the Modern Olympic Games.

The field for the 100 meters, however, was missing many top sprinters. The world's best in 1896 were Bernie Wefers of the United States and Charles Bradley of England. They had matched up in September 1895 at the London Athletic Club versus New York Athletic Club meet, with Wefers winning. Although Tom Burke was the U.S. champion at 400 meters, he had no real reputation in the short sprint. Conversely, the best Continental sprinter was probably Fritz Hofmann, who was present in Athens, and who in 1893 had scored a double victory (100 and 400 meters) at the "Championship of the Continent" in Berlin.

See Notes on pages 74–80.

The finals of the 100 meters were held on 10 April, four days after the heats. Five runners came to the starting line: Tom Burke and Frank Lane of the United States, Fritz Hofmann (GER), Alajos Szokolyi (HUN), and Greece's Alexandros Khalkokondilis. The start was even but Burke and Hofmann pulled away at 50 meters. Burke outran Hofmann over the last 50 meters, winning by about two meters in 12.0 seconds.

Final A: 5; C: 4; D: 10 April (29 March).

1.	Thomas Burke	USA	12[2]
2.	Fritz Hofmann	GER	at 2 m.[3]
=3.[4]	Alajos Szokolyi	HUN	at 4 m.[5]
	Francis Lane	USA	at 4 m.[6]
5.	Alexandros Khalkokondilis	GRE	at 4 m.[7]
	Thomas Curtis	USA	DNS[8,9]

Round One A: 15; C: 9; D: 6 April (25 March); F: First two in each heat advance to the finals.

Heat 1 A: 5[10]; C: 5.

1.	Francis Lane	USA	12⅕
2.	Alajos Szokolyi	HUN	12¾[11]
3.[12]	Charles Gmelin	GBR	at 1 m.
4.	Alphonse Grisel	FRA	
AC.	Kurt Doerry	GER	
	[13]		

Heat 2 A: 5[14]; C; 4.

1.	Thomas Curtis	USA[15]	12⅕
2.	Alexandros Khalkokondilis	GRE	12¾[16]
3.[17]	Launceston Elliot	GBR	at 1 m.
AC.	Eugen Schmidt	DEN	
	George Marshal	GBR	
	[18]		

Heat 3 A: 5[19]; C: 4.

1.	Thomas Burke	USA	11⅘[20]
2.	Fritz Hofmann	GER	12¾[21]
3.[22]	Friedrich Traun	GER	at 6 m.
AC.	Henrik Sjöberg	SWE	
	Georgios Gennimatas	GRE	
	[23,24]		

400 Meters

A: 7[25]; E: 19; C: 4; D: 6–7 April (25–26 March).

The two best one-lap runners in 1896 were Tom Burke of the United States and Edgar Bredin of Britain. Burke had beaten Bredin at the 1895 New York AC–London AC meet, but Bredin was the coholder of the world record with 48.5 for 440 yards. In early 1896, however, as so aptly put by Montague Shearman, Bredin "voluntarily joined the professional ranks, a step which was received with great surprise, as he was a gentleman by birth and education."

The heats of the 400 meters were held on 6 April. The race was slightly over one lap in length, with no lanes to separate the runners. There were two heats, with seven runners coming to the start. In heat one, Herbert Jamison (USA) won, defeating Fritz Hofmann and Kurt Doerry of Germany, trailed by France's Alphonse Grisel. There was a false start in this heat, and Hofmann and Grisel were penalized two yards for their indiscretion. The second heat was won by the favorite, Tom Burke, who defeated Britain's Charles Gmelin and Frantz Reichel of France.

The finals followed on the next day, 7 April. Burke won very easily, in 54.2, with Jamison trailing him by as much as 15 meters. Third-place is disputed in later sources, with some listing Gmelin and some Hofmann, but Gmelin definitely finished 3rd per 1896 sources.

Final A: 4; C: 3; D: 7 April (26 March).

1.	Thomas Burke	USA	54⅕[26]
2.	Herbert Jamison	USA	55⅕[27]
3.	Charles Gmelin	GBR	at 15–20 m.[28]
4.	Fritz Hofmann	GER	

Round One A: 7; C: 4; D: 6 April (25 March); F: First two in each heat advance to the final.

Heat 1 A: 4[29]; C: 3.

1.	Herbert Jamison	USA	56⅘
2.	Fritz Hofmann	GER[30]	58⅗[31]
AC.	Alphonse Grisel	FRA[32]	
	Kurt Doerry	GER	

[33]

Heat 2 A: 3[34]; C: 3.

1.	Thomas Burke	USA	58⅖[35]
2.	Charles Gmelin	GBR	at 15 yds.[36]
3.	Frantz Reichel	FRA	at 12 yds.

[37,38]

800 Meters

A: 9[39]; E: 15; C: 5; D: 6, 9 April (25, 28 March).

America's Charles Kilpatrick was the world record holder and easily the top ½-mile runner in the world, but he did not make the trip to Athens. This left the favorite's role to Australia's Edwin "Teddy" Flack, an accountant who was living and training in London in 1896.

The heats of the 800 meters were held on 6 April. Flack won heat one over Hungary's Nándor Dáni, with Friedrich Traun (GER) third, and France's Frantz Reichel finishing fourth and last. In heat two, Albin Lermusiaux (FRA) won narrowly over three Hellenes, led by Dimitrios Golemis.

The 800 meter finals were held three days later on 9 April. Lermusiaux chose not to start, presumably saving himself for the marathon which was to start the next day. Thus, only three runners contested the final — Flack, Dáni, and Golemis. Flack won by 10 meters in 2:11, easing up, with Dáni second, and Golemis over 100 meters behind Flack.

Final A: 3; C: 3; D: 9 April (28 March); T: 1430.

1.	Edwin Flack	AUS	2:11[40,41]
2.	Nándor Dáni	HUN	2:11⅘[42]
3.	Dimitrios Golemis	GRE	at 20–100 m.
	Albin Lermusiaux	FRA	DNS[43]

Round One A: 9; C: 5; D: 6 April (25 March); F: First two in each heat advance to the final.

Heat 1 A: 4; C: 4.

1.	Edwin Flack	AUS	2:10[44]
2.	Nándor Dáni	HUN	2:10⅕[45]
3.	Friedrich Traun	GER	at 20 m.
4.	George Marshal	GBR	[46]
	[47]		

Heat 2 A: 5; C: 4.

1.	Albin Lermusiaux	FRA	2:16⅗[48]
2.	Dimitrios Golemis	GRE	2:16⅘[49]
3.[50]	Georges De La Nézière	FRA	
AC.	Dimitrios Tomprof	SMY	
	Angelos Fetsis	GRE	[51]
	[52,53]		

1,500 Meters

A: 8[54]; E: 12: C: 5; D: 7 April (26 March).

The 1,500 meter race was run on 7 April. There were no heats, only a final. Eight runners started: Flack of Australia, Arthur Blake of the United States, Lermusiaux of France, Germany's Carl Galle, and four Greeks — Angelos Fetsis, Dimitrios Golemis, Konstantinos Karakatsanis, and Dimitrios Tomprof.

The runners stayed together for one lap, with the time at 300 meters being 52.2, at which time the four Greeks lost contact. Blake then took the lead, with 700 meters being passed in 2:08.2, but on the third lap Lermusiaux took over. He ran 1,100 meters in 3:25.2. At the bell, Flack and Blake passed him, easily drawing away. Flack defeated Blake by five meters in 4:33.2, with Lermusiaux another 15 meters back. Carl Galle finished fourth, trailed by the four Greeks.

1.	Edwin Flack	AUS	4:33⅕[55]
2.	Arthur Blake	USA	at 2–10 m.[56]
3.	Albin Lermusiaux	FRA	at 6–15 m.
4.[57]	Carl Galle	GER	
AC.	Angelos Fetsis	GRE	[58]

Dimitrios Golemis	GRE
Konstantinos Karakatsanis	GRE
Dimitrios Tomprof	SMY

59,60

Marathon

A: 17[61]; E: 25; C: 5; D: 10 April (29 March); T: 1400.

Prior to 1896, although distance running was popular as pedestrianism, a marathon-distance race had never been formally run. The origin of the modern marathon lies in the ancient legend of a Greek courier, normally seen as Pheidippides, but more likely actually Philippides. The primary source for the legend is the Greek historian Herodotus, who recorded the verbal history of men who had fought in the ancient battle of Marathon.

According to Herodotus, Philippides was sent to Sparta from Athens asking for help in the battle. After the battle, a runner, whose name was Pheidippides per Lucian and Eucles per Plutarch, was sent to Marathon from Athens to tell of the victory. Further details are sketchy, though modern legend has Pheidippides arriving in Athens to tell of victory in the battle with the words, "Rejoice, we conquer," and then dying from his effort. There is little ancient documentary evidence to support that part of the tale.

The modern marathon was suggested by the Frenchman Michael Bréal, a friend of Baron Pierre de Coubertin who accompanied Coubertin to Athens in planning the 1896 Olympics. Bréal wrote Coubertin thusly, "If the Organizing Committee of the Athens Olympics would be willing to revive the famous run of the Marathon soldier as part of the program of the Games, I would be glad to offer a prize for this new Marathon race." The idea was immediately accepted.

The marathon race was held on 10 April 1896, starting in the village of Marathon, with the runners covering the dusty dirt roads to Athens, a distance of about 40 kilometers. There were 17 starters, of whom 12 were Greek and 5 foreign. The race started at 1400 hours when Colonel Papadiamantopoulos fired the starter's pistol.

The leader for the first 20 km. was Albin Lermusiaux of France. At about this time, the heat, the uphill grade, and the dusty roads began to take their toll, and runners began to withdraw from the race. At the halfway mark, Greece's Spiridon Louis was in sixth place, trailing Lermusiaux, Edwin Flack (AUS), Arthur Blake (USA), Gyula Kellner (HUN), and the leading Greek, Georgios Lavrentis. Blake dropped out at 23 km. and the Greek favorite, Kharilaos Vasilakos, moved into third place.

Shortly thereafter, Lermusiaux tired and Flack took the lead. Lermusiaux would eventually retire at 32 km. At 32 km. Louis caught Flack and they ran together for about five kilometers. Louis finally dropped Flack near the village of Ambelokipi, and Flack dropped out on the outskirts of Athens.

At this time, various couriers who had negotiated the course on bicycles and horses entered the Panathenaic Stadium and informed the crowd of Louis's approach, announcing, "Hellene, Hellene!" (A Greek, a Greek!). Louis then entered the stadium, and Prince Nicholas and Prince Georgios accompanied him on his last circuit. He finished and won in 2 hours, 58 minutes and 50 seconds. Vasilakos was 2nd in 3-06:03, trailed by Kellner in 3-09:35. Greece's Spiridon Belokas was the original third-place finisher in 3-06:30, but following a Hungarian protest, he was disqualified when it was found he had taken a carriage for a short part of the race. Ten runners finished: eight Greeks (including Belokas), Kellner, and Lagoudakis.

1.	Spiridon Louis	GRE	2-58:50[62]
2.	Kharilaos Vasilakos	GRE	3-06:03[63]
3.[64]	Gyula Kellner	HUN	3-06:35[65]
4.	Ioannis Vrettos	GRE	
5.	Eleitherios Papasimeon	GRE	
6.	Dimitrios Deligiannis	GRE	
7.	Evangelos Gerakaris	GRE[66]	
8.	Stamatios Masouris	GRE	
9.	Sokratis Lagoudakis	FRA	
AB.	Edwin Flack	AUS	DNF[67]
	Albin Lermusiaux	FRA	DNF
	Ioannis Lavrentis	GRE	DNF
	Georgios Grigoriou	GRE	DNF
	Arthur Blake	USA	DNF
	Ilias Kafetzis	GRE	DNF
	Dimitrios Khristopoulos	GRE	DNF
DQ.	Spiridon Belokas	GRE	3-06:30[68,69]

[70]

110[71] Meter Hurdles

A: 8; E: 18; C: 6; D: 7, 10 April (26, 29 March).

A misprint in the 1896 Official Report has led some to believe that the distance was 100 meters. But there is little doubt that the race was contested over the standard distance of 110 meters. There was no real favorite, as the two top hurdlers in the world, Stephen Chase (USA) and Godfrey Shaw (GBR), elected not to make the trip. The Greeks felt their champion, Anastasios Andreou of Cyprus, was unbeatable. The British hurdler, Grantley Goulding, paraded around Athens wearing his medals on his coat, causing his American rival, Thomas Curtis, to remark, "I never met a more confident athlete."

Though four heats were scheduled, only two were contested, and they were held on 7 April. Goulding won the first heat easily in 18.4 over Hungary's Alajos Szokolyi, and Andreou. Curtis won the second heat in 18.0 over his teammate Welles Hoyt, France's Frantz Reichel, and Germany's Kurt Doerry.

Reichel and Hoyt, though qualified, elected not to contest the finals on 10 April, leaving only Goulding and Curtis to race for the championship. Hoyt most likely withdrew to concentrate on the pole vault. Reichel did not start because he was seconding Lermusiaux in the marathon race, held concurrent with the hurdle final. Goulding was noted to be a better technical hurdler but Curtis was much the faster runner. Goulding led at the last hurdle but lost on the run-in by centimeters, with Curtis timed in 17⅗ seconds.

Final A: 2; C: 2; D: 10 April (29 March).

1.	Thomas Curtis	USA	17⅗
2.	Grantley Goulding	GBR	at 5 cm.[72]
	Frantz Reichel	FRA	DNS
	Welles Hoyt	USA	DNS

Round One A: 8[73]; C: 6; D: 7 April (26 March); F: First two in each heat advance to the final.

Heat 1 A: 4; C: 4.

1.	Grantley Goulding	GBR	18²/₅
2.	Frantz Reichel	FRA	[74]
AC.	Alajos Szokolyi	HUN	[75]
	Anastasios Andreou	CYP	[76]

Heat 2 A: 4; C: 2.

1.	Thomas Curtis	USA	18[77]
2.	Welles Hoyt	USA	
AC.	Kurt Doerry	GER	
	Athanasios Skaltsogiannis	GRE	

[78]

High Jump

A: 5; E: 20[79]; C: 3; D: 10 April (29 March).

The world's top high jumper in 1896 was Mike Sweeney, who held the world record, but he turned professional in early 1896 and was not eligible. Five jumpers started. No Greeks were in the high jump, the only event in track & field in which the home team did not have a starter.

The high jump was contested on 10 April. The opening height was 1.50 meters[80], and all jumpers were required to jump at each height. The bar was initially raised 5 centimeters at a time; this interval was changed to 2.5 centimeters after 1.60 meters was negotiated.[81] Fritz Hofmann (GER) was the first to be eliminated, as he cleared 1.55 but failed at 1.60. Sweden's Henrik Sjöberg cleared 1.60 but went out at 1.625 and finished 4th, leaving the three Americans, Ellery Clark, James Connolly, and Robert Garrett.

Clark was the class of the field, and won the title easily. Garrett and Connolly tied for second, both clearing 1.65 meters. Clark cleared 1.675, 1.70, 1.75, and then had the bar raised to 1.81 meters, which he negotiated on the first try.

1.	Ellery Clark	USA	1.81[82]
=2.	Robert Garrett	USA	1.65[83]
	James Connolly	USA	1.65
4.	Henrik Sjöberg	SWE	1.60
5.	Fritz Hofmann	GER	1.55

[84]

Pole Vault

A: 5; E: 21; C: 2; D: 10 April (29 March).

There were 16 final entries but again only five competitors for the pole vault, which was held on 10 April. The starters were two Americans (Welles Hoyt and Albert Tyler) and three Greeks (Evangelos Damaskos, Ioannis Theodoropoulos, and Vasilios Xydas). Hoyt was the best known vaulter, as he had finished third at the 1895 ICAAAA Meet. Missing were America's world record holder Walter Rodenbaugh and Britain's five-time AAA champion, Richard Dickinson.

The opening height was 2.40 meters, which was cleared successfully by the three Greeks. Damaskos and Theodoropoulos cleared 2.50 and 2.60 meters before failing at 2.70. Thus, they tied for third. Hoyt and Tyler began vaulting at 2.80 meters, and both cleared each height successfully in 10 centimeter increments through 3.20 meters. At that time, the bar was raised to 3.25 meters and Tyler failed to clear. Hoyt did, and also went over the bar at 3.30 meters to win the championship. This event started while the marathon was being run and was interrupted by the frenzy of the crowd when Louis came into the stadium and won that event.

1.	Welles Hoyt	USA	3.30[85]
2.	Albert Tyler	USA	3.20[86]
=3.	Evangelos Damaskos	GRE	2.60[87]
	Ioannis Theodoropoulos	GRE	2.60
5.	Vasilios Xydas	GRE	2.40

[88]

Broad (Long) Jump

A: 9[89]; E: 23; C: 5; D: 7 April (26 March).

Among the 18 final entries, nine competitors started in the broad jump, now usually called the long jump. There were three Americans, two Greeks, two Frenchmen, one German, and one Sweden.

Very little is known about this competition except that it was won by Ellery Clark, who would later also win the high jump. His winning mark was 6.35 meters, with the USA sweeping the medals, Robert Garrett finishing second, and James Connolly third.

Clark made his winning leap on his last of three attempts, and wrote of it in his autobiography, *Reminiscences of an Athlete:* "It was little short of agony, I shall never forget my feelings as I stood at the end of the path for my third — and last — try. Five thousand miles, I reflected, I had come; and was it to end in this? Three fouls and then five thousand miles back again, with that for my memory of the Games."

1.	Ellery Clark	USA	6.35[90]	
2.	Robert Garrett	USA	6.00[91]	
3.	James Connolly	USA	5.84[92]	
4.	Alexandros Khalkokondilis	GRE	5.74[93]	
AC.	Alexandre Tufferi[94]	FRA[95]	[96]	
	Athanasios Skaltsogiannis	GRE		
	Henrik Sjöberg	SWE		
	Carl Schuhmann	GER		
	Alphonse Grisel	FRA	[97]	

[98]

Hop, Step and Jump (Triple Jump)

A: 7[99]; E: 11[100]; C: 5; D: 6 April (25 March).

The hop, step and jump was the first final contested at the 1896 Olympic Games. The competition occurred on 6 April 1896. The honor of being the first Modern Olympic Champion thus went to the winner of this event: James Connolly of Boston, Massachusetts, USA, the Suffolk Athletic Club, and briefly, Harvard University.

Connolly led a field of seven competitors, with France's Alexandre Tufferi finishing second, and Greece's Ioannis Persakis third. Tufferi was the first jumper and Connolly the last. There were no precise rules for required style. The styles of the medalists were described in *The Field* as follows: Connolly took two hops on his right foot and then a jump; Tufferi performed a hop, step and a jump in the standard English method; and Persakis used two steps and a jump. Persakis' method was apparently the common one used in Greece, where the event was popular and often held at various village festivals.

1.	James Connolly	USA	13.71
2.	Alexandre Tufferi	FRA	12.70[101]
3.	Ioannis Persakis	GRE	12.52[102]
4.	Alajos Szokolyi	HUN	11.26[103]
5.	Carl Schuhmann	GER	[104]
AC.	Khristos Zoumis	GRE	
	Fritz Hofmann	GER	
	[105]		

Putting the Weight (Shot Put)

A: 7[106]; E: 19; C: 4[107]; D: 7 April (26 March).

The shot put was held on 7 April, but only 7 of the 15 final entries actually started. The shot was put from a two-meter square. Robert Garrett (USA) won with a throw of 11.22 meters. Miltiades Gouskos (GRE) was second and Georgios Papasideris (GRE) was third. Garrett led from his first throw. Gouskos' best effort was on his last attempt and the Greek crowd cheered wildly, thinking he had beaten Garrett. The Greek crowd was very disappointed, especially when the official posting the scores made an error and initially listed Gouskos as the winner. The error was quickly corrected.

The distances were well off George Gray's (CAN) world record of 14.32, but George Robertson, a British athlete who competed in the discus throw, noted that this was due to the size of the square, which "corresponded with no known rules, although the event was purported to be held under English rules."

1.	Robert Garrett	USA	11.22
2.	Miltiadis Gouskos	GRE	11.03[108]
3.	Georgios Papsideris	GRE	10.36[109]
4.[110]	Viggo Jensen	DEN	[111,112]
AC.	Carl Schuhmann[113]	GER	*ca.* 10.00[114]
	Fritz Hofmann	GER	
	Ellery Clark	USA	
	[115]		

Discus Throw

A: 9[116]; E: 13; C: 6; D: 6 April (25 March).

The discus throw was held on the first day of athletics competition, 6 April 1896. It was the first time the discus was ever contested at a major athletics meeting. There were nine competitors who took three throws from a 2.50 meters square, with the top three receiving an additional three efforts. The Greeks felt that they had an unbeatable thrower in Panagiotis Paraskevopoulos, but he was beaten by Robert Garrett (USA) on Garrett's fifth, and last, attempt of 29.15 meters. Part of Paraskevopoulos' problem was that he attempted to strike poses reminiscent of the ancient Greek statues of "diskoboloi." Paraskevopoulos threw 28.955 meters, while Greece's Sotirios Versis finished third with 28.78 meters.

Garrett was a Princeton student who initially was not going to compete in the discus throw. He had heard of the event from his history professor at Princeton, William Milligan Sloane, the first IOC Member in the United States. Sloane had a discus made for Garrett and it weighed about 10 kilograms. Garrett's efforts reflected the enormous weight of the implement and which greatly discouraged him. Upon arriving in Athens, he saw that the real discus weighed only two kilograms, so he changed his mind and elected to compete.

1.	Robert Garrett	USA	29.15[117]
2.	Panagiotis Paraskevopoulos	GRE	28.955[118]
3.	Sotirios Versis	GRE	27.78[119]
4.[120]	George Stuart Robertson	GBR	25.20[121]
AC.	Henrik Sjöberg	SWE	
	Georgios Papasideris	GRE	
	Holger Nielsen[122]	DEN	[123]
	Viggo Jensen	DEN	[124]
	Alphonse Grisel	FRA	
	[125]		

NOTES

1. VK lists 17 competitors from 8 nations. FW has 19 competitors. EK has 18 competitors.
2. SV has 12⅕ sec.
3. Listed as 12.2, an estimated time, in EzM, EK, and VK.
4. Per SV, Szokolyi and Lane finished simultaneously. This is the only source mentioning 3rd place, and thus we have listed them as =3rd. However, all records since have listed Szokolyi as 3rd and Lane 4th, for unknown reasons.
5. Given as 12.6, an estimated time, in EzM, EK, and VK.
6. Given as 12.6, an estimated time, in EzM, EK, and VK.
7. Given as 12.6, an estimated time, in EzM, EK, and VK.
8. Thomas Curtis, who had qualified, did not start in the finals.
9. FW has Curtis racing and finishing 4th, with Lane 5th and Khalkokondilis 6th.
10. TF noted that "6 ran."
11. The time was 12¾ per the OR, Akrp, and Argy. It was 12⅗ in SV.
12. Gmelin is listed as 3rd in SV, the only 1896 source listing 3rd place.
13. Luis Subercaseaux (CHI) and Leonidasz Manno (HUN) were also entered in this heat. Some later sources claim that Subercaseaux did compete, but no 1896 reports confirm this. EzM has Manno 5th and Subercaseaux 6th. EzM did not list Grisel but had André Tournois (FRA) 3rd.
14. TF noted erroneously that "6 ran." A photograph of the start of the heat exists, showing five starters.
15. Curtis claimed in his article that he competed against a German, a Frenchman, a Briton, and two Greeks. Some sources erroneously list Tufferi as having competed, and EzM has him finishing 3rd in this heat.

16. EzM gives an estimated time of 12.6. The only 1896 source giving a time, Akrp, listed $12\frac{3}{4}$.

17. Elliot is listed as 3rd in SV and BDP, the only 1896 sources listing 3rd place.

18. Also entered in this heat, but not competing, were Alexandre Tufferi (FRA), André Tournois (FRA), and Nándor Dáni (HUN). SV notes that Tufferi competed, but did not list a finish. EzM has Tufferi 3rd, Elliot 4th, Schmidt 5th, and Kurt Doerry 6th. He did not list Marshal in this event.

19. TF noted erroneously that "6 ran."

20. The OR has 12 seconds, but all other sources list the time as $11\frac{4}{5}$.

21. EzM gives an estimated time of 12.0. The only 1896 sources giving a time were Akrp ($12\frac{3}{4}$) and SV ($12\frac{3}{5}$).

22. Traun is listed as 3rd in SV, the only 1896 source listing 3rd place.

23. Also entered in this heat, but not competing, were Alfred Flatow (GER), and Konstantinos Mouratis (SMY). EzM has Sjöberg 3rd, Nándor Dáni (HUN) 4th and Gennimatas 5th.

24. Also entered in this event, but not assigned to a definite heat, were the following, who were known not to be in Athens: István Zachar (HUN), Charles Vanoni (FRA), Ralph Derr (USA), Harald Andersson (SWE), and Louis Adler (FRA).

25. EK and VK list 11 competitors from 6 nations. FW has 16 competitors from 8 nations.

26. TfI claims the margins were 20 meters between 1st and 2nd and also between 2nd and 3rd. EK gives Jamison 2nd at 14 meters behind Burke. EzM and VK give estimates of 55.2, 55.6, and 55.6 for 2nd, 3rd, and 4th. The estimates for 3rd and 4th (and probably for 2nd) are unreasonably generous.

27. SV gave the time as $55\frac{1}{5}$, the only 1896 source giving a time. TF mentions the margin as about 15–20 yards.

28. There is some controversy over the 3rd and 4th place finishers. EK lists Hofmann as 3rd in his original *Encyclopædia*, but later reversed himself and had Gmelin 3rd. George Robertson, in his article in *Fortnightly Review* (see p. 54) gives Gmelin 3rd as did Carl Galle, an 1896 competitor, who was interviewed on the subject in the 1960s. TfI has Gmelin 3rd, and Balck explicitly states that Gmelin overtook Hofmann at the end of the race. EK, FW, ORev, and EzM have Hofmann 3rd. TF has Gmelin 3rd. FM has Gmelin 3rd.

29. EzM has six running in this heat but no 1896 source confirms this. He listed Launceston Elliot (GBR) in 5th and Charles Vanoni (FRA) in 6th. TF noted that four ran: 2 Germans, an American, and Frenchman.

30. Hofmann was penalized two meters for false starts.

31. EzM gives an estimate of 57.8. KLWT has 58.6 as given here, with the 1896 source being NS, the only source to give a time for Hofmann. TF gave the margin as 7 yards.

32. Grisel was penalized two meters for false starts.

33. Also entered in this heat, but not competing, were Friedrich Traun (GER), George Marshal (GBR), Edwin Flack (AUS), Luis Subercaseaux (CHI), and Konstantinos Mouratis (SMY). EzM has Grisel 4th, Launceston Elliot (GBR) 5th, and Charles Vanoni (FRA) 6th.

34. EzM again claimed that five ran in this heat, but 1896 evidence of this is lacking. EzM had Nándor Dáni (HUN) as 4th and Luis Subercaseaux (CHI) as 5th. Chilean sports historian Prof. Carlos Lopez von Vriessen (University of Valparaiso) also claims that Subercaseaux competed in the 400 meters and was 5th in this heat, but this is not supported in any 1896 source.

35. The time was given as $58\frac{3}{5}$ in SiB.

36. EzM gives an estimate of 60.0, which seems slightly generous.

37. Also entered in this heat, but not competing, were Grantley Goulding (GBR), Launceston Elliot (GBR), Georges De La Nézière (FRA), Nándor Dáni (HUN), and Leonidasz Manno (HUN). EzM has [Georges] De La Nézière 3rd, Nándor Dáni 4th, and Luis Subercaseaux (CHI) 5th.

38. Also entered in this event, but not assigned to a heat, and not in Athens, were István Zaborszky (HUN), and Charles Vanoni (FRA).

39. The OR claims that 14 ran, but this was probably based on the number of entries. FW also listed 14. VK listed 8 competitors.

40. Per TF, Flack's 400 meter split was 65.5.

41. The OR gave the time as 2:01.0, which is an obvious error not seen elsewhere. TF gave the mark as 2:10.0.

42. The only 1896 source giving a time was SV, which listed 2:11$\frac{4}{5}$. The margins between 2nd and 3rd are given variously. EK, EzM, and VK give the 2nd-place time of 2:11.8, but this is likely an estimate. EzM and VK also gave a 3rd-place time of 2:28.0, while EK states only that Golemis was 90 meters behind, apparently using TF as a source. TF gives the margins as 10 yds. between 1-2, and 100 yards between 2-3. Tfl lists 10 meters between 1-2 but notes that Golemis was more than 100 meters behind Dáni. The ORev gives the margin between 2nd and 3rd as 50 meters.

43. SV lists Lermusiaux as 3rd.

44. The OR gives the time as 2:11.

45. EzM gives estimated times of 2:11.4 and 2:14.0 for 2nd and 3rd. SV gave a time for Dáni of 2:10$\frac{1}{5}$, which seems most likely. SV also listed Traun as 3rd and Marshal 4th, the only source to give finishes this deep.

46. EzM has Frantz Reichel (FRA) in 4th and did not list Marshal as competing.

47. Also entered, but not competing, were Frantz Reichel (FRA), Fritz Hofmann (GER), and Thomas Burke (USA).

48. TF gives the time as 2:11$\frac{3}{5}$, which is not seen in any other source. Tfl gave 2:16$\frac{4}{5}$.

49. TF gives the margin as 1$\frac{1}{2}$ yards. Plng gave the time as 2:18. SV erroneously listed Fetsis as 2nd.

50. De La Nézière listed as 3rd in SV, the only 1896 source to list the 3rd place finisher.

51. EzM has Fetsis 3rd and Tomprof 4th, but this is not supported by any 1896 source.

52. Also entered, but not competing, were Kurt Doerry (GER), and Luis Subercaseaux (CHI).

53. István Zaborszky (HUN) was also entered but was not in Athens and was not assigned to a heat.

54. VK lists 7 competitors.

55. Multiple different times have been listed. The OR gives 4:35.2, which is seen in no other source. TF, Tfl, SiB, Hüppe, ASZ, Prsk, Plng, ToA, FM, SV, Gagalis, and ORev list the time as 4:33$\frac{1}{5}$. Akrp has the time as 4:33$\frac{2}{5}$. The time was given as 4:23 in Epth, an obvious error.

56. EzM, EK, VK, and OTAF all give times of 4:34.0, 4:36.0, and 4:39.0 for 2nd, 3rd, and 4th, but these are certainly estimates which are copied from one to another. SV has the margin as 30 meters and 10 meters on differing accounts. TF has Blake 5 yards behind Flack, and Lermusiaux 15 yards behind Blake.

57. Listed as 4th per SiB, the only 1896 source giving results that deep.

58. FW and EzM have Fetsis in 5th and Golemis in 6th, but no 1896 source gives results that deep, and it is not at all certain about placements after 4th.

59. Also entered, but not competing, in this event were George Marshal (GBR), Georges De La Nézière (FRA), and Nándor Dáni (HUN). Gyula Malcsiner (HUN) was also entered but was not in Athens.

60. It is not at all certain that Tomprof was the 8th runner, although the other 7 competitors are well established. Karakatsanis, Golemis, and Fetsis are listed as competitors in Akrp and Gagalis. No 1896 source lists Tomprof or gives the exact identity of the 8th runner. The only reference to Tomprof is from Manitakis, but that is from 1962. It is possible that the 8th runner was De La Nézière or Marshal. Dáni did not start per SV.

61. The number of starters is listed differently in many sources, but studying 1896 sources makes it quite certain that 17 is correct. Later sources give as follows: Pointu, VK—18; EK—17; FW, OTAF—25; and TMF—16.

62. Times given in 1896 sources as follows: 2-55 in Akrp, SV, Velo; 2-55:20 in SiB, Hüppe; 2-58:20 in NS and ASZ.

63. Times given in 1896 sources as follows: 2-57 in SV; 2-58 in Akrp; 2-58:20 in SiB and Velo.

64. Many sources list Belokas as 3rd, either disregarding or not knowing of his disqualification.

65. Kellner's time is given variously as 3-02 (SV); 3-06:35 (FM, TMF, EzM, OTAF); and 3-09:35 (Plng, Argy, Tfl, VK, ORev, Pointu, TF). OR, ToA, Prsk, and Smnds all note that Kellner was 5 seconds behind Belokas.

66. FW and EzM omitted Gerakaris, listing Masouris as 7th. They gave no further places.

67. The runners who dropped out, did so in the following order: Kafetzis at 9 km., Grigoriou and Lavrentis at 24 km., Lermusiaux at 32 km., and Flack at 37 km.

68. Time given as 2-59 in SV and 3-06:03 in Velo.

69. Following a Hungarian protest, Belokas was disqualified for having taken a carriage ride to the vicinity of the stadium when he was exhausted. He reentered the race at that time.

70. Also entered but not competing were Carl Galle (GER), –– Vathis (GRE), –– Vanitakis (GRE), Gyula Malcsiner (HUN), and Carlo Airoldi (ITA). Airoldi was not allowed to compete because his amateur status was not ratified after his arrival in Athens.

71. Based on a misprint in the OR, some later sources claim 100 meters, rather than 110 meters. Research done by British track & field historian Peter Lovesey, published in the *Olympic Review*, Vols. 121-122, p. 722, concludes that the distance was 110 meters.

72. TF gives the margin as half-a-yard, TfI as a couple of centimeters, while Curtis claims he won by only a few centimeters. EzM and OTAF both estimated the time as 18.0, which seems to be an overestimate. EK estimated it to 17.7 for Goulding, which seems about right.

73. The number of competitors and exact composition of the heats is quite controversial, and depends somewhat on one's interpretation of the various sources. Of the 18 available sources from 1896, only five mention all the participants. They do not agree. ToA and Prsk have 8 competitors, as follows: Heat 1 (4 competitors): Tufferi, Goulding, Andreou, and Reichel; Heat 2 (4 competitors): Curtis, Connolly, Doerry, and Hoyt. Akrp has 7 competitors, as follows: Heat 1 (4 competitors): Szokolyi, Goulding, Andreou, and Reichel; Heat 2 (3 competitors): Curtis, Hofmann, and Hoyt. SV has 8 competitors, as follows: Heat 1 (5 competitors): Tufferi, Szokolyi, Goulding, Andreou, and Reichel; Heat 2 (3 competitors): Curtis, Hofmann, and Hoyt. SV also notes that Sjöberg, Skaltsogiannis, Traun, Doerry, and Connolly DNS. Finally, BDP has 8 competitors, as follows: Heat 1 (4 competitors): Tufferi, Szokolyi, Goulding, and Andreou; Heat 2 (4 competitors): Sjöberg, Reichel, Skaltsogiannis, and Curtis.

It appears that Szokolyi, Goulding, Andreou and Reichel competed in heat one. What of Tufferi? He may have competed, based on the evidence, but it is less certain. SV has five competitors, including Tufferi, and Gagalis also mentions 5 competitors. Also, were there five or four competitors in heat one? Four seems more likely, though there is some support for five, as noted.

Heat two is more difficult. Curtis and Hoyt definitely took part. ToA and Prsk have Connolly, but no American source lists him as competing. ToA and Prsk have Doerry, Akrp and SV have Hofmann, Gagalis and BDP have Skaltsogiannis, and BDP lists Sjöberg and Reichel. Reichel started in heat one and is certainly incorrect. Per Viktor Balck (TfI), Sjöberg DNS. Walter Teutenberg maintains that Hofmann DNS because he wished to save himself for the final of the 400 meters, which followed one hour later. Thus it appears most likely that Doerry and Skaltsogiannis competed along with Curtis and Hoyt in heat two. There is also the question of four or three competitors, and four seems most likely. In addition, if we accept four competitors in heat one, most sources support eight total competitors in the event, making four in each heat most likely.

74. TF erroneously has Szokolyi in 2nd and 10 yards behind Goulding. OR repeats this error. SV specifically states that Szokolyi stumbled at the last hurdle, thereby missing the final. BDP also says that Szokolyi hit the last hurdle.

75. EzM has Reichel 3rd and Szokolyi 2nd. Only two 1896 sources listed the 3rd place finisher. SV listed 3rd as Szokolyi, and Salpigx listed Andreou. We cannot be certain and list them as also competing.

76. Listed as 3rd in Salpigx, as noted above.

77. TF noted that Curtis finished before the other hurdlers reached the last hurdle.

78. The heat composition is very confusing, as discussed above. There were originally four heats, with the following make-up: Heat 1: Tufferi, Szokolyi, Goulding, Andreou; Heat 2: Sjöberg, Reichel, Skaltsogiannis; Heat 3: Curtis, Traun, Hofmann; and Heat 4: Doerry, Connolly, Hoyt. Also originally entered but not in Athens, and not assigned to a definite heat after the draw, were Charles Vanoni (FRA), Pál Péthy (HUN), Konstantinos Mouratis (SMY), Frederick W. Lord (USA), and Harald Andersson (SWE). Because of the many withdrawals, the heats were rearranged. It appears that

Reichel was moved to heat one, with Tufferi most likely not competing. Heats 2-4 were then combined into the revised Heat 2.

79. There were 15 final entries and 20 in all.

80. This is per OR, TF, and TfI, but was 1.40 meters per Hüppe.

81. The source for this is the OR and Hüppe.

82. SV has the mark as 1.71. Hüppe notes that Clark cleared 1.70, 1.75, and 1.81.

83. There is much controversy over the heights cleared, except that all agree that Clark won with 1.81. EzM gives 1.72 (Connolly), 1.71 (Garrett), and 1.70 for Sjöberg and Hofmann. EK, VK, and OTAF give 1.625 for Sjöberg and Hofmann, with VK and OTAF probably copying EK in this case. OR, TfI, and TF, note that the opening height was 1.50 meters. The OR states that the bar was raised 5 centimeters at a time, until 1.60, at which time it was raised 2.5 centimeters at a time. TF states that Hofmann missed his third jump and Sjöberg missed his fourth, which makes these heights the most reasonable finish. TfI has Connolly 2nd, Sjöberg 3rd, and Hofmann 4th and does not mention Garrett. ORev has 1.76 for Connolly, 1.71 for Garrett, and 1.62 for Hofmann and Sjöberg in =4th.

84. Also entered and included in the final drawing of lots, but not competing, were Desiderius Wein (HUN), Alajos Szokolyi (HUN), Carl Schuhmann (GER), Gustav Schuft (GER), Fritz Manteuffel (GER), Gyula Kakas (HUN), Gustav Flatow (GER), Alfred Flatow (GER), Conrad Böcker (GER), and John Stanley Edwards (USA). Also entered, but not included in the drawing of the lots and not competing, were Harald Andersson (SWE), Louis Adler (FRA), Friedrich Traun (GER), Carl Galle (GER), and Kurt Doerry (GER).

85. Many sources, even from 1896, including OR, TF, TfI, ASZ, Akrp, Epth, Argy, Gagalis, and Prsk are in error, listing Tyler as the champion, with Hoyt second.

86. FM erroneously has the mark as 3.25.

87. There is much confusion over the heights cleared. The accounts of ToA and TF are the most detailed and thus accepted here as the most reliable. Various marks seen are as follows: Damaskos — 2.85 (EK, Chrysafis, OTAF), 2.80 (EzM, Prsk, Gagalis). 2.60 (TfI and lists him as sole 3rd, ToA, TF); Theodoropoulos — 2.80 (EK, Chrysafis, OTAF, Prsk, Gagalis), 2.85 (EzM), 2.60 (TfI and listed as sole 4th, ToA, TF); Xydas — 2.80 (EzM), 2.50 (EK), and 2.40 (Chrysafis, ToA, TF).

88. Also entered, but not competing, were Hermann Weingärtner (GER), Desiderius Wein (HUN), Momcsilló Topavicza (HUN), Alajos Szokolyi (HUN), Carl Schuhmann (GER), Karl Neukirch (GER), Fritz Manteuffel (GER), Gyula Kakas (HUN), Gustav Flatow (GER), Alfred Flatow (GER), Charles Champaud (SUI), Friedrich Traun (GER), Fritz Hofmann (GER), Carl Galle (GER), and Kurt Doerry (GER). Charles Vanoni (FRA) was entered but not included at the drawing of the lots.

89. The OR, ToA, Prsk, Akrp, and NS claim there were only 8 competitors. TF, SV, and SiB claim there were nine, with TF giving the national representation as listed.

90. Hüppe has the mark as 6.30.

91. Mallon gave 6.18 for Garrett, 6.11 for Connolly, and 5.98 for Tufferi in 4th, 5.83 for Grisel in 5th, 5.74 for Khalkokondilis in 6th, 5.70 for Schuhmann in 7th, and 5.64 for Wein in 8th. His source for this was EzM, but Widlund has pointed out that from the 18 available 1896 sources, no marks are given beyond 4th place, so we have not included any further marks. The mark for Garrett is 6.00 per OR, ToA, Prsk, and SV, but was 6.30 in NS.

92. SV has the mark as 5.82. ToA and Prsk give the 5.84 noted here. NS has 5.76.

93. Listed as 4th with 5.74 by SV, ToA, and Prsk. NS has 5.70.

94. Mallon listed Tuffer[e] 4th, Grisel 5th, and Khalkokondilis 6th, but this is not supported by 1896 sources.

95. EzM has Schuhmann 6th, Desider [*sic*] Wein 7th, and Khalkokondilis 8th. FW also gives Schuhmann 6th. This is not supported by any 1896 source.

96. EK listed Tufferi 4th with 5.98, Grisel 5th with 5.83, and Khalkokondilis 6th with 5.74, but no 1896 source confirms this.

97. EK has Grisel 5th with 5.83; again, not confirmed by 1896 sources.

98. Also entered, but not competing, were Hermann Weingärtner (GER), Momcsilló Topavicza (HUN), Alajos Szokolyi (HUN), Fritz Hofmann (GER), Alfred Flatow (GER), Kurt Doerry (GER),

Nándor Dáni (HUN), Thomas Curtis (USA), and Ralph Derr (USA). Also entered but not included in the drawing of lots were Konstantinos Mouratis (SMY), Carl Galle (GER), Pál Péthy (HUN), Harald Andersson (SWE), and Friedrich Traun (GER). SV has Flatow competing and not Grisel, but SiB specifically states that "of the Germans Schuhmann took part," which implies that he was the only German competitor.

99. EzM lists 10 competitors, giving three Germans as unplaced competitors: Fritz Hofmann, Gustav Felix Flatow, and Carl Schuhmann. FW and OR have 10 competitors, but this was the number of final entrants. VK lists 7 competitors.

100. There were 10 final entries and 11 altogether.

101. 12.62 in Hüppe and 12.60 in ASZ.

102. EK, OR, FM, EzM, ToA, Prsk, and ORev have the mark as 12.52, while SV has 12.565, and Hüppe has 12.53.

103. SV lists 11.26, but notes in our copy of SV have that crossed out and list 12.30 for Szokolyi. EK and ORev have the mark as 12.30.

104. Mallon listed Zoumis as 5th, Alexandros Khalkokondilis as 6th, and Alphonse Grisel as 7th. He did not list Schuhmann or Hofmann as competing. Schuhmann, in an interview years later, described himself as finishing 5th in this event.

105. Also entered, but not competing, were Friedrich Traun (GER), Alphonse Grisel (FRA), and Alfred Flatow (GER). Pál Péthy (HUN) was entered but was not in Athens.

106. The OR, ToA, NS, Chrysafis, Prsk, SV, VK, and EzM list 7; while TF, and Epth have 4 competitors; and Gagalis lists 5. ToA and Prsk have the best reports. They both mention Garrett, Gouskos, Papasideris and Jensen. Akrp mentions Garrett, Gouskos, Schuhmann, and Clark. Gavrilidou mentions Garrett, Gouskos, Schuhmann, Hofmann, and Clark. SV says Grisel, Nielsen, Flatow, Wein, Clark, Robertson, Topavicza, and Jensen did not start, implying that Garrett, Gouskos, Papasideris, Schuhmann, Hofmann, Weingärtner, and Böcker took part. Four Germans is unlikely and not supported by German sources. There was a likely a mix-up between Weingärtner/Böcker and Jensen/Clark.

107. VK has athletes from 5 nations competing.

108. Many different marks are seen in the 1896 sources for Gouskos, as follows: 11.20 (TF), 11.15 (Epth, Gavrilidou), 11.09 (Chrysafis), 11.08 (ASZ), 11.07 (Akrp), and 11.03 (ToA, Prsk, NS, SV, and Hüppe). Most more modern sources have 11.20 (EK, DW, SG, FM), but 11.15 is noted in EzM and FW.

109. Listed as 3rd in TF, TfI, and SV. Only SV gave a mark of 10.36.

110. OTAF lists the top 7 and EK lists the top 6. They both erroneously give 4-6 to George Stuart Robertson (GBR), Louis Adler (FRA), and Sotirios Versis (GRE). OTAF has Charles Winckler (DEN) in 7th. Danish expert Hans Larsen has spoken with Winckler's family and examined Danish sources from 1896 and emphatically denies Winckler's participation. He states that Winckler was not even in Athens.

111. TfI has Schuhmann 4th with no distance given.

112. Prsk notes that "four men, Garrett, Gouskos, Papasideris, and Jensen, remained in the competition." The rules stated that only the top three after three rounds advanced to the final three puts. This may imply that there was a tie for 3rd place after three rounds.

113. In a later interview, Schuhmann said he was 6th.

114. Hüppe notes that Schuhmann and Robertson "put between 10 and 11 meters." Robertson's participation is not mentioned even in his own article. TF notes that Robertson "stood out of the weight putting, in which he might be presumed to have made a respectable appearance. Probably his time was too much occupied by the composition of his Greek ode."

115. Also entered, but not competing, were Hermann Weingärtner (GER), Desiderius Wein (HUN), Momcsilló Topavicza (HUN), George Stuart Robertson (GBR), Holger Nielsen (DEN), Alphonse Grisel (FRA), Alfred Flatow (GER), and Conrad Böcker (GER). Also entered but not in Athens were Charles Winckler (DEN), Charles Vanoni (FRA), Pál Péthy (HUN), and Louis Adler (FRA).

116. The OR lists 11 competitors, which was the number of final entries, but TF states that there were 9, and gives the following breakdown: 3 GRE, 2 DEN, 1 SWE, 1 FRA, 1 GBR, and 1 USA. This

agrees with our results. OR has 11 competitors, giving as follows: 3 GRE, 3 DEN, 1 SWE, 1 GBR, 1 FRA, 1 USA, and 1 GER; but of these, Charles Winckler (DEN) [not in Athens] and Carl Schuhmann (GER) did not compete.

117. Garrett's series was 27.53, foul, unknown, 28.72, and 29.15. It was given in the notebooks of Francis Lane held at the Princeton University Archives.

118. Paraskevopoulos' series was 28.51, unknown, unknown, 28.88, and 28.955. It was given in the notebooks of Francis Lane held at the Princeton University Archives.

119. ToA and Prsk list the mark as 27.78, while NS has 27.48. TF has 88'6" (26.98).

120. EK, EzM, and ORev have A. [Louis] Adler (FRA) [not in Athens] in 4th, Papasideris in 5th, and Robertson in 6th. EzM also listed Sjöberg in 7th. They apparently copied one another.

121. Fourth was not known until recently, when Ian Buchanan unearthed a letter from Robertson stating that he had finished fourth and listing his mark as 82'8" (25.20).

122. Most sources lists Winckler and not Nielsen, but Winckler was not in Athens, per Danish expert Hans Larsen.

123. Danish sources (*Olympiadebogen*) note that Nielsen threw *circa* 27 meters. This does not correlate well with Robertson's letter stating he finished 4th with 25.20.

124. Danish sources (*Olympiadebogen*) note that Jensen threw *circa* 26 meters. This does not correlate well with Robertson's letter stating he finished 4th with 25.20.

125. Also in the final entry list, but not competing, were Carl Schuhmann (GER), and Charles Winckler (DEN). Also entered, but not in Athens, were the Frenchmen Charles Vanoni and Louis Adler.

Cycling

The 1896 cycling events were held on the Neo Phaliron Velodrome, which was built specially for the Olympics near the sea in Piraeus. The Neo Phaliron Velodrome was fairly modern in appearance with banked turns, and measured 333⅓ meters, or ⅓ kilometer, in length. Seating was available for 7,000 spectators. The velodrome was built at a cost of 100,000 Greek drachma. Coubertin had looked in Paris for the design of the velodrome, but before he could find one, Crown Prince Konstantinos of Greece had found a design in Copenhagen, and used it to design and build the track, which was built by the Greek Vellinis. The Velodrome also contained tennis courts within the infield, where some of the 1896 tennis matches were played. The 1896 cycling events were not well attended by cyclists, as only five nations took part. However, photographs of the events do exist, and it appears that very large crowds watched the 1896 cycling competitions.

A royal box was constructed on the west side of the stadium, from which King Georgios watched the events. He was accompanied by Prince Konstantinos, King Alexandros of Serbia, Queen Olga, and Prince Andreas.

Site:	Neo Phaliron Velodrome
Dates:	8, 11–13 April (27 March, 30 March–1 April)
Events:	6
Competitors:	19 (19 Men)
Nations:	6

	Competitors	1st	2nd	3rd	Places
Austria	1	1	–	2	3
France	2	4	1	1	6
Germany	5	–	1	–	1
Great Britain	2	–	1	1	2
Greece	8	1	3	–	4
Smyrna	1	–	–	–	–
Totals	19	6	6	4	16
Nations	5	3	4	5	5

TRACK EVENTS

One Lap (333⅓ meters) Time Trial

A: 8; E: ?[1]*; C: 5[2]; D: 11 April (30 March); F: 333⅓ meters flying start.

Paul Masson was not related to the Paul Masson who started the famous wine company. Masson had won a number of races in France since 1894 and was well known. In 1894 he had won a major international race against 12 rivals over 5,000 meters which had been organized by the Union Vélocipédique de France. He attempted to take part in the World Championships in 1895 but his entry was not accepted. At the end of the year, after winning races in Ostend and Antwerp, he was finally admitted to the French national team.

After the Olympics Masson turned professional, adopting the name Paul Nossam (Masson spelled backwards). His only significant performance as Paul Nossam was third in the world professional sprint championship in 1897.

Nikolopoulos and Schmal tied for 2nd initially with the same times of 26 seconds. In a race-off for second place, Nikolopoulos won the final medal position with a time 25⅖ seconds versus 26⅗ for Schmal.

1.	Paul Masson	FRA	24	
2.	Stamatios Nikolopoulos	GRE	26[3]	25⅖
3.	Adolf Schmal	AUT	26[4]	26⅗
4.	E. Battel[5]	GBR	26⅕[6]	
=5.	F. Keeping	GBR	27	
	Theodor Leupold	GER	27[7]	
	Léon Flameng	FRA	27[8]	
8.	Joseph Rosemeyer	GER	27⅕[9]	

2,000 meter Sprint

A: 4[10]; E: 21[11]; C: 3; D: 11 April (30 March); T: 1707.

It was very cold on this day. There was only one final heat of the four competitors, with no qualifying rounds. There were no pacemakers. It was a very slow race until the finish when Masson won easily.

1.	Paul Masson	FRA	4:58⅕[12]
2.	Stamatios Nikolopoulos	GRE	5:00⅕[13]
3.	Léon Flameng	FRA	
4.	Joseph Rosemeyer	GER	
	[14]		

10,000 meters

A: 6; E: 16[15]; C: 4; D: 11 April (30 March); T: 1530.

It was noted to be a very cold day. Only a final race took place, with no pacemakers allowed. The two French cyclists, Masson and Flameng, were the class of the cycling events at the 1896

*See Notes on pages 85–86.

Olympics. In the 10 kilometer race on the track they battled very closely, with Masson narrowly winning in a sprint. On the 20th lap, Kolettis and Konstantinidis collided and both fell. They both remounted and continued, but shortly thereafter Kolettis withdrew because of injuries sustained during the fall. It is uncertain if Konstantinidis finished or not.

1.	Paul Masson	FRA	17:54⅕
2.	Léon Flameng	FRA	17:54⅘[16]
3.	Adolf Schmal	AUT	
4.	Joseph Rosemeyer	GER	
AC.	Aristidis Konstantinidis[17]	GRE	
AB.	Georgios Kolettis	GRE	DNF[18]

[19]

100 kilometers

A: 9[20]; E: 22; C: 5; D: 8 April (27 March).

The race was a mass start and required 300 laps of the 333⅓ meter track. The riders were paced throughout by cyclists or tandems who would join up and lead out the riders for a few laps. However, only the Greek and French riders had pacemakers, and the others quickly dropped out when they realized they could not keep pace without pacers. Kolettis had a mechanical problem in mid-race, but Flameng stopped and got off his bike, waiting until Kolettis' bike was repaired. He also fell near the end of the race but won quite easily. Flameng raced with a French flag tied around his leg. In August 1895, Flameng had achieved some measure of fame by cycling 3,000 kilometers across France. However, he was not a well-known cyclist prior to the 1896 Olympics. He never placed at the world championships. Paul Masson did not start this race, although he was entered, but served as one of the pacemakers for Flameng.

1.	Léon Flameng	FRA	3-08:19⅕
2.	Georgios Kolettis	GRE	at 11 laps[21]
AB.	Bernhard Knubel	GER	DNF[22]
	Theodor Leupold	GER	DNF[23]
	E. Battel	GBR	DNF[24]
	Aristidis Konstantinidis	GRE	DNF[25]
	Joseph Welzenbacher	GER	DNF[26]
	Adolf Schmal	AUT	DNF
	Joseph Rosemeyer	GER	DNF

[27]

12-hours race

A: 7[28]; E: 17[29]; C: 4; D: 13 April (1 April).

The race was a mass start which began at 7:20 A.M. (0720).[30] Pacemakers were allowed. The weather was noted to be the worst of the Olympics, with cold, wind, and rain. Snow was noted on the mountains outside of Athens. Rowing events, which were scheduled for this day, had to be cancelled. This was the last event held at the Games of the Ist Olympiad.

Early in the race, Adolf Schmal, who was better known as a fencer, jumped the field and gained a lap early, lapping the Greeks at 5 laps, the German at 7 laps, and Keeping at 10 laps. He then rode with the pack until one by one the riders dropped out. At 1200, the two remaining riders, Schmal and Keeping, took a 10 minute break. Schmal rode directly behind Keeping's wheel throughout, never allowing himself to be dropped, and won by the one lap that he had gained early in the race. Keeping made occasional bursts to regain the lost lap, but to no avail. On the last lap, Schmal opened a small gap over Keeping, in addition to the extra lap gained.

1.	Adolf Schmal	AUT	295.300 km.[31]
2.	F. Keeping	GBR	at 354 m.[32]
AB.	Georgios Paraskevopoulos[33]	GRE	DNF[34]
	Joseph Welzenbacher[35]	GER	DNF[36]
	A. Tryfiatis-Tripiaris	GRE	DNF[37]
	–– Loverdos	SMY	DNF[38]
	Konstantinos Konstantinou	GRE	DNF[39]
40			

ROAD EVENT

Road Race, Individual

A: 7[41]; E: 26; C: 3; D: 12 April (31 March); T: 1217; F: 87 kilometers, from Athens to Marathon and then return to Athens.

This race was held on the same course as the running marathon, but consisted of riding that course twice, on an out-and-back course. The riders started in Athens on the Odos Kifisia, rode to Marathon, and then returned to Athens, finishing at the velodrome at Neo Phaliron. In Marathon they were required to sign a document in the presence of an official, verifying that they had arrived there.

The pack rode together most of the way to Marathon. On the return, the pack split due to many falls. Konstantinidis fell three times; Goedrich also fell and had to stop to borrow a new bike because of damage to his original. Konstantinidis flatted near Athens and was overtaken by Battel. Konstantinidis borrowed a bicycle and continued, but crashed just as he caught up to Battel. He borrowed yet another bike and caught Battel, who was exhausted from the effort of staying ahead of Konstantinidis and ended up barely finishing.

Battel was a servant at the British Embassy in Athens. Some British officials attempted to prevent him from entering the Olympic cycling events on the grounds that his job disqualified him as a gentleman, and thus he could not be an amateur.

1.	Aristidis Konstantinidis	GRE	3-21:10[42]
2.	August Goedrich	GER	3-31:14[43]
3.	E. Battel[44]	GBR	
AC.	Georgios Paraskevopoulos	GRE[45]	
	Konstantinos Konstantinou	GRE	
	Miltiades Iatrou	GRE	
	Georgios Aspiotis	GRE	
46			

NOTES

1. We know of no other entrants who did not compete. The program for this event has not been found.

2. VK lists 4 nations.

3. The following times are also seen: OR, Akrp, Epth, ToA, Prsk, TF, SiB, and Velo — 25⅖ (these appear to be using the time for the race-off in error); TfI — 24⅖; ORev — 25; RW — 25⅗.

4. The following time is also seen: Akrp, Epth — 26⅗.

5. Spelled Battle in Hüppe, which may be a more normal Anglicized spelling. Battel may be an incorrect transliteration from the Greek.

6. The places for Battel and Keeping are uncertain. Their names may be reversed, and it may be that Keeping finished 4th in 26⅕ and Battel was =5th in 27 seconds. The following times for the two in these places are also seen: Keeping — Akrp, Velo — 26⅕; Epth — 27. Battel — Epth — 26⅕; Akrp, Velo — 27.

7. Noted in Akrp and Velo.

8. Noted in Akrp and Velo.

9. Given as 27⅕ in Velo, but as 27 seconds in Akrp and Epth.

10. Four participants per OR, ToA, Epth, NS, Argy, and TF.

11. Per Epth, there were 21 entries but only 18 have been identified.

12. The mark is 4:56.0 per FM, VB, and TF, but 4:58⅕ per OR, Akrp, Epth, NS, Argy, Gavrilidou, Gagalis, Velo, and RW.

13. 5:00½ in Epth, but 5:00⅕ in OR, Akrp, and Argy.

14. Also entered, but not competing, were Joseph Welzenbacher (GER), Adolf Schmal (AUT), Fritz Manteuffel (GER), Theodor Leupold (GER), Aristidis Konstantinidis (GRE), Georgios Kolettis (GRE), Bernhard Knubel (GER), and E. Battel (GBR). Also entered, but known not to be in Athens, were Luis Subercaseaux (CHI), Angelo Porciatti (ITA), Ray MacDonald (USA), John Johnson (USA), Jules Hatté (FRA), and Gustave De Lafreté (FRA).

15. The number of entries is not listed in any source, but has been deduced from the entry lists in Velo and SV, and reports in Greek papers and books.

16. Marks seen in 1896 source are as follows: Gavrilidou, Gagalis —17:54⅘; FM —17:54⅕; Akrp —17:54⅗; NS —17:58⅕; Prsk —17:64½ (likely a misprint for 17:54½).

17. The identity of this cyclist is somewhat in question. The OR, ToA, NS, Chrysafis, and Prsk call him Konstantinidis. Akrp, Epth, Gavrilidou, and Gagalis call him Konstantinos Konstantinou. Velo and RW list him as Stamatios Nikolopoulos, which seems unlikely when considering the sources.

18. Kolettis abandoned at about 7 km.

19. Also entered, but not competing, were Joseph Welzenbacher (GER), Fritz Manteuffel (GER), Theodor Leupold (GER), and Bernhard Knubel (GER). Also entered, not competing and known not to be in Athens, were Luis Subercaseaux (CHI), Angelo Porciatti (ITA), Ray MacDonald (USA), John Johnson (USA), Jules Hatté (FRA), and Gustave De Lafreté (FRA).

20. Akrp, Epth, NS, Pronoia, Argy, TF, and TfI list 9. OR, FW, ToA, AGS, and Gagalis have 10 competitors. RW has 11 competitors.

21. At 5-6 laps per TF, but 11 per OR and ToA. It is not certain if Kolettis went on to finish or simply stopped riding when Flameng finished 100 km. No time was recorded for Kolettis.

22. Retired at 123 laps or 41 km.

23. Retired at 113 laps or 37 km.

24. Retired at 51 laps or 17 km.

25. Retired at 50 laps or 16 km.

26. It is not known when Welzenbacher, Schmal, and Rosemeyer abandoned the race.

27. OR and ToA also list Georgios Aspiotis as competing, and Gagalis lists Miltiades Iatrou as competing; but these are unlikely, as there is no record of their abandonment in any 1896 source describing the race. Also in the final entry list, but not competing, were Paul Masson (FRA), Fritz Manteuffel (GER), Konstantinos Konstantinou (GRE), F. Keeping (GBR), Miltiades Iatrou (GRE), August Goedrich (GER), Georgios Aspiotis (GRE), Ray MacDonald (USA), John Johnson (USA),

and S. Antoniadis (GRE). Also entered, not competing and known not to be in Athens, were Luis Subercaseaux (CHI), Angelo Porciatti (ITA), and Gustave De Lafreté (FRA).

28. ToA, TF, TfI, SiB, and Velo have 7 competitors. OR, FW, and RW have 6 competitors.

29. ToA, TF, and TfI noted 12 entries, without listing them. The entry lists of Velo and SV and the Greek papers and books list 17 names.

30. The starting time is disputed, with the following times seen: AT — 5 A.M. (0500); Gagalis — 7:30 A.M. (0730); OR — 6 A.M. (0600); and TfI, TF, RW, SiB — 7 A.M. (0700).

31. This is the distance given in the OR, but it is highly disputed. The following are seen: OR — 295.300 km.; FM — 314.997 km.; Argy — 298 km.; Gagalis — 296 km.; ASZ — 296 km.; TF, TfI, SiB, RW, ToA, Prsk — 315 km.

32. The margin is disputed. The following gaps are seen: OR — slightly more than one lap; TF, ToA, SiB, and TfI — 354 meters; RW —1¼ laps; Argy — 348 meters.

33. FM lists this athlete as Panagiotis Paraskevopoulos (the discus thrower), and has him finishing the race, in 3rd, with a distance of 313.300 km.

34. Retired at 5:15 P.M. (1715) after 9-55, and 231 km.

35. Prsk has Bernhard Knubel instead of Welzenbacher.

36. Retired after *circa* 3 hrs.

37. Retired after *circa* 3 hrs. per RW.

38. Retired after *circa* 3 hrs. per RW

39. Retired after *circa* 3 hrs. per RW

40. Also entered, but not competing, were Joseph Rosemeyer (GER), Fritz Manteuffel (GER), Theodor Leupold (GER), Aristidis Konstantinidis (GRE), and Bernhard Knubel (GER). Also entered, not competing and known not to be in Athens, were Luis Subercaseaux (CHI), Angelo Porciatti (ITA), Ray MacDonald (USA), John Johnson (USA), and Gustave De Lafreté (FRA).

41. FW, ToA, OR, TF, SiB, and VK have 6 competitors, not listing Georgios Paraskevopoulos. Akrp, NS, and Argy have 7.

42. Multiple different times are seen, as follows: Gagalis — 3-21:10; TF, OR, NS, Argy, TfI, EK, FW, FM, and ORev — 3-22:31; Gavrilidou — 3-18; RW — 3-24; ToA, Chrysafis, Prsk, and SiB — 3-13; Epth — 3:21. Gagalis seems the best source, as it is the only 1896 source giving the time to the second for both Konstantinidis and Goedrich.

43. Multiple other times are seen: ORev — 3-42:30; FM — 3-42:31; EK and FW — 3-42:18; RW — 3-30; Epth — 3-31; OR, TF, SiB, and TfI — *circa* 20 minutes after Konstantinidis.

44. SiB has Keeping in 3rd.

45. ORev lists Konstantinou in 4th, Aspiotis in 5th, and Iatrou in 6th. Paraskevopoulos is not in the final entry list, but Akrp lists him as participating.

46. Also in the final entry list, but not competing, were A. Tryfiatis-Trypiaris (GRE), Adolf Schmal (AUT), Joseph Rosemeyer (GER), Stamatios Nikolopoulos (GRE), Paul Masson (FRA), Fritz Manteuffel (GER), Theodor Leupold (GER), Georgios Kolettis (GRE), Gyula Kellner (HUN), F. Keeping (GBR), Léon Flameng (FRA), Gustave De Lafreté (FRA), and Epamaindos Kharilaos (GRE). Also entered, not competing and known not to be in Athens, were Luis Subercaseaux (CHI), Angelo Porciatti (ITA), Ray MacDonald (USA), John Johnson (USA), Joseph Welzenbacher (GER), and Bernhard Knubel (GER). Knubel, Kolettis, and Welzenbacher were provisionally entered, but were not in the final entry lists.

Fencing

The 1896 fencing events were held in the Zappeion, which was a large exhibition hall built in 1888 and named for Evangelos Zappas, an early benefactor of the Olympic idea. King Georgios watched the Olympic fencing matches. The sabre matches started prior to his arrival, but those matches were disregarded and the competition restarted after his appearance in the Zappeion. The bouts were conducted until one fencer scored three touches.

Events were conducted in foil, sabre, and foil for masters — or professionals. The professional fencing matches were known by Coubertin and the Olympic officials, and in fact were approved, as fencings masters (or teachers) were very popular athletes in France at that time. An épée event was also scheduled but did not take place.

Site:	Zappeion	
Dates:	7, 9 April	
Events:	3	
Competitors:	15 (15 Men)	
Nations:	4	

	Competitors	1st	2nd	3rd	Places
Austria	1	–	–	–	–
Denmark	1	–	–	1	1
France	4	1	2	–	3
Greece	9	2	1	2	5
Totals	15	3	3	3	9
Nations	4	2	2	2	3

Foil[1]*

A: 8; E: 15; C: 2; D: 7 April (26 March).

The format of this event was two round-robin pools of four fencers each. The first to score three touches in each match was the winner. The winners of each pool, Eugene-Henri Grav-

See Notes on pages 89–90.

elotte and Henri Callot, both Frenchmen, then met in the finals to determine the champion. There is no record of other matches being held to determine the other positions. Gravelotte was a medical student who celebrated his victory that night by drinking a glass of retzina (wine) at the Akropolis.

1.	Eugene-Henri Gravelotte	FRA
2.	Henri Callot	FRA
=3.	Athanasios Vouros	GRE[2]
	Periklis Pierrakos-Mauromikhalis	GRE
=5.	Konstantinos Komninos-Miliotis	GRE
	Henri Delaborde	FRA
=7.	Ioannis Poulos	GRE
	Georgios Balakakis	GRE

[3]

Final A: 2; C: 1; D: 7 April (26 March).

1.	Eugene-Henri Gravelotte	FRA	3–2
2.	Henri Callot	FRA	

Round One A: 8; C: ; D: 7 April (26 March)

Pool A A: 4; C: 2.

			hc	ppm	hd	ip	W	L	Hits
1.	Henri Callot	FRA	--	3–1[4]	3–1	3–2	3	0	9–4
2.	Periklis Pierrakos-Mauromikhalis	GRE	1–3[5]	--	3–1	3–0	2	1	7–4
3.	Henri Delaborde	FRA	1–3	1–3	--	3–2[6]	1	2	5–8
4.	Ioannis Poulos	GRE	2–3	0–3	2–3[7]	--	0	3	4–9

Pool B A: 4; C: 2.

			ehg	av	kmk	gb	W	L	Hits
1.	Eugene-Henri Gravelotte	FRA	--	3–2[8]	3–2	3–1[9]	3	0	9–5
2.	Athanasios Vouros	GRE	2–3[10]	--	wo[11]	3–1	2	1	5–4 (8–4)
3.	Konstantinos Komninos-Miliotis	GRE	2–3	wo	--	3–1	1	2	5–4 (5–7)
4.	Georgios Balakakis	GRE	1–3[12]	1–3	1–3	--	0	3	3–9

Sabre

A: 5; E: 10; C: 3; D: 9 April (28 March)[13].

Adolf Schmal was considered to be one of the favorites but he succeeded in winning only one match. After two rounds, Schmal had two victories against Georgiadis (3–0) and Nielsen (3–1). The King, the Crown Prince and their entourage then arrived. The officials decided to restart the competition, abandoning the earlier results so that the Royal Family could watch the entire tournament. Schmal succeeded in winning only one match in the restarted competition.

			ig	tk	hn	as	gi	W	L	Hits
1.	Ioannis Georgiadis	GRE	--	3–2	3–2	3–2	3–0	4	0	12–6
2.	Tilemakhos Karakalos	GRE	2–3	--	3–2	3–0	3–0[14]	3	1	11–5
3.	Holger Nielsen	DEN	2–3	2–3	--	3–2	3–1	2	2	10–9

4.	Adolf Schmal	AUT	2–3	0–3	2–3	––	3–2	1	3	7–11
5.	Georgios Iatridis	GRE	0–3	0–3[15]	1–3	2–3	––	0	4	3–12
	16									

Foil Fencing for Masters[17]

A: 2; E: 2; C: 2; D: 7 April (26 March).

With his victory in this event, Leonidas Pyrgos became the first Greek in modern times to win an Olympic championship.

1.	Leonidas Pyrgos	GRE	3–1
2.	Jean Perronet	FRA	
	18		

SCHEDULED EVENT, NOT CONTESTED

Épée[19]

E: 3; D: 7 April (26 March).

This event was postponed because the foil took such a long time to complete on 7 April (26 March). We have no record as to why the épée event was eventually cancelled. There were three known entries, all from Greece: Ioannis Poulos, Periklis Pierrakos-Mauromikhalis, and Konstantinos Komninos-Miliotis.

NOTES

1. FW notes that foil fencing was not held in 1896 at Athens. It definitely was. FW gave the results of an épée event with the same results as for the foil, obviously confusing the two events.
2. ORev have Pierrakos-Mavromikhalis in 3rd, Poulos 4th, Vouros 5th, and Komninos-Miliotis [*sic*] in 6th. FM also has Perrakos solely in 3rd. EK has Mavromikhalis-Pierrakos [*sic*] as sole 3rd, with Poulos, Vouros, and Komninos-Miliotis as equal 4th.
3. Also entered, but not competing, were Cyrille Verbrugge (BEL), István Szabo Kisgeszeni (HUN), Jean-Joseph Renaud (FRA), Fred Hellen (USA), Giuseppe Caruso (ITA), Vincenzo Baroni (ITA), and Holger Nielsen (DEN).
4. Prsk has the score as 3–2.
5. Prsk has the score as 2–3.
6. This match score was 3–1 per TF, 3–2 per TfI, Prsk, and 1–3 per OR and Argy.
7. This match score was 1–3 per TF, 2–3 per TfI, Prsk, and 3–1 per OR and Argy.
8. TF has the score as 2–3, with Vouros winning.
9. This match score was 3–0 per VB.
10. TF has the score as 3–2, with Vouros winning.
11. Komninos-Miliotis refused to fence against Vouros because he was upset at the judge's decision in his match against Gravelotte. The officials did not press him to fence, as it was the last match of the pool and neither he nor Vouros could win the pool.
12. This match score was 0–3 per VB.

13. Originally scheduled as the last event on 7 April (26 March), it was postponed when the foil took so long to complete.

14. TfI has the score as 0–3, Iatridis winning.

15. TfI has the score as 3–0, Iatridis winning.

16. Also entered, but not competing, were István Szabo Kisgeszeni (HUN), Giuseppe Caruso (ITA), Vincenzo Baroni (ITA), Eugene-Henri Gravelotte (FRA), and Henri Delaborde (FRA).

17. This event was not listed in FW.

18. EK and ORev list Konstantinos Komninos-Miliotis in 3rd place, but there is no evidence that Konstantinos Komninos-Miliotis competed. He was also not a fencing master; thus, he could not have taken part in this event.

19. FW gave the results of an épée event with the same results as above for the foil, obviously confusing the two events.

Gymnastics

The 1896 gymnastics events were conducted in the Panathenaic Stadium, in the infield of the track. They were basically contests among the Greeks and the Germans, although there were several other nations who had one or two competitors.

The Germans competed amidst controversy back home, as the Deutsche Turnerschaft, the German gymnastics association, did not want them to appear. The German gymnasts were threatened with suspension if they competed in Athens, but this suspension was not carried out.

In the two team events, the Germans won easily. Only the Germans competed on the horizontal bar for teams. The team events allowed each team an exercise of up to four minutes in length. Teams were required to have at least ten members, and there was no limit on the number of gymnasts on a team. Germany had a 10-man team, while the two Greek teams had 32 and 18 gymnasts. Unfortunately, the names of most of the Greek gymnastics teams have not survived.

In the individual events, the performances on each apparatus lasted up to two minutes in length. There were seven judges, including Prince Georgios as referee in all events. The judges were to evaluate the performance as to: 1) body control and power, and 2) agility and mobility. The average of the two components gave the final points. The number of points in all the events has not survived. There were no compulsory exercises, only voluntary, which, according to the Germans, made the judging difficult.

Site:	Panathenaic Stadium					
Dates:	9–11 April (28–31 March)					
Events:	8					
Competitors:	28 Known; 71 Estimated (28/71 Men)					
Nations:	8					

	Known Competitors	*Est. Comp.*	*1st*	*2nd*	*3rd*	*Places*
Denmark	1	1	–	–	–	–
France	1	1	–	–	–	–
Germany	11	11	5	3	2	10
Great Britain	1	1	–	–	–	–
Greece	9	52	2	2	2	6

	Known Competitors	Est. Comp.	1st	2nd	3rd	Places
Hungary	2	2	–	–	–	–
Sweden	1	1	–	–	–	–
Switzerland	2	2	1	2	–	3
Totals	28	71	8	7	4	19
Nations	8	8	3	3	2	3

Parallel Bars, Teams

A: 63[1]*; C: 2; D: 9 April (28 March)

There were ten sets of parallel bars available for use. The judges gave points for the following components: 1) execution, 2) rhythm, and 3) technical difficulty.

1. Germany
    (10 Men + Team Leader Fritz Hofmann)
    [Carl Schuhmann, Conrad Böcker, Alfred Flatow, Gustav Flatow, Fritz Manteuffel, Karl Neukirch, Richard Röstel, Gustav Schuft, Hermann Weingärtner, Georg Hillmar]
2. Greece (Panellinios Gymnastikos Syllogos)
    (32 Men + Team Leader Sotirios Athanasopoulos[2])
3. Greece (Ethnikos Gymnastikos Syllogos)[3]
    (18 Men + Team Leader Ioannis Chrysafis)
    [Filippos Karvelas, Dimitrios Loundras]

Horizontal Bar, Teams

A: 11; C: 1; D: 9 April (28 March)

There were ten sets of horizontal bars available for use. The judges gave points for the following components: 1) execution, 2) rhythm, and 3) technical difficulty.

1. Germany
    (10 Men + Team Leader Fritz Hofmann)
    [Carl Schuhmann, Conrad Böcker, Alfred Flatow, Gustav Flatow, Fritz Manteuffel, Karl Neukirch, Richard Röstel, Gustav Schuft, Hermann Weingärtner, Georg Hillmar]

Horse Vault

A: 15[4]; E: 21; C: 4; D: 9 April (28 March).

In the two available minutes, the gymnasts could do as many jumps as they wished. The victory of the very popular Schuhmann was "greeted with ovations that would never end."

See Notes on pages 95–96.

1.	Carl Schuhmann	GER
2.	Louis Zutter	SUI
3.	Hermann Weingärtner	GER
AC.	Desiderius Wein	HUN
	Henrik Sjöberg	SWE
	Gustav Schuft	GER
	Richard Röstel	GER
	Karl Neukirch	GER
	Fritz Manteuffel	GER
	Gyula Kakas	HUN
	Georg Hillmar	GER
	Gustav Flatow	GER
	Alfred Flatow	GER
	Charles Champaud	SUI
	Conrad Böcker	GER

5

Pommelled Horse

A: 15[6]; E: 21; C: 4; D: 9 April (28 March).

1.	Louis Zutter	SUI
2.	Hermann Weingärtner	GER
AC.	Carl Schuhmann	GER[7]
	Gustav Schuft	GER
	Richard Röstel	GER
	Aristovoulos Petmezas	GRE
	Karl Neukirch	GER
	Fritz Manteuffel	GER
	Gyula Kakas	HUN
	Georg Hillmar	GER
	Gustav Flatow	GER
	Alfred Flatow	GER
	Charles Champaud	SUI
	Conrad Böcker	GER

8

Rings

A: 8[9]; E: 13; C: 3; D: 9 April (28 March).

The ring exercise was of two minutes in length. The result was a split decision in which three judges had Mitropoulos first and three had Weingärtner first. Prince Georgios cast the deciding vote in favor of Mitropoulos. The Official Report noted of Mitropoulos's victory, "Before the result is officially announced one of the judges shouts in French, 'Vive la Grèce.' A few minutes later the number of Mitropoulos is put up and the Greek flag is hoisted. He is the first Greek Olympic winner in the stadium. The enthusiasm bursts forth beyond control; tears damp the eyes, hats are hurled into the air, and handkerchiefs are waved frenziedly. The cheers and the endless applause of which the signal is given by the Royal Family constitute an indescribable composite sound."

1.	Ioannis Mitropoulos	GRE
2.	Hermann Weingärtner	GER
3.	Petros Persakis[10]	GRE
4.	[11]	
5.	Carl Schuhmann	GER
AC.	Desiderius Wein	HUN
	Gustav Flatow	GER
	Alfred Flatow	GER
	Conrad Böcker	GER
	[12]	

Horizontal Bar

A: 15[13]; E: 21; C: 4; D: 9 April (28 March).

Schuhmann gave a performance full of circus tricks, which the crowd loved, and they could not understand why he was not given first place. Two judges had him in first place, but per Hüppe, "they only displayed their ignorance of gymnastics."

1.	Hermann Weingärtner	GER
2.	Alfred Flatow	GER
AC.	Conrad Böcker	GER[14]
	Carl Schuhmann	GER
	Louis Zutter	SUI
	Desiderius Wein	HUN
	Leonidas Tsiklitiras	GRE
	Gustav Schuft	GER
	Richard Röstel	GER
	Antonios Papaigannou	GRE
	Karl Neukirch	GER
	Fritz Manteuffel	GER
	Gyula Kakas	HUN
	Georg Hillmar	GER
	Gustav Flatow	GER
	[15]	

Parallel Bars

A: 18[16]; E: 21; C: 5[17]; D: 10 April (29 March).[18]

Alfred Flatow competed in Athens with his cousin, Gustav Felix Flatow. Both were Jewish. During World War II, both were victims of Hitler's "final solution," perishing in concentration camps, Alfred in 1942 and Felix in 1945.

1.	Alfred Flatow	GER
2.	Louis Zutter	SUI
AC.	Hermann Weingärtner	GER[19]
	Conrad Böcker	GER
	Carl Schuhmann	GER[20]
	Desiderius Wein	HUN
	Gustav Schuft	GER
	Richard Röstel	GER
	Antonios Papaioannou	GRE
	Karl Neukirch	GER
	Ioannis Mitropoulos	GRE
	Fritz Manteuffel	GER
	Filippos Karvelas	GRE
	Gyula Kakas	HUN
	Georg Hillmar	GER
	Alphonse Grisel	FRA
	Gustav Flatow	GER
	Charles Champaud	SUI

[21]

Rope Climbing (14 meters)

A: 5[22]; E: 11; C: 4; D: 10 April (29 March).[23]

The rope climbing event was conducted outdoors on a rope hung from a specially designed frame. It was 14 meters in height. The winner was supposed to be based on who climbed the rope the quickest and with the best style. In the event that nobody was best in both time and style, the competitor with the most total points was the winner. In the event that no competitor reached the top of the rope, the winner was to be the climber achieving the greatest height. Thus, not reaching the top did not necessarily constitute a did not finish (DNF). Point scores have not survived.

Only the two Greeks, Andriakopoulos and Xenakis, succeeded in climbing all the way to the top, with Andriakopoulos winning the championship based on a faster time, although Xenakis's time is not recorded. Andriakopoulos was the first to climb, followed by Xenakis, Hofmann, Elliot, and Jensen, in that order. Hofmann, Elliot, and Jensen stopped climbing when they realized they could not beat the Greek climbers.

1.	Nikolaos Andriakopoulos	GRE	14.0 meters	23⅖[24]
2.	Thomas Xenakis	GRE	14.0 meters[25]	
3.	Fritz Hofmann	GER	12.5 meters[26]	
4.[27]	Viggo Jensen	DEN		
5.	Launceston Elliot	GBR		

[28]

NOTES

1. Various numbers are seen: VK has 71.
2. Listed as Sot[irios] Athanasopoulos in OR and Spyr[idon] Athanasopoulos in Chrysafis.

There were 36 team members per TF and 32 in Epth, Plng, and Argy. There is no information available as to the composition of the team members.

3. The Ethnikos team was obviously a very youthful one. Per Chrysafis the team members were boys from 14–17 years of age, per Prsk they were 14–18, and per ToA from 10–20. SiB and Hüppe noted they were boys from Athenian schools.

4. FW, OR, and Prsk have 17 competitors. Gagalis has 14. Epth has 15. There is only one entry list for the two horse events, and it may be that 17 is the total number of competitors in the two events.

5. The following were also entered: Momcsilló Topavicza (HUN), Aristovoulos Petmezas (GRE), Viggo Jensen (DEN), Fritz Hofmann (GER), Alphonse Grisel (FRA), and Harald Andersson (SWE). Andersson was not in Athens.

6. FW and VK have 17 athletes from 5 nations.

7. VK has Gyula Kakas (HUN) in 3rd, Aristovoulos Petmesas (GRE) in 4th, and Charles Champaud (SUI) in 5th. This is not supported in any 1896 source. No 1896 source lists any place winners after second.

8. The following were also entered, but did not compete: Desiderius Wein (HUN), Momcsilló Topavicza (HUN), Henrik Sjöberg (SWE), Viggo Jensen (DEN), Fritz Hofmann (GER), and Alphonse Grisel (FRA).

9. FW and VK have 12 competitors from 3 nations. TF and ToA noted that 8 competed — 5 Germans, 2 Greeks, and a Hungarian.

10. Listed as 3rd in Prsk, the only source giving a 3rd place finisher.

11. It is known that Schuhmann finished 5th, but the 4th-place finisher is not mentioned in any source.

12. The following were also entered, but did not compete: Fritz Manteuffel (GER), Gyula Kakas (HUN), Viggo Jensen (DEN), Alphonse Grisel (FRA), and Edward Lawrence Levy (GBR).

13. FW, OR, and VK have 16 competitors. TF noted that there were 15 competitors — 10 Germans, 2 Greeks, 2 Hungarians, and 1 Swiss, which is our listing. Prsk has 16 competitors — 11 Germans, 2 Greeks, 2 Hungarians and 1 Swiss. Epth has 14 participants, of which 2 were noted to be Greek.

14. VK and ORev erroneously list [Aristovoulos] Petmezas (GRE) as 3rd, but he fell ill just before the event and could not compete.

15. The following were also entered, but did not compete: Aristovoulos Petmezas (GRE), Viggo Jensen (DEN), Fritz Hofmann (GER), Alphonse Grisel (FRA), Robert Garrett (USA), and Ralph Derr (USA).

16. There were 18 competitors per OR, ToA, Argy, and TF.

17. VK lists 3 nations.

18. Originally scheduled for 9 April (28 March), it was postponed due to darkness.

19. EK, VK, and ORev have Weingärtner 3rd, but no evidence of 3rd place has been found in any 1896 source.

20. In a later interview, Schuhmann said that there were 3 Germans in front of him in this event — Weingärtner, Flatow, and Böcker. The only non–German good enough to split the German block was Zutter. Böcker and Weingärtner were most likely 3rd and 4th and Schuhmann 5th.

21. The following were also entered, but did not compete: Momcsilló Topavicza (HUN), Viggo Jensen (DEN), and Fritz Hofmann (GER).

22. VK lists 15 competitors, which does not even correspond to the number of entrants, and we are not certain of his source.

23. Originally scheduled for 9 April (29 March) but postponed to the next day due to darkness.

24. The time is from Hüppe, the only source which gave a time.

25. No time has been found for Xenakis.

26. Hofmann is listed as 3rd in SV, and his mark is listed as 12½ meters in SiB and *circa* 12 meters in Hüppe.

27. Danish sources list Jensen as 4th.

28. The following were also entered, but did not compete: Hermann Weingärtner (GER), Richard Röstel (GER), Karl Neukirch (GER), Fritz Manteuffel (GER), Alphonse Grisel (FRA), and Alfred Flatow (GER).

Shooting

The shooting events were contested at a specially built shooting gallery at Kallithea. It was inaugurated on the morning of the opening of the shooting events, 8 April 1896 (27 March). The ceremony began with a short benediction by Bishop Kompothekras of Cefallonia. Queen Olga of Greece arrived at the range at 1030 hours accompanied by the Princess Maria and her fiancé, Grand Duke George. A ceremony was performed, at the end of which the Queen fired a single shot from a rifle. The Royal Family then departed and the events began.

The most difficult thing to understand about the 1896 shooting events was the scoring system. In all the events, the competition was broken up into four strings of 10 shots in rifle events, and five strings of six shots in pistol events. The total score for each string was calculated by multiplying the number of hits for the string times the score for the shots done in that string. This was then repeated for each string, and the final score was the total of the calculated score for each string. This severely penalized missing the target entirely, as both no score was registered, and the multiplier was decreased as well. As an example, six scoring shots, each worth one point, would normally give a total of 6 points. But this was multiplied by the six hits, to give a score of 36 points. Another shooter, only hitting the target three times, but scoring in the 4-ring each time for 12 points, would also get only 36 points, as he had only three scoring hits. This method of scoring was used in all the events.

Site:	Shooting Range at Kalithea
Dates:	8–12 April (27–31 March)
Events:	5
Competitors:	39 Known; 61 Estimated (39/61 Men)
Nations:	7

	Known Competitors	*Est. Comp.*	*1st*	*2nd*	*3rd*	*Places*
Denmark	3	3	–	1	2	3
France	1	1	–	–	–	–
Great Britain	2	2	–	–	–	–
Greece	28	50	3	3	3	9
Italy	1	1	–	–	–	–

	Known Competitors	Est. Comp.	1st	2nd	3rd	Places
Switzerland	1	1	–	–	–	–
United States	3	3	2	1	–	3
Totals	39	61	5	5	5	15
Nations	7	7	2	3	2	3

Military Rifle (200 meters)

A: 42[1]*; E: 160; C: 7; D: 8–9 April (27–28 March); F: Two sighting shots were allowed. The competition consisted of four 10-shot strings. Two strings were shot each day.

Pantelis Karasevdas was a law student. He won the military rifle competition by a huge margin, as he was successful in hitting the target on all 40 of his shots.

			Hits	Total	Strings	String Scores
1.	Pantelis Karasevdas	GRE	40	2,350	[2](480– – –)	(10x48 + 10x + 10x + 10x)
2.	Paulos Paulidis	GRE	38	1,978[3]		
3.	Nikolaos Trikoupis	GRE	34	1,713[4]		
4.	Anastasios Metaxas	GRE		1,701		
5.	Georgios Orfanidis	GRE		1,698[5]		
6.	Viggo Jensen	DEN	30	1,640		
7.	Georgios Diamantis	GRE		1,456	([6]–384– –)	(+ 8x48 + +)
8.	A. Baumann	SUI		1,294		
9.	Ioannis Theofilakis	GRE		1,261	(–312– –)	(+ 8x39 + +)
10.	Sidney Merlin	GBR		1,156	(477– – –)	(9x53 + + +)
11.	Alexios Fetsios	GRE		894	(–272– –)	(+ 8x34 + +)
=12.	Eugen Schmidt	DEN	26	845[7]		
	Spiridon Stais	GRE[8]				
AC.	Charles Waldstein	USA			(354–154– –)	(6x59 + 7x22 + +)
	– – Machonet[9]	GBR			(8x + + +)	
	– – Rivabella	ITA				
	Aristovoulos Petmezas	GRE				
	Albin Lermusiaux	FRA				
	G. Karagiannopoulos	GRE				
AB.	Holger Nielsen	DEN		DNF[10]		
[11]						

Free Rifle (300 meters)

A: 20[12]; E: 25; C: 3; D: 11–12 April (30–31 March)[13]; F: Two sighting shots were allowed. The competition consisted of four 10-shot strings.

Georgios Orfanidis was the son of a university professor, D. Orfanidis. The event began on 11 April but was postponed at the request of the competitors when they were unable to finish the competition before darkness.

*See Notes on pages 101–102.

			Hits	Total	Strings	String Scores
1.	Georgios Orfanidis	GRE	37	1,583	(328–520–420–315)	(8x41+10x52+10x42+9x35)
2.	Ioannis Frangoudis	GRE	31	1,312	(470–192–440–210)	(10x47+6x32+8x55+7x30)
3.	Viggo Jensen	DEN	31	1,305	(392–423–280–210)	(7x56+9x47+8x35+7x30)
4.	Anastasios Metaxas	GRE		1,102		
5.	Pantelis Karasevdas	GRE		1,039		
AC.	Zenon Mikhailidis	GRE			(68– – –)[14]	
	Nikolaos Trikoupis	GRE				
	Ioannis Theofilakis	GRE				
	Alexandros Theofilakis	GRE				
	Paulos Paulidis	GRE				
	–– Moustakopoulos	GRE				
	Sidney Merlin	GBR				
	Nikolaos Levidis	GRE				
	–– Karakatsanis	GRE				
	Alexios Fetsios	GRE				
	Georgios Diamantis	GRE				
	–– Khatzidakis	GRE				
	–– Antelothanasis	GRE				
AB.	Ioannis Vourakis	GRE	DNF			
	Leonidas Langakis	GRE	DNF			

15

Military Pistol (25 meters)

A: 16[16]; E: 17; C: 4[17]; D: 10 April (29 March); T: 0900–1300; F: Two sighting shots allowed. The competition consisted of five strings of six shots each. There were six scoring rings, counting from 1–6. 180 possible string scores, 1,080 possible total score.

John and Sumner Paine were brothers. John Paine had heard of the Olympic Games in Boston, where he was a member of the Boston Athletic Association (BAA). He elected to sail to Athens with other members of the BAA. However, he sailed first, going to Paris to meet his brother, Sumner, who was shooting that summer in the Gastinne-Renette Galleries. They were unable to find out much about the competitions, except that one event was to be a revolver contest over 30 meters. Sumner Paine brought along everything he could find in Paris, including a Colt Army revolver, a Smith & Wesson Russian revolver, and a pocket gun for each of them, as well as John's .22 caliber Stevens pistol and Sumner's .22 Wurfflein pistol. They also brought along 3,500 rounds of ammunition, which proved to be ample, as they eventually only fired a total of 96 rounds.

The Colt Army revolver, the famous gun of the Old West, was also known as the Frontier Six-Shooter. The Smith & Wesson Russian, or No. 3 Single Action revolver, was usually the choice of the knowledgable pistol shooter of the era. The gun was made in large quantities, as the Smith & Wesson plant had received huge orders from Russia beginning in 1870, and almost 250,000 had been manufactured by the time of the Athens Olympics. The Wurfflein pistol was a single-shot pistol with a tip-up barrel, hinged at the front end of the frame. They were popular in shooting events in the 19th century, winning many matches and setting many records.

The shooters shot in groups of three. The first group was Pantelis Karasevdas, Sidney Merlin and Sumner Paine. The second group was Sanidis, Aristovoulos Petmezas, and John Paine. The composition of the subsequent groups is not known.

This was the first pistol event of the 1896 Olympics, and the Paines outclassed their competitors, despite the fact that they had difficulty with the conditions. The sunlight was almost blinding and they had problems seeing the black target with its white center. In addition, both of their pistols had been sighted for 50 yards, not 25 meters, and they had to make some minor sighting adjustments.

			Hits	*Total*
1.	John Paine	USA	25	442[18]
2.	Sumner Paine	USA	23	380[19]
3.	Nikolaos Dorakis[20]	GRE		205
4.	Ioannis Frangoudis	GRE		
5.	Holger Nielsen	DEN		
AC.	–– Vavis	GRE		
	–– Platis	GRE		
	Aristovoulos Petmezas	GRE		
	Paulos Paulidis	GRE		
	–– Patsouris	GRE		
	–– Pantazidis	GRE		
	Georgios Orfanidis	GRE		
	Zenon Mikhailidis	GRE		
AB.	–– Sanidis	GRE		DNF[21]
	Sidney Merlin	GBR		DNF[22]
	Pantelis Karasevdas	GRE		DNF[23]
	[24]			

Pistol (25 meters)[25]

A: 4; E: [26]; C: 3[27]; D: 11 April[28] (30 March); F: Two sighting shots allowed. The competition consisted of five strings of six shots each.

This event was to be for "pistols of usual caliber." The Paine brothers expected to compete using their .22 caliber handguns. However, the guns were ruled out as being not of usual caliber. The other contestants used muzzle-loading pistols of about .45 caliber. The Greeks offered to allow the Paine brothers to use their pistols, but the Paines elected not to compete.

			Hits	*Total*	*Strings*
1.	Ioannis Frangoudis	GRE	23	344	92 points
2.	Georgios Orfanidis	GRE	20	249	
3.	Holger Nielsen	DEN			
AB.	Sidney Merlin	GBR		DNF[29]	
	[30]				

Free Pistol (30 meters)

A: 5[31]; E: 10[32]; C: 3; D: 11 April (30 March); F: Two sighting shots allowed. The competition consisted of five strings of six shots each. There were six scoring rings, counting from 1–6. 180 possible scores, 1,080 possible total score.

After the first pistol event of the 1896 shooting competition, the Paine brothers realized that they were far superior to the competition, mostly consisting of Greek shooters. They elected that whoever had won the first event (military pistol, John Paine) would sit out any future events, so that they would not embarrass their Greek hosts. Oddly, Sumner Paine won this event with the exact same score (442) that John had scored the day before in the military pistol event.

			Hits	Total	Strings	String Score
1.	Sumner Paine	USA	24	442[33]	(76–64–80–120–102)	(4x19+4x16+5x16+5x24+6x17)[34]
2.[35]	Holger Nielsen	DEN		285[36]	(12–85–64–24–100)	(+5x17+4x16+ +5x20)[37]
3.	Ioannis Frangoudis	GRE				
4.	Leonidas Morakis	GRE				
5.	Georgios Orfanidis	GRE				

[38]

NOTES

1. VK has 160 competitors, which was the number of entrants.

2. TF, Akrp, ToA, Prsk, Gagalis, and Gavrilidou list the mark as 2,350. The OR has 2,320.

3. OR, Akrp, and Gavrilidou give 1,978; while ToA, Prsk, Gagalis, and TF have 1,970.

4. TF, ToA, and Prsk list the mark as 1,713. Gagalis has 1,763, and Akrp has 1,773.

5. The score is given as 1,692 in Akrp, but as 1,698 in ToA, Prsk, and TF.

6. The first series score for Diamantis is given in Akrp and Prsk as 394, which cannot be correct because of the system of scoring used. It could be 392 (8x49 or 7x56), 396 (9x44), or 384 (8x48).

7. Schimdt listed as 12th in Akrp with the score of 26/845.

8. Stais listed as 12th in Epth, but with no score given.

9. Also seen spelled as "Mokchoinet." Both spellings are unusual Anglo-Saxon names and are likely misspellings from the Greek.

10. Nielsen did not appear for the second day of competition.

11. Roberto Minervini of Italy is the only known entrant who did not compete. The other 22 competitors in this event cannot be identified.

12. VK has 25 competitors, which was the number of entrants.

13. The four series were all to be shot in one day, but all the shooters could not finish because of darkness, and finished the next day (12 April [31 March]). Four shooters (Orfanidis, Mikhailidis, Vourakis, and Langakis) finished on the second day.

14. The score of some mark in the 680's is given in Akrp, but the last digit is not legible.

15. Also entered, but not competing in this event, were Roberto Minervini (ITA), Charles Waldstein (USA), Eugen Schmidt (DEN), and Holger Nielsen (DEN).

16. TF stated that there were only 16 competitors, the two Americans, a Dane, and 13 Greeks. The 16 competitors were given in ToA by name. They also noted that one German competed, but no German is listed in other sources, including by the German experts. Merlin, a Brit living in Greece, is apparently considered a Greek entrant by TF.

17. VK lists athletes competing from only 3 nations.

18. John Paine's "raw" score for points was noted to be 85 in the article they authored in AATM.

19. Sumner Paine's "raw" score for points was noted to be 79 in the article they authored in AATM.

20. Usually seen as Mourakis. Third place is listed as "Mourakis" in Akrp, "Corporal Mourakis" in Prsk, "Captain Mourakis" in TF, "Corporal Bramis" in Gagalis, and "Nikolaos Dorakis" in Epth. We have used "Nikolaos Dorakis" from Epth, as it is the only source giving both names.

21. Retired after two series.

22. Retired after two series.

23. Retired after two series.

24. Charles Waldstein (USA) was also entered but did not compete.

25. This event is often listed only as a "Pistol Match." It was apparently open to pistols of the "usual caliber," i.e., muzzle-loading pistols of about .45 caliber.

26. The number of entrants is not known.

27. VK has only two nations competing, and lists Merlin as Danish.

28. TF erroneously has the date as 10 April (29 March).

29. Merlin is listed as 4th in ORev.

30. Also entered, but not competing, in this event were Charles Waldstein (USA), and Roberto Minervini (ITA).

31. VK has 6 competitors, which was the number of entrants.

32. Argy listed the number of entrants as 10. OR listed 6. Viggo Jensen (DEN) was probably also entered but competed instead in the Free Rifle (300 meters), which was held concurrently. John Paine (USA) was also entered but withdrew. Thus, we know of 7 entries and prefer to believe that 10 entrants is correct.

33. Erroneously 452 in Akrp, Argy, and Gavrilidou.

34. The exact hits and scores per string are not known for each string. For strings 1, 2, and 5, there is only one alternative given the scoring system. In the 3rd and 4th strings there are two alternatives — 4x20=80 (3rd) and 6x20=120 (4th), or as given above [5x16=80 (3rd) and 5x24=120 [4th]). Both give total hits and score for the two strings of 10 and 200, respectively.

35. ORev has Jensen in 2nd (with 285), Nielsen in 3rd, Morakis in 4th, and Frangoudis in 5th.

36. Erroneously 385 in Akrp and Gavrilidou.

37. The exact number of hits is not recorded and cannot be determined with precision, but it can be deduced that Nielsen must have had between 19–21 hits on target. Possible scores for strings one and four are as follows: 1) 2x6=12 or 3x4=12, and 4) 3x8=24, or 4x6=24. In those two strings the total hits could thus be 5, 6, or 7, with the total score still equalling 36. This would give the correct total points of 285, with either 19, 20, or 21 hits on target.

38. Charles Waldstein (USA) was also entered but did not compete. Not listed as entered is John Paine (USA), but he surely was, as he describes the fact that he elected not to compete after winning another pistol event on the day before.

Swimming

The swimming events took place in the Bay of Zea, off the coast of Piraeus. All four events were conducted in one day, and because of this no amphitheatre was conducted, only a few temporary buildings. However, as many as 20,000 spectators were listed as watching the swimming events on this Saturday. King Georgios I arrived at about 1030 and watched the races, which began at 1100.

The water was noted to be frigid, between 12–14° C. (53–57° F.), with the air temperature 18° C. (64° F.). One story, which is most likely apocryphal, involved the only American swimmer entered, Gardner Williams. Supposedly, he jumped into the water for the start of the 100 meters, and then scrambled back to shore, yelling out, "Jesus Christ, it's freezing." The story was reported by American team member Thomas Curtis in an article he wrote 36 years later. However, it is highly unlikely that Williams did not venture into the water until the day of the races. Possibly it occurred during training. Secondly, Williams could not have scrambled back to shore, as the 100 meter freestyle began out in the Bay and the swimmers swam toward the shore.

Site:	Bay of Zea, off Piraeus	
Dates:	11 April (31 March)	
Events:	4	
Competitors:	13 Known; 19 Estimated (13/19 Men)	
Nations:	4	

	Known Competitors	*Est. Comp.*	*1st*	*2nd*	*3rd*	*Places*
Austria	2	2	1	1	–	2
Greece	9	15	1	3	2	6
Hungary	1	1	2	–	–	2
United States	1	1	–	–	–	–
Totals	13	19	4	4	2	10
Nations	4	4	3	2	1	3

100 meter freestyle

A: 10[1]*; E: 34; C: 4; D: 11 April (30 March).

A ship transported the swimmers out into the Bay of Zea for the start of this event in the open sea. The starting line was placed between two buoys. The swimmers swam towards the shore, where the finish line was marked by a red flag. The course was laid out by a series of hollow pumpkins which marked it, but which floated and moved on the water, making the course difficult to follow.

The race between Herschmann and Hajós saw Hajós winning by ½ meter. The others were noted to be far behind. Prince Georgios hoisted the Hungarian flag himself and the band began to play the Austrian national anthem, but the Hungarians began to sing "their" national anthem, and the band stopped playing.

Alfréd Hajós began swimming after his father drowned in the Danube. In 1895 he had been European Champion in the 100 meters in Vienna. He later became a member of the Hungarian national football team. In 1924 he won a second Olympic medal in the art contests, winning the designs for town planning class, for the plan of a stadium. In 1953 he was awarded the Olympic Diploma by the IOC for his contributions to the Olympic ideal.

1.	Alfréd Hajós	HUN	1:22⅕[2]
2.	Otto Herschmann	AUT	1:22⅘[3,4]
AC.	Gardner Williams	USA	
	Alexandros Khrisafos	GRE	
	Evstathios Khorafas	GRE	
	Georgios Anninos	GRE	
	[5,6]		

500 meter freestyle

A: 3; E: 29[7]; C: 2; D: 11 April (30 March).

The race also started out in the Bay, with the swimmers swimming into shore. The swimmers were transported out to the starting line by a steamer, shortly after the finish of the 100 metres. Only Khorafas of the 100 meter swimmers competed, because of the proximity of the races and the chill they received from the water. This time, the boat took them out into the Saronic Gulf for the start of the race. Neumann won by a huge margin.

1.	Paul Neumann	AUT	8:12⅗[8]
2.	Antonios Pepanos	GRE	9:57⅗
3.	Evstathios Khorafas	GRE	
	[9]		

1,200 meter freestyle

A: 9[10]; E: [11]; C: 4; D: 11 April (30 March).

*See Notes on pages 105–106.

Hajós had hoped to enter, and win, all three swimming races open to all competitors. However, the 500 meters started immediately after the 100 meters, so he had to wait for the 1,200 to start so he could recover. Alfréd Hajós was born Arnold Guttmann, but he changed his name on the occasion of the 1,000th anniversary of the Magyar Empire. "Hajós" means "sailor" in Hungarian.

1.	Alfréd Hajós	HUN	18:22⅕[12]
2.	Ioannis Andreou	GRE	21:03⅖[13]
AC.	Gardner Williams	USA[14]	
	–– Katravas	GRE[15]	
	Evstathios Khorafas	GRE	
AB.	Paul Neumann	AUT	DNF
	[16]		

100 meter freestyle for sailors[17]

A: 3; E: 11[18]; C: 1; D: 11 April (30 March).

There were 11 entrants but only the three finishers eventually started the race. Because this race was exclusively for sailors from the Greek navy, its inclusion in the Olympic records is dubious at best.

1.	Ioannis Malokinis	GRE	2:20⅖
2.	Spiridon Khazapis	GRE	
3.	Dimitrios Drivas	GRE	
	[19]		

NOTES

1. FW, OR, ToA, Akrp, Epth, Prsk, Chrysafis, Argy, Gavrilidou, and TF have 13 competing. ASZ and Gagalis have 10 competing. SS listed 11–7 Greeks, Hajós, Herschmann, Nielsen, and Williams. But Nielsen definitely did not compete, as he was competing in shooting, which was held concurrently. This would reduce the number of competitors to 10.

2. The time is 1:22⅕ in all 1896 sources except ToA and Prsk, which list 1:22½.

3. FW, VK, and ORev list the time for 2nd as 1:23.0, giving the swimmer as Khorafas. The only 1896 sources to give the time for 2nd were Hüppe, which gave 1:22⅘, and ASZ, which gave 1:23.

4. EK, FW, OR, VK, TF, TfI, and ORev have Evstathios Khorafas (GRE) in 2nd and Herschmann 3rd. VK and FW further lists Anninos as 4th, Williams 5th, and Khrysafos 6th. FM and SV erroneously have Williams 2nd and Herschmann 3rd. TfI has Khorafas 3rd.

5. There were four other Greek competitors who are not known.

6. The following were entered: V. Mangourakis (GRE), Merk. Lerias (GRE), Sav. Laskaridis (GRE), Georg. Lamprakis (GRE), P. F. Koukoudakis (GRE), Theod. Kontos (GRE), –– Katravas (GRE), G. K. Karagiannis (GRE), Georg. Gaitanos (GRE), D. Frangopoulos (GRE), I. Dontis (GRE), Ag. Diamantopoulos (GRE), V. Khatzis (GRE), Georgios Valakakis (GRE), Holger Nielsen (DEN), Frantz Reichel (FRA), Alphonse Grisel (FRA), Johan Bergman (SWE), Charles Winckler (DEN), H. F. Suter (GBR), and Ferenc Szöreny Reich (HUN), Sol. Xenopoulos (GRE), Ir. Vlachos (GRE), Emm. Valetsiotis (GRE), Fil. Pathilos (GRE), Georg. Petrou (GRE), Pan. Nastos (GRE), G. Marnezos (GRE), and I. Markou (GRE). Four of the Greeks must have taken part. No exact source of entrants

for 1896 swimming is available, and we have listed names found in various sources, but this yields 35 names for 34 entries.

7. There were 29 entrants in OR, ToA, Epth, and Prsk, but 30 per Akrp and Argy.

8. The mark is 8:12¾ per the OR, ToA, and Prsk, but is 8:12⅗ in TF, VB, Akrp, Epth, Argy, and Hüppe.

9. The following were entered, but did not compete: A. Zanos (GRE), Sol. Xenopoulos (GRE), N. Stournaras (GRE), D. Santanis (GRE), K. Salouros (GRE), Fill. Pothitos (GRE), Pan. Nastos (GRE), P. Mikhalopoulos (GRE), G. Mazoukas (GRE), G. Marnezos (GRE), I. Markou (GRE), U. Mangourakis (GRE), Merk. Lerias (GRE), Sav. Laskaridis (GRE), K. Kourkoulas (GRE), Nik. Kourakos (GRE), Theod. Kontos (GRE), -- Katravas (GRE), I. Georgiadis (GRE), Georg. Gaitanos (GRE), D. Frangopoulos (GRE), I. Dontis (GRE), Ag. Diamantopoulos (GRE), D. Khristopoulos (GRE), V. Khatzis (GRE), A. Grigoriadis (GRE), Holger Nielsen (DEN), Frantz Reichel (FRA), Otto Herschmann (AUT), Alfréd Hajós (HUN), Alphonse Grisel (FRA), Charles Winckler (DEN), H. F. Suter (GBR), and Ferenc Szöreny Reich (HUN).

10. OR, Akrp, Epth, Argy, and Gagalis stated that 9 competed.

11. No 1896 source listed the number of entrants. In different lists of competitors and entrants, at least 24 names are given, however.

12. The mark is given variously: TF, ToA, Prsk, and SS—18:22⅕; OR, Argy, VB, Gagalis—18:22½; NS—18:22⅖; SV—18:02⅖; Hüppe—18:28⅗; and ASZ—17:53.

13. Time given variously as follows: OR, Akrp, Argy—21:03⅖; NS—21:03⅕; and listed as 3:21⅕ behind Hajós (=21:43⅖) in ToA. Also, Hüppe gave 2nd as 21:03⅖, but listed the swimmer as Katravas.

14. EK, FW, VK, and ORev have Khorafas 3rd and Williams 4th, but there is no evidence of that in 1896 sources.

15. Hüppe has Katravas in 2nd place with 21:03⅖.

16. The following were entered: Sol. Xenopoulos (GRE), Emm. Valetsiotis (GRE), A. Romantzas (GRE), Antonios Pepanos (GRE), Pan. Nastos (GRE), Merk. Lerias (GRE), Sav. Laskaridis (GRE), P. F. Koukoudakis (GRE), Theod. Kontos (GRE), D. Frangopoulos (GRE), I. Dontis (GRE), Ag. Diamantopoulos (GRE), V. Khatzis (GRE), G. Athanasiou (GRE), Holger Nielsen (DEN), Alphonse Grisel (FRA), and Charles Winckler (DEN). Three of the Greeks must have competed to fill out the field of 9.

17. This event was not listed in FW.

18. OR, Akrp, and Argy have 11, while ToA and Prsk have 14.

19. The following were entered, but did not compete: N. Stournaras (GRE), D. Santanis (GRE), K. Salouros (GRE), P. Mikhalopoulos (GRE), K. Kourkoulas (GRE), and Nik. Kourakos (GRE). There were two other entrants whose names have not been found.

Tennis (Lawn)

The tennis events of the 1896 Olympics were held at the cycling velodrome, the Neo Phaliron, and at the Athens Lawn Tennis Club, near the Ilissos River. Two tennis courts were constructed in the infield of the velodrome and a few matches were contested there. The tennis tournament had none of the top players in the world, who were mostly the Brits who starred at Wimbledon. No Americans competed either.

Site:	Infield of the Neo Phaliron Velodrome, near Piraeus; and also at the Athens Lawn Tennis Club, near the Ilissos
Dates:	8–11 April (27–30 March)
Events:	2
Competitors:	13 (13 Men)
Nations:	7

By Nations

	Competitors	1st	2nd	3rd	Places
Australia	1	–	–	½	½
Egypt	1	–	1½	–	1½
France	1	–	–	–	–
Germany	1	½	–	–	½
Great Britain	2	1½	–	½	2
Greece	6	–	½	1	1½
Hungary	1	–	–	1	1
Totals	13	2	2	3	7
Nations	7	2	2	4	6

Places By Teams

	1st	2nd	3rd	Places
Egypt	–	1	–	1
Great Britain	1	–	–	1

Great Britain/Australia	–	–	1	1
Great Britain/Germany	1	–	–	1
Greece	–	–	1	1
Greece/Egypt	–	1	–	1
Hungary	–	–	1	1
Totals	2	2	3	7
Teams	2	2	3	7

Men's Singles

A: 13[1]*; E: 16; C: 7; D: 8–11 April (27–30 March).

This tournament was essentially a single-elimination event, although the Greek organizers split the 15-person draw into four "groups," A, B, G, and D[2], with the winner of each group advancing to the semi-finals. The groups were played by a single-elimination system. The reason for four groups was to guarantee four semi-finalists, a situation which did not occur in wrestling nor in the men's doubles. A player who withdrew would then affect only the matches within the group. According to the ancient Greek system for elimination tournaments, a new draw was made for each round with all the remaining participants. If there was an odd number remaining, someone would receive a bye.

The results of the early matches are not known, with the exception of when John Boland defeated Fritz Traun, 3 sets to 2. John Boland was a student at Christ's College, Oxford, in 1894 when he invited a Greek friend, Konstantinos Manos, to speak at the Oxford Union. Manos invited Boland to spend the 1896 Easter holiday in Greece during the Olympics. Boland then entered the tennis tournament, although he was not a well-known tournament player. Boland, an Irishman, later became a member of the British parliament for South Kerry from 1900 to 1918.

1.	John Pius Boland	GBR
2.	Dionysios Kasdaglis	EGY
=3.	Momcsilló Topavicza	HUN
	Konstantinos Paspatis	GRE
=5.	Aristidis Akratopoulos	GRE
	E. Rallis	GRE
	Konstantinos Akratopoulos	GRE
=8.	D. Frangopoulos	GRE
	–– Defert	FRA
	Friedrich Traun	GER
	Dimitrios Petrokokkinos	GRE
	George Stuart Robertson	GBR
	Edwin Flack	AUS
	3,4	

Tournament Summary

	Match Result	Date	Site
Group A	A. Akratopoulos d. Flack	8 April	Neo Phaliron
	Paspatis d. Robertson	9 April	Ilissos

	Paspatis d. A. Akratopoulos	9 April	Ilissos
Group B	Rallis d. Petrokokkinos	8 April	Ilissos
	Boland d. Traun (3–2)	8 April	Neo Phaliron
	Boland d. Rallis (6–0, 2–6, 6–2)	9 April	Ilissos
Group G	F. Marshal v. G. Marshal[5] (not played)	8 April	Ilissos
	Topavicza d. Frangopoulos	8 April	Ilissos
Group D	Kasdaglis d. Defert	9 April	Ilissos
	Kasdaglis d. K. Akratopoulos	10 April	Ilissos
Semi-finals	Boland d. Paspatis	10 April	Ilissos (0900)
	Kasdaglis d. Topavicza	10 April	Ilissos
Final	Boland d. Kasdaglis (6–2, 6–2)[6]	11 April	Ilissos

Men's Doubles

A: 10[7]; E: 14[8]; C: 5; D: 8–11 April (27–30 March).

Fritz Traun was supposed to enter the tennis doubles with a partner whose name has not survived, but who withdrew from an injury. He then competed with John Boland, who had defeated him in the singles, and they won the championship. No records of any of the match results, other than the final, exist.

Traun was a good German athlete, but was primarily a runner. Between 1893 and 1894 he set several German records at distances from 880 yards up to 2 miles. He competed in the 800 meters in Athens but did not qualify for the finals.

1. John Pius Boland (GBR)	Friedrich Traun (GER)	GBR/GER
2. Dimitrios Petrokokkinos (GRE)	Dionysios Kasdaglis (EGY)	GRE/EGY
3. George Stuart Robertson (GBR)	Edwin Flack (AUS)	GBR/AUS
=4. E. Rallis	Konstantinos Paspatis	GRE
Konstantinos Akratopoulos 9,10	Aristidis Akratopoulos	GRE

Tournament Summary

	Match Result	Date	Site
First Round	Flack/Robertson v. Marshal/Marshal[11]	8 April	Ilissos (1600)
	Kasdaglis/Petrokokkinos d. Paspatis/Rallis	8 April	Neo Phaliron
	Boland/Traun d. Akratopoulos/Akratopoulos	9 April	Ilissos
Semi-finals	Kasdaglis/Petrokokkinos d. Flack/Robertson	9 April	Ilissos
	Boland/Traun — bye		
Final	Boland/Traun d. Kasdaglis/Petrokokkinos 5–7, 6–3, 6–3[12]	11 April	Ilissos

NOTES

1. VK has 16 competitors from 6 nations. The OR also notes 16 players, with 6 Greeks. The two Marshals definitely did not compete, although they were scheduled to do so. Velo noted that two Frenchmen were entered, Defert and Vacherot. No other source lists Vacherot, but he must have been the 16th entrant.

2. A, β, Γ, and Δ are the first four Greek letters — alpha, beta, gamma, and delta.

3. The following were entered but did not compete: George Marshal (GBR), Frank Marshal (GBR), and —— Vacherot (FRA).

4. No match results have been found, except for the final. However, it is possible to draw conclusions as to the development of the tournament by way of newspaper notices. Match reports are missing.

5. According to Akrp, the match between F. Marshal–G. Marshal was never played, as neither of them appeared.

6. From 1896 sources, only Velo has the score, 6–3, 6–1, with Boland winning. EK, FW, FM, and ORev give the match score as 7–5, 6–4, 6–1, but no 1896 source supports that. Our result, 6–2, 6–2, is from Boland's personal diaries.

7. VK has 8 competitors from 4 nations.

8. No source mentioned how many pairs were entered. Akrp has the draw up to the final, showing six pairs participating. But according to Velo, the French pair, Defert/Vacherot, was also entered. Thus, seven pairs were entered.

9. The following pairs were entered but did not compete: George Marshal and Frank Marshal (GBR), and —— Vacherot and —— Defert (FRA).

10. No match results have been found, except for the final. However, it is possible to draw conclusions as to the development of the tournament by way of newspaper notices. Match reports are missing.

11. This match was scheduled but did not take place. Frank and George Marshal did not compete in tennis.

12. EK, FW, FM, and ORev give the match score as 6–2, 6–4, but this is not supported by any 1896 source. Of 1896 sources, only Velo gives the score, which they listed as 5–7, 6–4, 6–1. Our score is from Boland's personal diary.

Weightlifting

The 1896 weightlifting events were conducted outdoors in the infield of the Panathenaic Stadium. In 1896, there were no internationally accepted rules or classifications for weightlifting. Dumbbells were used for the one-handed lift, with competitors required to "snatch" from ground to arm's length with or without stopping at the shoulder, and for the two-handed lift a barbell was used. A two-handed event with dumbbells was often contested in that era. Its absence from the program upset the British team greatly, and after being advised by Prince Georgios of Greece that the conditions of the contests were immutable, Great Britain's Lawrence Levy withdrew. This, however, was not the end of Levy's involvement, as he joined Prince Georgios as one of the judges of the competitions and served as an assistant to the British lifter, Launceston Elliot.

The competitors had three attempts. After three lifts the three best lifters had another three attempts. In the event that lifters tied at the same weight, the one with the better style, as noted by the judges, was determined to be the winner.[1]*

The lifting order was different from that used now. The lifters started in the order of their start numbers, and could ask for any weight. The next lifters could ask for lower weights. All did their first round of lifts before the next round started.

Site:	Panathenaic Stadium	
Dates	7 April (26 March)	
Events:	2	
Competitors:	7 (7 Men)	
Nations:	5	

	Competitors	*1st*	*2nd*	*3rd*	*Places*
Denmark	1	1	1	–	2
Germany	1	–	–	–	–
Great Britain	1	1	1	–	2
Greece	3	–	–	2	2
Hungary	1	–	–	–	–
Totals	7	2	2	2	6
Nations	5	2	2	2	4

*See Notes on pages 113–114.

Unlimited Class, Two Hands Clean & Jerk

A: 6[2,3]; E: 15; C: 5; D: 7 April (26 March).

This event, lifting a barbell with two hands, was the first held of the two weightlifting competitions. Elliot and Jensen tied for first place but Jensen was awarded first place by the judges, based on his having lifted in a better style. Apparently Elliot moved one foot while lifting his weight. Ian Buchanan has described this well in his article on Launceston Elliot in *Citius, Altius, Fortius*[4]:

"The two-handed lift came first on the program and, after a long drawn out contest, Viggo Jensen of Denmark and Elliot had both lifted 110 kg., but Prince George awarded the Dane first place for having done so in better style. Jensen's lift was accomplished with a superb clean lift whereas Elliot had certainly encountered difficulty but to award the Olympic title on the basis of 'style' was a decision to which Lawrence Levy, understandably, took exception.

"Levy's main objection was that, as both contestants had lifted the same weight, they should now each be given the chance to lift a heavier weight in accordance with all known weightlifting protocol. Prince George then agreed with Levy's view but the decision was rendered academic by the rider to the judgment that there were, in fact, no heavier weights available. Levy stood his ground and eventually plates were screwed onto the barbell and lifting was resumed. After Jensen had raised the bar, Levy again objected, this time on the grounds that Jensen's method was not in accordance with the rules.

"Again Prince George sided against Levy and once more lifting was resumed, by which time most of the spectators had left but they didn't miss a great deal as, eventually, the original result based on 'style' was allowed to stand. By contrast, the one-handed event was a short, sharp event. Elliot declined Prince George's courteous offer of a rest break but he asked that he might this time lift after Jensen, as in the two-handed event the Dane had the advantage of lifting after Elliot. The request was granted although the order of lifting was not to have a material effect on the result. Elliot raised 71.0 kg. without difficulty whereas Jensen, who had injured his shoulder trying to raise 112.5 kg. in the two-handed event, could only manage 57.0 kg. and Britain's first Olympic champion was crowned.

"One feature that stands out from the judging of the competition is the inherent courtesy exercised by Prince George throughout the proceedings. Despite the constant protests of Lawrence Levy, the Prince sought him out that evening at an illumination display at the Royal Palace, and smilingly enquired 'Are you calmer now, Mr. Levy?'"

Levy was apparently unaware of the rules stating that the tie-breaker was the style of the lift.

1.	Viggo Jensen	DEN	111.5 kg.
2.	Launceston Elliot	GBR	111.5 kg.[5]
3.	Sotirios Versis	GRE	90.0 kg.[6]
=4.	Georgios Papasideris[7]	GRE	90.0 kg.[8]
	Carl Schuhmann	GER	90.0 kg.[9]
6.	Momcsilló Topavicza	HUN	80.0 kg.[10]
	[11]		

Unlimited Class, One Hand

A: 4[12]; E: 15; C: 3; D: 7 April (26 March).

In the one-hand lift the lifters had to lift the weight with each hand separately. Launceston Elliot won this dumbbell lift, reversing the order of the barbell event. It was a simple win for Elliot, who picked 71 kg. for his first lift, and cleared the weight to win easily. The Greeks clearly took a great liking to the handsome Launceston Elliot. One source reported "This young gentleman attracted universal attention by his uncommon type of beauty. He was of imposing stature, tall, well proportioned, his hair and complexion of surprising fairness." Another wrote of "…the finest man of English birth" and he received an offer of marriage from a "highly placed lady admirer."

At the end of the dumbbell event, the strength of Prince Georgios was demonstrated. The Prince had been the lead judge for the weightlifting events and was renowned for his strength. One of the aides attempted to move one of the weights but without success. The Prince bent over and picked it up with ease. The *Official Report* noted, "The public admires and claps with enthusiasm and cheers."

Jensen was hampered by an injury sustained during his last attempt of 112½ kg. in the two-hand lift. He lifted 57 kg. with each hand, while Nikolopoulos apparently lifted 57 kg. with only one hand.

1.	Launceston Elliot	GBR	71.0 kg.
2.	Viggo Jensen	DEN	57.0 kg.[13]
3.	Alexandros Nikolopoulos	GRE	57.0 kg.[14]
4.	Sotirios Versis[15]	GRE	40.0 kg.[16]
	[17]		

NOTES

1. Description from Chrysafis.

2. VK has 10 competitors from 6 nations.

3. The lifting order was by entry numbers as follows: Elliot (#2), Papasideris (#3), Topavicza (#5), Jensen (#7), Versis (#11), and Schuhmann (#12).

4. "Launceston Elliot," in *Citius, Altius, Fortius*, Vol. 3, No. 1, p. 20.

5. Elliot is listed with a mark of 103 kg. in SV, but in the next issue it is corrected to 111.5 kg., and his series of lifts is given — 99, 110, 111.5 kg. FW and ORev listed Elliot's mark as 111 kg.

6 VK has Versis 3rd with 100.0, Schuhmann 4th with 90.0, Momcsilló T*a*pavicza [sic] 5th with 80.0, and Alexandros Nikolopoulos (GRE) 6th with no weight listed. EK, FM, and ORev have Versis' mark as 110 kg. and list him as 3rd. Versis is listed as 3rd in SV, the only 1896 source noting the 3rd-place finisher. SV also lists his mark as 110 kg., but no other 1896 source gives this, and if he was that close to Jensen and Elliot, it is likely this would have been mentioned.

7. It is possible that the 2nd Greek lifter was Alexandros Nikolopoulos. The only definite evidence supporting Papasideris is that he defeated Nikolopoulos in the Greek trials.

8. SV has Alphonse Grisel (FRA) competing and does not list Papasideris. FW has Alexandros Nikolopoulos (GRE) 3rd with 110.0.

9. SV has Schuhmann's mark as 96 kg., but this is likely a misprint, as no other 1896 source supports this mark.

10. Topavicza's mark is given in SV, who said that Topavicza refrained from further lifting after clearing 80 kg.

11. The following were also entered but did not compete: Alexandros Nikolopoulos (GRE), Louis Zutter (SUI), Hermann Weingärtner (GER), Sidney Merlin (GBR), Alphonse Grisel (FRA), Alfred Flatow (GER), Edward Lawrence Levy (GBR), Charles Winckler (DEN), and Fritz Manteuffel (GER). Winckler was known not to be in Athens.

12. VK has 10 competitors from 6 nations.

13. EK, FW, FM, VK, and ORev give Jensen and Nikolopoulos 57.2 kg., but this is not supported in any 1896 source.

14. Nikolopoulos is listed as 3rd in ToA and Prsk with 57.0 kg.

15. It is not absolutely certain if this lifter was Versis or Georgios Papasideris. No 1896 source gives any definite clue from the competition itself. We have opted for Versis because he bettered Papasideris in the Greek trials.

16. According to SV, no one except Jensen and Elliot lifted more than 40.0 kg. We have interpreted this to mean that the 4th-place lifter (choosing Versis) lifted 40.0 kg. For Nikolopoulos' mark of 57.0 kg., see the above footnote.

17. The following were also entered but did not compete: Louis Zutter (SUI), Hermann Weingärtner (GER), Momcsilló Topavicza (HUN), Carl Schuhmann (GER), Georgios Papasideris (GRE), Sidney Merlin (GBR), Alphonse Grisel (FRA), Alfred Flatow (GER), Edward Lawrence Levy (GBR), Charles Winckler (DEN), and Fritz Manteuffel (GER). Winckler was known not to be in Athens.

Wrestling

The 1896 wrestling competition consisted of a single event. It was contested basically in the Greco-Roman style, although some legholds were allowed. No weight limit was placed. The matches took place in the infield of the Panathenaic Stadium, on a sand-covered circle near the Splendone end of the stadium. There was no time limit, with a wrestler losing if he was thrown onto his back.

Britain's Launceston Elliot, already popular with the Greeks because of his performance in weightlifting, was thought to be a favorite. He was much larger than his opponent, Germany's Carl Schuhmann, but Schuhmann defeated him easily. Elliot took his defeat badly, claiming that only one of his shoulders touched the ground, not both as required by the rules, and after refusing to accept the judge's decision, he had to be escorted from the field by the Royal Princes.

The Greeks were upset when their two wrestlers, Georgios Tsitas and Stefanos Khristopoulos, met each other in the only semi-final. Tsitas won when Khristopoulos had to retire with a broken shoulder.

The matches had started in the late afternoon on a Friday. After the semi-final, this left Carl Schuhmann to wrestle against Georgios Tsitas in the final. After 40 minutes of wrestling, no decision had been reached and it was now quite dark. The match was postponed to 0900 Saturday morning, although Schuhmann protested, stating that it would take him only a few more minutes to defeat Tsitas. It took Schuhmann 15 minutes more on Saturday morning to defeat Tsitas with an armpull and a pressed-down bridge. He became the first known Olympic wrestling champion since Aurelius Aelix of Phoenicia in 213 A.D.

Site:	Panathenaic Stadium	
Dates:	10–11 April (29–30 March)	
Events:	1	
Competitors:	5 (5 Men)	
Nations:	4	

	Competitors	1st	2nd	3rd	Places
Germany	1	1	–	–	1
Great Britain	1	–	–	–	–
Greece	2	–	1	1	2

	Competitors	1st	2nd	3rd	Places
Hungary	1	–	–	–	–
Totals	5	1	1	1	3
Nations	4	1	1	1	2

Unlimited Class (Greco-Roman Style)

A: 5; E: 10; C: 4; D: 10–11 April (29–30 March); T: 0900 (11 April [30 March]).

1.	Carl Schuhmann	GER
2.	Georgios Tsitas	GRE
3.	Stefanos Khristopoulos	GRE
=4.	Momcsilló Topavicza	HUN[1]*
	Launceston Elliot	GBR

2

Tournament Summary

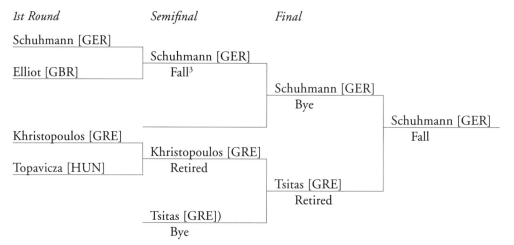

1st Round   *Semifinal*   *Final*

Schuhmann [GER]

Elliot [GBR]

Schuhmann [GER]
Fall[3]

Schuhmann [GER]
Bye

Schuhmann [GER]
Fall

Khristopoulos [GRE]

Topavicza [HUN]

Khristopoulos [GRE]
Retired

Tsitas [GRE]
Retired

Tsitas [GRE])
Bye

NOTES

1. ORev has Elliot as 4th and Topavicza in 5th.

2. The following were also entered, but did not compete: Viggo Jensen (DEN), Nikolaj De Ritter (RUS), Louis Zutter (SUI), Charles Champaud (SUI), and Charles Winckler (DEN). De Ritter and Winckler were not in Athens.

3. At 2 minutes in SiB and ½ minute in Hüppe.

*See Notes above.

Other Sports and Events

There were several other sports scheduled to be contested at the 1896 Olympic Games which were not held. Several events were also scheduled but not contested. In addition, early programs and schedules mentioned sports which did not appear on the final program. Following is an analysis of these events and sports which never took place.

Cricket

Cricket was listed as one of the sports to be conducted in the first *Bulletin du Comité International des Jeux Olympiques*, published in January 1895. It was listed under "Jeux Athlétiques" in the "Programme des Jeux Olympiqes de 1896," which was published in the third edition (January 1895) of the *Bulletin du Comité International des Jeux Olympiques*. It was to be conducted using the rules of the Marylebone Cricket Club; however, it was not held at the 1896 Olympics for reasons unknown.

Equestrian Events

Equestrian events were also listed in the January 1895 edition of the *Bulletin du Comité International des Jeux Olympiques*. The events mentioned were dressage, with and without a carriage; show jumping; figure riding; and high jumping. In addition, equestrian events were listed by the Sorbonne Congress Commission on the Olympic Games as one of the sports which should be conducted at the Olympics Games. The sport was not again mentioned in the plans and did not take place in 1896.

Fencing

Foil and sabre fencing, as well as a masters' foil competition, were conducted as events in 1896. Épée fencing was also scheduled but the event did not take place. It was scheduled for 7 April (26 March) and was postponed when the foil took a long time to complete, but the reasons for its eventual cancellation have not been found. It was listed in the program published in the third edition (January 1895) of the *Bulletin du Comité International des Jeux Olympiques*.

Football (Soccer)

Football is sometimes listed as having been contested in 1896 as an exhibition sport or demonstration sport at the Olympic Games, although no such designation existed at the time of the 1896 Olympics. Supposedly, a match between a Greek club and a Danish club was conducted. No 1896 source supports this, and we think this is most likely an error which has been perpetrated in multiple texts. No such match occurred.

Ice Skating

Ice skating was listed by the Commission on the Olympic Games of the Sorbonne Congress as one of the sports which should be conducted at the Olympic Games. This idea was not mentioned again for 1896, and skating did not appear in the Olympics until 1908. It is not certain if "patinage" (ice skating) referred to speed skating or figure skating, though it is most likely that it referred to figure skating.

Mountaineering

The Commission on the Olympic Games of the Sorbonne Congress concluded that a "prize should be awarded to the best mountaineering since the last celebration of the Olympic Games." This was never given.

Paume

Paume was listed in the first edition of the *Bulletin du Comité International des Jeux Olympiques* as one of the "Jeux Athlétiques" which should be conducted at the 1896 Olympic Games. This did not take place. It is unclear if this sport was to be jeu de paume (court or royal tennis), courte paume, or longue paume.

Pentathlon

The conclusions by the Commission on Olympic Games of the Sorbonne Congress noted that "There should be instituted a general championship of athletics under the name 'pentathlon.'" It never was organized, and this idea was not again mentioned in the plans for the 1896 Olympics. It is not certain which five events were to be contested in the pentathlon. It is likely that it would have had primarily track & field athletics events, but perhaps wrestling would have also have been on the schedule, as in the Ancient Olympic Games.

Polo

Polo events were listed in the first edition of the *Bulletin du Comité International des Jeux Olympiques* as a possible sport which could be conducted. This was also listed under the conclusions of the Commission on the Olympic Games of the Sorbonne Congress, but polo events were never conducted in 1896.

Rowing

Rowing was on the 1896 Olympic program and represents the sport which came the closest to being held at the 1st Olympics, without that actually occurring. Seven rowing events were scheduled, all to be conducted on 13 April (1 April). The weather that day was horrid, with high wind, almost freezing rain, and very rough seas. Because of the weather and the dangerous seas, the rowing events were rescheduled from 1000 to 1500. As the weather was no better in the afternoon, and the rowing events were the last scheduled events of the 1896 Olympics, they were cancelled. The rules for the rowing were to be those of the Rowing Club Italiano. The start was to be at the Palaio (Old) Phaliron and finish at the Neo Phaliron.

The *Official Report* noted, "The wind, however, continually strengthens and the contestants are hesitant in coming forward. In spite of this it is decided that only the four-oar boats contest should take place, and they are transported to Old Phaliron drawn by steam launches, to the starting point which is marked by the boats of the Syra Rowing Club and that of the Panhellenic Club of Athens. The bad weather, however, turns into rough seas making their rowing impossible. Owing to this the contest is postponed until 3 PM. Yet as the bad weather continued up to then, indeed with greater violence, and the boats and barges were swept ashore, the contest both of rowing and of the naval boats were definitely cancelled."

The following events were scheduled:

> Single sculls over 2,000 meters[1]* (one known entrant — Berthold Küttner [GER])
> Double sculls over 2,000 meters[2] (one known boat entered — Berthold Küttner and Alfred Jaeger [GER])
> Coxed pairs over 2,000 meters[3] (one known boat entered — Ruderklub Piraeus [GRE])
> Coxed fours[4] (two known boats entered — Ruderverein Hermopolis [GRE], Panhellenischer Turnverein [GRE])

And the following events for Naval boats:

> Gigs over 2 nautical miles (7 boats entered — Hydra [GRE], Spetzai [GRE], Psara [GRE], Hellas [GRE], a Greek panzerfregatte [GRE], Devastation [FRA], San Francisco [USA])
> Skiffs over 2 nautical miles (unknown entries)
> Ship's boats of 10-14 oars over 2 nautical miles (5 boats entered — Hydra [GRE], Spetzai [GRE], Psara [GRE], Devastation [FRA], San Francisco [USA])
> Ship's boats of 16-20 oars over 2 nautical miles (3 boats entered — Hydra [GRE], Spetzai [GRE], Psara [GRE]).

Water Polo

Water polo was listed as a sport which would be conducted in a March 1896 edition of *Le Messager d'Athènes*. It had also been listed in the "Programme des Jeux Olympiqes de 1896," which

*See Notes on page 120.

was published in the third edition (January 1895) of the *Bulletin du Comité International des Jeux Olympiques*. The sport was not held at the 1896 Olympic Games.

Yachting

Yachting events were mentioned several times during the plans for the 1896 Olympics and were even discussed in the *Official Report*. In the *Official Program*, these events were scheduled for 12 April (31 March). The first edition of the *Bulletin du Comité International des Jeux Olympiques* listed them as a scheduled sport under the larger category "Other Sports and Events Nautiques." They were again mentioned in the third edition of the Bulletin, with no details given concerning the events scheduled.

Five events were listed on the first known program, dated 12/24 November 1894. Four of these were for yachts less than 3 tons over 5 miles, from 3-10 tons over 10 miles, from 10-20 tons over 10 miles, and yachts over 20 tons over 10 miles. The rules were to be those of the Yacht Racing Association of Great Britain. A fifth event, for steam yachts over 10 miles, was to be conducted under the rules of the Cercle de la Voile de Paris. The next known program, which appeared in the *Bulletin du Comité International des Jeux Olympiques* edition of January 1895, listed only "Yachting: Courses à la voile.—L'Union des Yachts Français a élaboré un règlement spécial."

The *Official Report* noted that "The sailing races were cancelled since we had no proper boats for this, nor did any foreign ones appear for the contest." There were three groups of events scheduled—those for yachts, those of merchant yachts, and those for steam yachts. The events finally scheduled were as follows:

Yachts—0-3 tons over 10 nautical miles; 3-10 tons over 15 nautical miles; 10-20 tons over 20 nautical miles; and 20+ tons over 20 nautical miles. The events were to be held under the rating rule of the L'Union des Yachts Français of 5 November 1892. The course was a triangular one starting and finishing at the Neo Phaliron, with one race for each event. Only one entrant is known in all—"Callux," of Mehmed Ali-Pasha Halim of Egypt, in the 20+ ton class.

Merchant Yachts—Aegina (-class), with 3 equally high masts and lanterns, 5-6 picheos (ells) long, over 5 nautical miles; Syros (-class), with 3 equally high masts and lanterns, 6-7 picheos (ells) long, over 5 nautical miles; and merchant yachts with 3 equally high masts and lanterns over 5 nautical miles. These races were to be over a straight course with the finish at the Neo Phaliron. There were no known entrants.[5]

Steam Yachts—one class only, over 10 nautical miles, with 3 races to decide the event. The races were to be over a straight course with start at Flivas and finish at Neo Phaliron. The rules were to be those of the Cercle de la Voile de Paris. Nothing is known about the size, displacement, power, or other ratings of the yachts.

NOTES

1. Under the rules of the Rowing Club Italiano.
2. Under the rules of the Rowing Club Italiano.
3. Under the rules of the Rowing Club Italiano.
4. Under the rules of the Rowing Club Italiano.
5. We have been unable to discover the length of a picheo.

Appendix I
1896 Program

| *Gregorian* *Julian* | | | | |
Date	*Date*	*Site*	*Time*	*Event*
5 April	24 March	Panathenaic Stadium	1100	Inauguration of the statue of Georgios Averoff
6 April	25 March	Panathenaic Stadium	1500	Opening Ceremony
			1530	Athletics, 100 meters; 3 heats
			1540	Athletics, Triple jump
			1615	Athletics, 800 meters; 2 heats
			1625	Athletics, Discus throw
			1710	Athletics, 400 meters; 2 heats
		Athens	Night	Light Feast
7 April	26 March	Zappeion	1000	Fencing, Foil; 2 pools
				Fencing, Sabre (postponed to 9 April/28 March)
				Fencing, Épée (postponed, later cancelled)
				Fencing, Foil for fencing masters
				Fencing, Foil; Final
		Panathenaic Stadium	1430	Athletics, 110 meter hurdles; 2 heats
			1440	Athletics, Long jump
			1530	Athletics, 400 meters; final
			1540	Athletics, Shot put
			1630	Weightlifting, Two hands
				Weightlifting, One hand
				Athletics, 1,500 meters
		Athens	2130	Akropolis illuminated
8 April	27 March	Kallithea	1030	Inauguration of the Shooting Range
				Shooting, Military Rifle, 200 meters (continued to next day)

		Ilissos	AM	Tennis, Singles; Group play
				Tennis, Doubles; 1st round
		Neo Phaliron	1300	Cycling, 100 km. track race
			1600	Tennis, Singles; Group play
				Tennis, Doubles; 1st round
9 April	28 March	Kallithea	0900	Shooting, Military Rifle, 200 meters
		Ilissos	AM	Tennis, Singles; Group play
				Tennis, Doubles; 1st round and one semifinal
		Zappeion	1000	Sabre (originally scheduled for 26 March/7 April)
		Panathenaic Stadium	1430	Athletics, 800 meters; final
			1440	Gymnastics, Parallel bars, teams
				Gymnastics, Horizontal bar, teams
				Gymnastics, Vaulting horse
				Gymnastics, Pommelled horse
				Gymnastics, Rings
				Gymnastics, Horizontal bar
				Gymnastics, Parallel bars (postponed to next day due to darkness)
				Gymnastics, Rope climbing (postponed to next day due to darkness)
		Mega Theatro	Night	Concert by the Athens Philharmonic Orchestra
10 April	29 March	Ilissos	0900	Tennis, Singles; Group play and semifinals
		Kallithea	0900	Shooting, Military Pistol, 25 meters
		Panathenaic Stadium	1000	Gymnastics, Parallel bars (originally scheduled 28 March/9 April)
				Gymnastics, Rope climbing (originally scheduled 28 March/9 April)
		Marathon	1400	Athletics, Marathon start
		Panathenaic Stadium	1430	Athletics, 100 meters; final
			1440	Athletics, High jump
			1530	Athletics, 110 meter hurdles; final
			1540	Athletics, Pole vault
			1630	Wrestling (not finished due to darkness)
			1655	Athletics, Marathon finish
		Piraeus	2130	Venetian Feast
			2200	Torchlight Procession
			2245	Fireworks
11 April	30 March	Panathenaic Stadium	0900	Wrestling, final
		Kallithea	0900	Shooting, Free Pistol, 30 meters
				Shooting, Free Rifle, 300 meters (finished the following day)
			1330	Shooting, Pistol, 25 meters
		Piraeus	1030	Swimming, 100 meter freestyle
				Swimming, 100 meters for sailors

				Swimming, 500 meter freestyle
				Swimming, 1,200 meter freestyle
		Neo Phaliron	1500	Cycling, 2 km. track race
				Cycling, 10 km. track race
				Cycling, 1 lap time trial
		Ilissos	PM	Tennis, Singles; final
				Tennis, Doubles; final
		Mega Theatro	Night	Antigone by Sophocles
12 April	31 March	Kallithea	Morning	Shooting, Free Rifle, 300 meters (continued from 30 March/11 April)
		The Royal Palace	1130	Dinner for participants and officials
		Odos Kifisia	1217	Cycling, Road race; start
		Phaliron	1500	Yachting (cancelled due to too few entrants)
			1500	Competition for orchestras (cancelled)
		Neo Phaliron	1539	Cycling, Road race; finish
		Odos Athinas	2100	Torchlight Procession
13 April	1 April	Neo Phaliron	0720	Cycling, 12 hour track race
		Phaliron	1000	Rowing (postponed to 1500 due to strong wind and high waves)
		Grand Hotel Phaliron	1200	Dinner given by President of Comité International des Jeux Olympiques
		Phaliron	1500	Rowing (cancelled due to strong wind and high waves)
14 April	2 April	Panathenaic Stadium	1430	Awards Ceremony (postponed to next day due to rain)
15 April	3 April	Panathenaic Stadium	1030	Awards Ceremony
				Closing Ceremony

PROGRAMME

DES

JEUX OLYMPIQUES DE 1896

ATHÈNES

5-15 Avril 1896.—(24 mars-3 avril, Style grec).

SOUS LA PRÉSIDENCE DE

S. A. R. Monseigneur le Prince Royal de Grèce

A. – SPORTS ATHLÉTIQUES

Courses à pied : 100 mètres, 400 mètres, 800 mètres et 1,500 mètres plat, 110 mètres haies. – Les règlements seront ceux de l' *Union des Sociétés françaises de Sports Athlétiques*.

Concours : Sauts en longueur et en hauteur *(running long et high jump)* ; Saut à la perche *(Pole jump)* ; Lancement du poids *(Putting the weihgt)* et du disque. – Les règlements seront ceux de l'*Amateur Athletic Association d'Angleterre*.

Course à pied, dite de Marathon, sur la distance de 42 kilomètres, de Marathon à Athènes, pour la coupe offerte par M. Michel Bréal, membre de l'Institut de France.

Le but de cette course sera au Stade Panathénaïque, restauré par la munificence du citoyen hellène Georges Avéroff.

C'est au «Stade Panathénaïque» qu'auront lieu aussi les sports Athlétiques et Gymnastiques.

B. – GYMNASTIQUE

Exercices individuels : Corde lisse en traction de bras. – Rétablissements divers à la barre fixe. – Mouvements aux anneaux. – Barres parallèles profondes. – Saut au cheval. – Travail des poids.

Mouvements d'ensemble : (Les Sociétés ne pourront présenter d'équipes inférieures à 10 gymnastes).

C. – ESCRIME ET LUTTE

Assauts de fleuret, sabre et épée : Amateurs ; Professeurs (civils et militaires). Un règlement spécial a été élaboré par la *Société d'encouragement d'Escrime* (Paris).

Lutte : romaine et grecque.

D. – TIR

Tir à l'arme de guerre et à l'arme libre 200 et 300 mètres. – Revolver d'ordonnance 25 mètres. – Revolver libre 30 mètres. – Pistolet 25 mètres.

E. – SPORTS NAUTIQUES

Yachting. (Avant-programme) : Course de steam-yachts sous le règlement du *Cercle de la Voile de Paris*. Distance : 10 milles.

Courses à la voile, jauge et règlements du *Yacht Racing Association d'Angleterre*.

1° Bateaux n'excédant pas 3 tonneaux (Divisible au besoin en 2 séries). Distance : 5 milles.

2° Bateaux de 3 à 10 tonneaux. Distance : 10 milles.

3° Bateaux de 10 à 20 tonneaux. Distance : 10 milles.

4° Bateaux au-dessus de 20 tonneaux. Distance : 10 milles.

Des courses seront en outre réservées aux embarcations et aux marins du pays.

Avirons : Un rameur : 2,000 mètres, sans virage, skiffs.

Deux rameurs de couple, sans virage, yoles et outriggers.

Quatre rameurs de pointe, sans virage, yoles.

Une course spéciale sera organisée pour les équipages des escadres.

Les règlements seront ceux du *Rowing Club Italiano*.

Natation : Vitesse : 100 mètres. Fond et vitesse : 500 mètres. Fond : 1,000 mètres.

Jeu de water-polo.

F. – VÉLOCIPÉDIE

Vitesse : 2,000 mètres, sur piste, sans entraîneurs, 10,000 mètres, sur piste, sans entraîneurs.

Fond : 100 kilomètres sur piste avec entraîneurs.

Course de 12 heures sur piste, avec entraîneurs.

Les règlements suivis seront ceux de l'*International Cyclist's Association*.

G. – JEUX ATHLÉTIQUES

Lawn tennis : Simple. Double.

Cricket : Les règlements seront ceux de la *All' England Lawn Tennis Association* et du *Marylebone Cricket Club*.

Football. Rugby et Association.

Fait à Athènes, le 12|24 novembre 1894.

N. Délyanni, président du Conseil des Ministres ; L. Déligeorges, A. Zaïmis, C. Carapanos, anciens ministres ; colonel Th. Mano ; K. Mavromichalis, ancien député ; colonel N. Métaxas, ministre de l'Intérieur ; Th. Retzinas, maire du Pirée ; G. Roma, ancien vice-président de la Chambre des députés ; Al. Skouzés, ancien député ; commandant A. Soutzo ; G. Kozakis-Typaldo, ancien député, *membres du Conseil du Comité Hellène* ; T. Philémon, ancien maire d'Athènes, *secrétaire-général* ; C. Mano, George Mélas, G. Streit, A. Mercati, *secrétaires*.

Approuvé :

D. Bikélas, *président du Comité International*. – Baron Pierre de Coubertin, *secrétaire général*.

A. Callot, *trésorier*.

The Initial 1896 Official Program

2ᵉ Année. — Nᵒ 3.   Janvier 1895.

BULLETIN DU COMITÉ INTERNATIONAL

DES

JEUX OLYMPIQUES

PARIS, 229, Rue Saint-Honoré   *Citius — Fortius — Altius*   Rue Saint-Honoré, 229, PARIS

PROGRAMME

DES

JEUX OLYMPIQUES DE 1896

ATHÈNES

5-15 AVRIL 1896. — *(24 mars-3 avril, Style grec).*

SOUS LA PRÉSIDENCE DE

S. A. R. Monseigneur le Prince Royal, duc de Sparte

A. — SPORTS ATHLÉTIQUES

Courses à pied : 100 mètres, 400 mètres, 800 mètres et 1,500 mètres plat, 110 mètres haies. — Les règlements seront ceux de l'*Union des Sociétés françaises de Sports Athlétiques*.

Concours : Sauts en longueur et en hauteur *(running long et high jump)*; Saut à la perche *(Pole vault)*; Lancement du poids *(Putting the weight)* et du disque. — Les règlements seront ceux de l'*Amateur Athletic Association d'Angleterre*.

Course à pied, dite de Marathon, sur la distance de 48 kilomètres, de Marathon à Athènes, pour la coupe offerte par M. Michel Bréal, membre de l'Institut de France.

B. — GYMNASTIQUE

Exercices individuels : Corde lisse en traction de bras. — Rétablissements divers à la barre fixe. — Mouvements aux anneaux. — Barres parallèles profondes. — Saut au cheval. — Travail des poids.

Mouvements d'ensemble : (Les Sociétés ne pourront présenter d'équipes inférieures à 10 gymnastes).

C. — ESCRIME ET LUTTE

Assauts de fleuret, sabre et épée : Amateurs; Professeurs (civils et militaires). — Un règlement spécial a été élaboré par la *Société d'encouragement de l'Escrime* (Paris).

Lutte : romaine et grecque.

D. — TIR

Par suite d'une difficulté imprévue, le programme du Tir ne pourra être publié qu'un peu plus tard.

E. — SPORTS NAUTIQUES

Yachting : Courses à la voile. — L'*Union des Yachts Français* a élaboré un règlement spécial

Aviron : Un rameur : 2,000 mètres, sans virage, skiffs.
Deux rameurs de couple, sans virage, yoles et outriggers.
Quatre rameurs de pointe, sans virage, yoles.
Une course spéciale sera organisée pour les équipages des escadres.
Les règlements seront ceux du *Rowing Club Italiano*.

Natation : Vitesse : 100 mètres. Fond et vitesse : 500 mètres. Fond : 1,000 mètres.
Jeu de water-polo.

F. — VÉLOCIPÉDIE

Vitesse : 2,000 mètres, sur piste, sans entraîneurs. 10,000 mètres, sur piste, sans entraîneurs.

Fond : 100 kilomètres sur piste avec entraîneurs.

Course de 12 heures sur piste, avec entraîneurs.

Les règlement suivis seront ceux de l'*International Cyclist's Association*.

G. — EQUITATION

Concours d'équitation : reprise de manège, avec et sans étriers, saut d'obstacles, voltige, haute école.
(Il ne sera tenu compte que de l'aptitude du cavalier et non de la valeur du cheval).

H. — JEUX ATHLÉTIQUES

Lawn tennis : Simple. Double.

Cricket : Les règlements seront ceux de la *All England Lawn Tennis Association* et du *Marylebone Cricket Club*.

Fait à Athènes, le 12/24 novembre 1894.

Colonel MANO;
ETIENNE SCOULOUDIS, député, ancien ministre;
A.-D. SOUTZO, chef d'escadron de cavalerie;
RETZINAS, maire du Pirée,
   vice-présidents du Comité hellène.
PAUL SKOUSÈS, *trésorier.*
ALEXANDRE MERCATI, GEORGES M. MELAS, *secrétaires.*

APPROUVÉ :

D. BIKELAS, *président du Comité International.*
Baron PIERRE DE COUBERTIN, *secrétaire général.*
A. CALLOT, *trésorier.*

The Final 1896 Official Program

Appendix II
Competitors (by Country)

In the following we have tried to give precise biographical information concerning full names, complete date of birth and death (where known), and club affiliations (where known). Also given are all events in which the competitors competed and their placement. In events where competitors were eliminated prior to a final, the following notation serves as an example to explain the results:

4h3r1/2 = 4th in heat 3, round 1 of 2

Australia [1].

Athletics [1].
> Flack, Edwin Harold. (Victoria AAA) [b.5 November 1873–d.10 January 1935]. 800 [1]; 1,500 [1]; Marathon [dnf]. [See also Tennis (Lawn)].

Tennis (Lawn) [1].
> Flack, Edwin Harold. (Melbourne LTC) [b.5 November 1873–d.10 January 1935]. Men's Singles [=8]; Men's Doubles [3]. [See also Athletics].

Austria [3].

Cycling [1].
> Schmal, Adolf. (Akademisch-Technische Radfahrer-Verein) [b.18 September 1872–d.28 August 1919]. One lap time trial [3]; 10 kilometers [3]; 100 kilometers [dnf]; 12 hr. [1]. [See also Fencing].

Fencing [1].
> Schmal, Adolf. (Akademisch-Technische Radfahrer-Verein) [b.18 September 1872–d.28 August 1919]. Sabre [4]. [See also Cycling].

Swimming [2].

Herschmann, Otto. (Wiener Amateur-Schwimmclub) [b.4 January 1877–d.14 June 1942]. 100 freestyle [2].

Neumann, Paul. (Wiener Amateur-Schwimmclub) [b.13 June 1875–d.9 February 1932]. 500 freestyle [1]; 1,200 freestyle [dnf].

Cyprus [1].

Athletics [1].

Andreou, Anastasios. (Gymnastikos Syllogos Olympia Kyprou). 110 meter hurdles [4h1r1/2].

Denmark [3].

Athletics [3].

Jensen, Alexander Viggo. (Handelsstandens Athletklub) [b.22 June 1874–d.2 November 1930]. Shot Put [4]; Discus Throw [ac]. [See also Gymnastics, Shooting, and Weightlifting].

Nielsen, Holger Louis. (Københavns Fodsports-Forening) [b.18 December 1866–d.26 January 1955]. Discus Throw [ac]. [See also Fencing and Shooting].

Schmidt, Eugen Stahl. (Københavns Roklub) [b.17 February 1862–d.7 October 1931]. 100 meters [ac/h2r1/2]. [See also Shooting].

Fencing [1].

Nielsen, Holger Louis. (Københavns Fægteklub) [b.18 December 1866–d.26 January 1955]. Sabre [3]. [See also Athletics and Shooting].

Gymnastics [1].

Jensen, Alexander Viggo. (Handelsstandens Athletklub) [b.22 June 1874–d.2 November 1930]. Rope Climbing [4]. [See also Athletics, Shooting, and Weightlifting].

Shooting [3].

Jensen, Alexander Viggo. (Handelsstandens Athletklub) [b.22 June 1874–d.2 November 1930]. Free Rifle (300 meters) [3]; Military Rifle (200 meters) [6]. [See also Athletics, Gymnastics, and Weightlifting].

Nielsen, Holger Louis. (Københavns Fodsports-Forening) [b.18 December 1866–d.26 January 1955]. Military Pistol [5]; Pistol (25 meters) [3]; Free Pistol (30 meters) [2]; Military Rifle (200 meters) [dnf]. [See also Athletics and Fencing].

Schmidt, Eugen Stahl. (Københavns Roklub) [b.17 February 1862–d.7 October 1931]. Military Rifle (200 meters) [=12]. [See also Athletics].

Weightlifting [1].

Jensen, Alexander Viggo. (Handelsstandens Athletklub) [b.22 June 1874–d.2 November 1930]. Unlimited class, one-hand [2]; Unlimited class, two-hands [1]. [See also Athletics, Gymnastics, and Shooting].

Egypt [1].

Tennis (Lawn) [1].
  Kasdaglis, Dionysios. (Alexandria) Men's Doubles [2]; Men's Singles [2].

France [13].

Athletics [6].
  De La Nézière, Georges. (Stade Français) 800 meters [3h2r1/2].
  Grisel, Alphonse. (Racing Club de France) 100 [4h1r1/2]; 400 meters [ac/h1r1/2]; Long Jump [ac]; Discus Throw [ac]. [See also Gymnastics].
  Lagoudakis, Sokratis. Marathon [9].
  Lermusiaux, Albin. (Racing Club de France) [b.9 April 1874–d.1940]. 800 meters [ac/r2/2]; 1,500 meters [3]; Marathon [dnf]. [See also Shooting].
  Reichel, Frantz. (Racing Club de France) [b.16 March 1871–d.24 March 1932]. 400 meters [3h2r1/2]; 110 meter hurdles [dns/r2/2].
  Tufferi, Alexandre. (Panellinios Gymnastikos Syllogos) [b.8 June 1876–d.14 March 1958]. Long Jump [ac]; Triple Jump [2].

Cycling [2].
  Flameng, Léon. (Association Vélocipédique Internationale) [b.1877–d.1917]. One Lap Time Trial [=5]; 2,000 meter sprint [3]; 10 kilometers [2]; 100 kilometers [1].
  Masson, Paul. (Association Vélocipédique Internationale) [b.1874–d.1945]. One Lap Time Trial [1]; 2,000 meter sprint [1]; 10 kilometers [1].

Fencing [4].
  Callot, Henri. (Union des Sociétés Françaises de Sports Athlétiques) Foil [2].
  Delaborde, Henri. Foil [=5].
  Gravelotte, Eugene-Henri. (Corichon) [b.6 February 1876–d.28 August 1939]. Foil [1].
  Perronet, Jean. Foil for Masters [2].

Gymnastics [1].
  Grisel, Alphonse. (Racing Club de France) Parallel Bars [ac]. [See also Athletics (Track & Field)].

Shooting [1].
  Lermusiaux, Albin. (Racing Club de France) [b.9 April 1874–d.1940]. Military Rifle (200 meters) [ac]. [See also Athletics (Track & Field)].
Tennis (Lawn) [1].
  Defert, ––. (Racing Club de France) Men's Singles [=8].

Germany [19].

Athletics [5].
  Doerry, Kurt. (Verein Sport-Exelsior) [b.24 September 1874–d.4 January 1947]. 100 meters [dnf/h1r1/2]; 400 meters [ac/h1r1/2]; 110 meter hurdles [ach2r1/2].

Galle, Carl. (Berliner Fußballklub Germania 88) [b.5 October 1872–d.18 April 1963]. 1,500 meters [4].

Hofmann, Fritz. (Turngemeinde im Berlin) [b.19 June 1871–d.14 July 1927]. 100 meters [2]; 400 meters [4]; High Jump [5]; Triple Jump [ac]; Shot Put [ac]. [See also Gymnastics].

Schuhmann, Carl. (Berliner Turnerschaft) [b.12 May 1869–d.24 March 1946]. Long Jump [ac]; Triple Jump [5]; Shot Put [ac]. [See also Gymnastics, Weightlifting, and Wrestling].

Traun, Friedrich Adolf "Fritz." (Sportsclub Germania, Hamburg) [b.29 March 1876–d.11 July 1908]. 100 meters [3h3r1/2]; 800 meters [3h1r1/2]. [See also Tennis (Lawn)].

Cycling [5].

Goedrich, August. (Athens) [b.1859–d.after 1936]. Road Race [2].

Knubel, Bernhard. (Radsportverein 1895 Münster) [b.13 November 1872–d.14 April 1957]. 100 kilometers [dnf].

Leupold, Theodor. (Radfahrverein 1884 Zittau). One Lap Time Trial [=5]; 100 kilometers [dnf].

Rosemeyer, Joseph. (Radfahrerverein Lingen) [b.13 March 1872–d.1 December 1919]. One Lap Time Trial [8]; 2,000 meter sprint [4]; 10 kilometers [4]; 100 kilometers [dnf].

Welzenbacher, Joseph. (Velocipedisten-Club Bavaria). 100 kilometers [dnf]; 12-hour race [dnf].

Gymnastics [11].

Böcker, Conrad. (Turngemeinde in Berlin) [b.1871–d.April 1936]. Horizontal Bar [ac]; Horse Vault [ac]; Parallel Bars [ac]; Pommelled Horse [ac]; Rings [ac]; Horizontal Bar, Teams [1]; Parallel Bars, Teams [1].

Flatow, Alfred. (Berliner Turnerschaft) [b.3 October 1869–d.28 December 1942]. Horizontal Bar [2]; Horse Vault [ac]; Parallel Bars [1]; Pommelled Horse [ac]; Rings [ac]; Horizontal Bar, Teams [1]; Parallel Bars, Teams [1].

Flatow, Gustav "Felix." (Berliner Turnverein) [b.7 January 1875–d.29 January 1945]. Horizontal Bar [ac]; Horse Vault [ac]; Parallel Bars [ac]; Pommelled Horse [ac]; Rings [ac]; Horizontal Bar, Teams [1]; Parallel Bars, Teams [1].

Hillmar, Georg. (Turngemeinde in Berlin) [b.1876–d.ca1936]. Horizontal Bar [ac]; Horse Vault [ac]; Parallel Bars [ac]; Pommelled Horse [ac]; Horizontal Bar, Teams [1]; Parallel Bars, Teams [1].

Hofmann, Fritz. (Turngemeinde in Berlin) [b.19 June 1871–d.14 July 1927]. Rope Climbing [3]. [See also Athletics (Track & Field)].

Manteuffel, Fritz. (Berliner Turnrat) [b.11 January 1875–d.21 April 1941]. Horizontal Bar [ac]; Horse Vault [ac]; Parallel Bars [ac]; Pommelled Horse [ac]; Horizontal Bar, Teams [1]; Parallel Bars, Teams [1].

Neukirch, Karl. (Berliner Turnerschaft) [b.3 November 1864–d.26 June 1941]. Horizontal Bar [ac]; Horse Vault [ac]; Parallel Bars [ac]; Pommelled Horse [ac]; Horizontal Bar, Teams [1]; Parallel Bars, Teams [1].

Röstel, Richard. (Turngemeinde in Berlin). [b.1872]. Horizontal Bar [ac]; Horse Vault [ac]; Parallel Bars [ac]; Pommelled Horse [ac]; Horizontal Bar, Teams [1]; Parallel Bars, Teams [1].

Schuft, Gustav. (Turngemeinde in Berlin) [b.16 June 1876–d.8 February 1948]. Horizontal Bar [ac]; Horse Vault [ac]; Parallel Bars [ac]; Pommelled Horse [ac]; Horizontal Bar, Teams [1]; Parallel Bars, Teams [1].

Schuhmann, Carl. (Berliner Turnerschaft) [b.12 May 1869–d.24 March 1946]. Horizontal Bar [ac]; Horse Vault [1]; Parallel Bars [ac]; Pommelled Horse [ac]; Rings [5]; Horizontal Bar, Teams [1]; Parallel Bars, Teams [1]. [See also Athletics (Track & Field), Weightlifting, and Wrestling].

Weingärtner, Hermann. (Berliner Turnerschaft) [b.27 August 1864–d.22 December 1919].
  Horizontal Bar [1]; Horse Vault [3]; Parallel Bars [ac]; Pommelled Horse [2]; Rings [2]; Horizontal Bar, Teams [1]; Parallel Bars, Teams [1].

Tennis (Lawn) [1].
  Traun, Friedrich Adolf "Fritz." (Sportsclub Germania, Hamburg) [b.29 March 1876–d.11 July
  1908]. Men's Singles [=8]; Men's Doubles [1]. [See also Athletics (Track & Field)].

Weightlifting [1].
  Schuhmann, Carl. (Berliner Turnerschaft) [b.12 May 1869–d.24 March 1946]. Unlimited
  Class — two-hands [4]. [See also Athletics (Track & Field), Gymnastics, and Wrestling].

Wrestling [1].
  Schuhmann, Carl. (Berliner Turnerschaft) [b.12 May 1869–d.24 March 1946]. Unlimited Class,
  Greco-Roman [1]. [See also Athletics (Track & Field), Gymnastics, and Weightlifting].

Great Britain and Ireland [10].

Athletics [5].
  Elliot, Launceston. (b.9 June 1874–d.8 August 1930) [London Amateur Weightlifting Club]
  100 meters [3h2r1/2]. [See also Gymnastics, Weightlifting, and Wrestling].
  Gmelin, Charles Henry Stuart. (b.28 May 1872–d.12 October 1950) [Oxford University Ath-
  letic Club (Keble College)] 100 meters [3h1r1/2]; 400 meters [3].
  Goulding, Grantley Thomas Smart. (b.23 March 1874) [Gloucester Athletic Club] 110 meter
  hurdles [2].
  Marshal, George. [Panakhaikos Gymnastikos Syllogos] 100 [ac/h2r1/2]; 800 meters [4h1r1/2].
  Robertson, George Stuart. (b.25 May 1872–d.29 January 1967) [Oxford University Athletic
  Club (New College)] Discus Throw [ac]. [See also Tennis (Lawn)].

Cycling [2].
  Battel, E.[1]* [British Embassy, Athens] 100 kilometers [dnf]; One Lap Time Trial [4]; Road Race
  [3].
  Keeping, F.[2] [British Embassy, Athens] One Lap Time Trial [=5]; 12-hour race [2].

Gymnastics [1].
  Elliot, Launceston. (b.9 June 1874–d.8 August 1930) [London Amateur Weightlifting Club]
  Rope Climbing [5]. [See also Athletics (Track & Field), Weightlifting, and Wrestling].

Shooting [2].
  Machonet, ——.[3] Military Rifle (200 meters) [ac].
  Merlin, Sidney Louis Walter. (b.26 April 1856–d.1952) Pistol (25 meters) [dnf]; Military Pis-
  tol [dnf]; Military Rifle (200 meters) [10]; Free Rifle (300 meters) [ac].

Tennis (Lawn) [2].
  Boland, John Mary Pius. (b.16 September 1870–d.17 March 1958) [Oxford University Ath-
  letic Club (Christ Church College)] Men's Singles [1]; Men's Doubles [1].
  Robertson, George Stuart. (b.25 May 1872–d.29 January 1967) [Oxford University Athletic Club
  (New College)] Men's Singles [=8]; Men's Doubles [3]. [See also Athletics (Track & Field)].

*See Notes on page 141.

Weightlifting [1].
   Elliot, Launceston. (b.9 June 1874–d.8 August 1930) [London Amateur Weightlifting Club]
      Unlimited Class — one-hand [1]; Unlimited Class — two-hands [2]. [See also Athletics
      (Track & Field), Gymnastics, and Wrestling].

Wrestling [1].
   Elliot, Launceston. (b.9 June 1874–d.8 August 1930) [London Amateur Weightlifting Club]
      Unlimited Class, Greco-Roman [=4]. [See also Athletics (Track & Field), Gymnastics, and
      Weightlifting].

Greece [98].[4]

Athletics [27].
   Belokas, Spiridon. (Athlitikos Omilos Athinon). Marathon [DQ].
   Damaskos, Evangelos. (Ethnikos Gymnastikos Syllogos). Pole Vault [=3].
   Deligiannis, Dimitrios. (Panellinios Gymnastikos Syllogos). Marathon [6].
   Fetsis, Angelos. (Athlitikos Omilos Athinon). 800 meters [ac/h2r1/2]; 1,500 meters [ac].
   Gennimatas, Georgios. (Panellinios Gymnastikos Syllogos). 100 meters [ac/h3r1/2].
   Gerakaris, Evangelos. (Panellinios Gymnastikos Syllogos). Marathon [7].
   Golemis, Dimitrios. (Athlitikos Omilos Athinon) [b.1877–d.1941]. 800 meters [3]; 1,500
      meters [ac].
   Gouskos, Miltiadis. (Panellinios Gymnastikos Syllogos) [b.1877–d.1904]. Shot Put [2].
   Grigoriou, Georgios. (Ethnikos Gymnastikos Syllogos). Marathon [dnf].
   Kafetzis, Ilias. (Chalandri). Marathon [dnf].
   Karakatsanis, Konstantinos. (Panellinios Gymnastikos Syllogos). 1,500 meters [ac].
   Khalkokondilis, Alexandros. (Athlitikos Omilos Athinon). 100 meters [5]; Long Jump [4].
   Khristopoulos, Dimitrios. (Gymnastiki Etaireia Patron). Marathon [dnf].
   Lavrentis, Ioannis. (Amarousi). Marathon [dnf].
   Louis, Spiridon. (Amarousi) [b.12 January 1873–d.26 March 1940]. Marathon [1].
   Masouris, Stamatios. (Amarousi). Marathon [8].
   Papasideris, Georgios. (Ethnikos Gymnastikos Syllogos). Shot Put [3]; Discus Throw [ac]. [See
      also Weightlifting].
   Papasimeon, Eleitherios. (Amarousi). Marathon [5].
   Paraskevopoulos, Panagiotis. (Athlitikos Omilos Athinon) [b.1875]. Discus Throw [2].
   Persakis, Ioannis. (Panellinios Gymnastikos Syllogos) [b.1877–d.1943]. Triple Jump [3].
   Skaltsogiannis, Athanasios. (Ethnikos Gymnastikos Syllogos). [b.1878]. 110 meter hurdles
      [ach2r1/2]; Long Jump [ac].
   Theodoropoulos, Ioannis. (Ethnikos Gymnastikos Syllogos). Pole Vault [=3].
   Vasilakos, Kharilaos. (Panellinios Gymnastikos Syllogos) [b.1877–d.1963]. Marathon [2].
   Versis, Sotirios. (Panellinios Gymnastikos Syllogos) [b.1876–d.1919]. Discus Throw [3]. [See
      also Weightlifting].
   Vrettos, Ioannis. (Chalandri). Marathon [4].
   Xydas, Vasilios. (Athlitikos Omilos Athinon). Pole Vault [5].
   Zoumis, Khristos. (Athlitikos Omilos Athinon). [b.1875]. Triple Jump [ac].

Cycling [8].
   Aspiotis, Georgios. (Kerkyra). Road Race [ac].
   Iatrou, Miltiades. Road Race [ac].

Kolettis, Georgios. 10 kilometers [dnf]; 100 kilometers [2].
Konstantinidis, Aristidis. 10 kilometers [ac]; 100 kilometers [dnf]; Road Race [1].
Konstantinou, Konstantinos. Road Race [ac]; 12-hour race [dnf].
Nikolopoulos, Stamatios. (Podilatikos Syllogos Athinon). One Lap Time Trial [2]; 2,000
     meter sprint [2].
Paraskevopoulos, Georgios. Road Race [ac]; 12-hour race [dnf].
Tryfiatis-Tripiaris, A. 12-hour race [dnf].

Fencing [9].
Balakakis, Georgios. Foil [=7].
Georgiadis, Ioannis. (Athinaiki Leschi) [b.29 March 1876–d.1960]. Sabre [1].
Iatridis, Georgios. Sabre [5].
Karakalos, Tilemakhos. (Athinaiki Leschi) [b.1868–d.1904]. Sabre [2].
Komninos-Miliotis, Konstantinos. (Athinaiki Leschi) [b.1874]. Foil [=5].
Pierrakos-Mauromikhalis, Periklis. (Athinaiki Leschi) [b.1863–d.1938] Foil [=3].
Poulos, Ioannis. (Athinaiki Leschi) Foil [=7].
Pyrgos, Leonidas. Foil for Masters [1].
Vouros, Athanasios. (Athinaiki Leschi) Foil [=3].

Gymnastics [9].
Andriakopoulos, Nikolaos. (Panakhaikos Gymnastikos Syllogos) [b.1878]. Rope Climbing [1].
Karvelas, Filippos. (Ethnikos Gymnastikos Syllogos) [b.1877–d.1952]. Parallel Bars [ac]; Par-
     allel Bars, Teams [3].
Loundras, Dimitrios. (Ethnikos Gymnastikos Syllogos) [b.6 September 1885–d.15 February
     1970]. Parallel Bars, Teams [3].
Mitropoulos, Ioannis. (Ethnikos Gymnastikos Syllogos) [b.1874]. Parallel Bars [ac]; Rings [1].
Papaigannou, Antonios. (Gymnastiki Etaireia Patron). Horizontal Bar [ac]; Parallel Bars [ac].
Persakis, Petros. (Panellinios Gymnastikos Syllogos). Rings [3].
Petmezas, Aristovoulos. (Panakhaikos Gymnastikos Syllogos). Pommelled Horse [ac]. [See
     also Shooting].
Tsiklitiras, Leonidas. (Panakhaikos Gymnastikos Syllogos). Horizontal Bar [ac].
Xenakis, Thomas. (Ethnikos Gymnastikos Syllogos). Rope Climbing [2].

Shooting [28].
Antelothanasis, ––. Free Rifle (300 meters) [ac].
Diamantis, Georgios. Military Rifle (200 meters) [7]; Free Rifle (300 meters) [ac].
Dorakis, Nikolaos. Military Pistol [3].
Fetsios, Alexios. Military Rifle (200 meters) [11]; Free Rifle (300 meters) [ac].
Frangoudis, Ioannis. Military Pistol [4]; Pistol (25 meters) [1]; Free Pistol (30 meters) [3];
     Free Rifle (300 meters) [2].
Karagiannopoulos, G. Military Rifle (200 meters) [ac].
Karakatsanis, ––. Free Rifle (300 meters) [ac].
Karasevdas, Pantelis. (Akadimiki Leschi) [b.1877–d.1946]. Military Pistol [dnf]; Military Rifle
     (200 meters) [1]; Free Rifle (300 meters) [5].
Khatzidakis, ––. Free Rifle (300 meters) [ac].
Langakis, Leonidas. Free Rifle (300 meters) [dnf].
Levidis, Nikolaos. [b.1868]. Free Rifle (300 meters) [ac].
Metaxas, Anastasios. [b.1862]. Military Rifle (200 meters) [4]; Free Rifle (300 meters) [4].

Mikhailidis, Zenon. Free Rifle (300 meters) [ac]; Military Pistol [ac].

Morakis, Leonidas. Free Pistol (30 meters) [4].

Moustakopoulos, ––. Free Rifle (300 meters) [ac].

Orfanidis, Georgios. [b.1859]. Military Pistol [ac]; Pistol (25 meters) [2]; Free Pistol (30 meters) [5]; Military Rifle (200 meters) [5]; Free Rifle (300 meters) [1].

Pantazidis, ––. Military Pistol [ac].

Patsouris, ––. Military Pistol [ac].

Paulidis, Paulos. [d.1968]. Military Pistol [ac]; Military Rifle (200 meters) [2]; Free Rifle (300 meters) [ac].

Petmezas, Aristovoulos. Military Pistol [ac]; Military Rifle (200 meters) [ac]. [See also Gymnastics].

Platis, ––. Military Pistol [ac].

Sanidis, ––. Military Pistol [dnf].

Stais, Spiridon. Military Rifle (200 meters) [=12].

Theofilakis, Alexandros. (Panellinios Skopeutiki Etairia) [b.1879]. Free Rifle (300 meters) [ac].

Theofilakis, Ioannis. (Sparti) [b.1882]. Military Rifle (200 meters) [9]; Free Rifle (300 meters) [ac].

Trikoupis, Nikolaos. (Axiom Ell. Str.) Military Rifle (200 meters) [3]; Free Rifle (300 meters) [ac].

Vavis, ––. Military Pistol [ac].

Vourakis, Ioannis. Free Rifle (300 meters) [dnf].

Swimming [9].

Andreou, Ioannis. (Omolos ton Pezoporon Peiraios). 1,200 meter freestyle [2].

Anninos, Georgios. 100 meter freestyle [ac].

Drivas, Dimitrios. (Spetses). 100 meter freestyle for sailors [3].

Katravas, ––. (Ethnikos Gymnastikos Syllogos) 1,200 meter freestyle [ac].

Khazapis, Spiridon. (Andros). 100 meter freestyle for sailors [2].

Khorafas, Evstathios. (Kefallinia). 100 meter freestyle [ac]; 500 meter freestyle [3]; 1,200 meter freestyle [ac].

Khrisafos, Alexandros. 100 meter freestyle [ac].

Malokinis, Ioannis. (Spetses — Hydra) [b.1880–d.1942]. 100 meter freestyle for sailors [1].

Pepanos, Antonios. (Gymnastiki Etaireia Patron). 500 meter freestyle [2].

Tennis (Lawn) [6].

Akratopoulos, Aristidis. (Panellinios Gymnastikos Syllogos). Men's Singles [=5]; Men's Doubles [=4].

Akratopoulos, Konstantinos. (Panellinios Gymnastikos Syllogos). Men's Singles [=5]; Men's Doubles [=4].

Frangopoulos, D. (Panakhaikos Syllogos Patron). Men's Singles [=8].

Paspatis, Konstantinos. (Athinai Lawn Tennis Club). Men's Singles [=3]; Men's Doubles [=4].

Petrokokkinos, Dimitrios. (Athinai Lawn Tennis Club) [b.1878]. Men's Singles [=8]; Men's Doubles [2].

Rallis, E. (Athinai Lawn Tennis Club). Men's Singles [=5]; Men's Doubles [=4].

Weightlifting [3].

Nikolopoulos, Alexandros. (Athlitikos Omilos Athinon) [b.1875]. Unlimited Class — one-hand [3].

Papasideris, Georgios. (Ethnikos Gymnastikos Syllogos). Unlimited Class — two-hands [=3]. [See also Athletics (Track & Field)].

Versis, Sotirios. (Panellinios Gymnastikos Syllogos) [b.1876–d.1919]. Unlimited Class — one-hand [4]; Unlimited Class — two-hands [=3]. [See also Athletics (Track & Field)].

Wrestling [2].

Khristopoulos, Stefanos. (Gymnastiki Etaireia Patron). Unlimited Class, Greco-Roman [3].

Tsitas, Georgios. (Panellinios Gymnastikos Syllogos) [b.1872]. Unlimited Class, Greco-Roman [2].

Hungary [7].

Athletics [3].

Dáni, Nándor. (Magyar Athletikai Club) [b.30 May 1871–d.31 December 1949]. 800 meters [2].

Kellner, Gyula. (Budapesti Torna Club) [b.11 April 1871–d.28 July 1940]. Marathon [3].

Szokolyi, Alajos.[5] (Magyar Athletikai Club) [b.19 June 1871–d.9 September 1932]. 100 meters [=3]; 110 meter hurdles [3h1r1/2]; Triple Jump [4].

Gymnastics [2].

Kakas, Gyula. (Magyar Testgyakorlok Köre) Horizontal Bar [ac]; Horse Vault [ac]; Parallel Bars [ac]; Pommelled Horse [ac].

Wein, Desiderius. (Budapesti Torna Egylet). Horizontal Bar [ac]; Horse Vault [ac]; Parallel Bars [ac]; Rings [ac].

Swimming [1].

Hajós, Alfréd. (Budapesti Torna Club) [b.1 February 1878–d.12 November 1955]. 100 meter freestyle [1]; 1,200 meter freestyle [1].

Tennis (Lawn) [1].

Topavicza, Momcsilló.[6] (Nemzeti Torna Egylet) [b.14 October 1872–d.10 January 1949]. Men's Singles [=3]. [See also Weightlifting and Wrestling].

Weightlifting [1].

Topavicza, Momcsilló. (Nemzeti Torna Egylet) [b.14 October 1872–d.10 January 1949]. Unlimited class, two-hands [6]. [See also Tennis (Lawn) and Wrestling].

Wrestling [1].

Topavicza, Momcsilló. (Nemzeti Torna Egylet) [b.14 October 1872–d.10 January 1949]. Unlimited, Greco-Roman [=4]. [See also Tennis (Lawn) and Weightlifting].

Italy [1].

Shooting [1].

Rivabella, ––. Military Rifle (200 meters) [ac].

Smyrna [2].

Athletics [1].
  Tomprof, Dimitrios. (Athlitikos Omilos Orfeus) 800 meters [ac/h2r1/2]; 1,500 meters [ac].

Cycling [1].
  Loverdos, ––. 12-hour race [dnf].

Sweden [1].

Athletics [1].
  Sjöberg, Henrik. (Stockholms Amatörförening) [b.20 January 1875–d.1 August 1905]. 100
  meter [ac/h3r1/2]; Long Jump [ac]; Discus Throw [ac]; HJ [4]. [See also Gymnastics].

Gymnastics [1].
  Sjöberg, Henrik. (Stockholms Amatörförening) [b.20 January 1875–d.1 August 1905]. Horse
  Vault [ac]. [See also Athletics].

Switzerland [3].

Gymnastics [2].
  Champaud, Charles. (Junak, Sofia) Horse Vault [ac]; Parallel Bars [ac]; Pommelled Horse [ac].
  Zutter, Louis. (Amis Gymnastes de Neuchâtel) [b.2 December 1865–d.10 November 1946].
  Horizontal Bar [ac]; Horse Vault [2]; Parallel Bars [2]; Pommelled Horse [1].

Shooting [1].
  Baumann, A. Military Rifle (200 meters) [8].

United States [14].

Athletics [10].
  Blake, Arthur Charles. (Boston Athletic Association) [b.26 January 1872–d.23 October 1944].
  1,500 meters [2]; Marathon [dnf].
  Burke, Thomas Edward. (Boston Athletic Association) [b.15 January 1875–d.14 February
  1929]. 100 meters [1]; 400 meters [1].
  Clark, Ellery Harding. (Boston Athletic Association) [b.13 March 1874–d.27 July 1949]. High
  Jump [1]; Long Jump [1]; Shot Put [ac].
  Connolly, James Brenden Bennet. (Suffolk Athletic Club) [b.28 November 1868–d.20 Janu-
  ary 1957]. High Jump [=2]; Long Jump [3]; Triple Jump [1].
  Curtis, Thomas Pelham. (Boston Athletic Association) [b.7 September 1870–d.23 May 1944].
  100 meters [ac/r2/2]; 110 meter hurdles [1].
  Garrett, Robert. (Princeton University) [b.24 June 1875–d.25 April 1961]. High Jump [=2];
  Long Jump [2]; Shot Put [1]; Discus Throw [1].
  Hoyt, William Welles. (Boston Athletic Association) [b.7 May 1875–d.1 December 1954]. 110
  meter hurdles [dnsr2/2]; Pole Vault [1].

Jamison, Herbert Brotherson. (Princeton University) [b.17 September 1875–d.22 June 1938]. 400 meters [2].

Lane, Francis Adonijah. (Princeton University) [b.23 September 1874–d.17 February 1927]. 100 meters [=3].

Tyler, Albert Clinton. (Princeton University) [b.4 January 1872–d.25 July 1945]. Pole Vault [2].

Shooting [3].

Paine, John. (Boston Athletic Association) [b.8 April 1870–d.2 August 1951]. Military Pistol [1].

Paine, Sumner. (Gastinne-Renette Galleries, Paris) [b.13 May 1868–d.18 April 1904]. Military Pistol [2]; Free Pistol (30 meters) [1].

Waldstein, Charles. (American School in Athens) (b.30 March 1856–d.March 1927) Military Rifle (200 meters) [ac].

Swimming [1].

Williams, Gardner Boyd. (Boston Athletic Association) (b.19 April 1877–d.14 December 1933) 100 meter freestyle [ac]; 1,200 meter freestyle [ac].

NON-COMPETITORS BY SPORT AND EVENTS

Following is a list of all athletes who were entered, but did not take part in, events in the 1896 Olympic Games. Those athletes listed in *italics* did not take part in any event at the 1896 Olympics. Note that three nations — Belgium, Chile, and Russia — had athletes entered in events in 1896, but none of them actually competed.

We have included full names, club affiliations, and, where known, dates of birth and death for those athletes who did not compete in the 1896 Olympic Games. For athletes who competed in events other than those listed, full biographical details are found in the previous list of competitors.

Australia

Flack, Edwin Harold. Athletics — 400 meters.

Austria

Herschmann, Otto. Swimming — 500 meter freestyle.
Schmal, Adolf. Cycling — 2,000 meter sprint; Road race.

Belgium

Verbrugge, Cyrille. [Voenno Uchilishche Na Ntv, Sofia.] (b.9 November 1866–d.1929) Fencing — Foil.

Chile

Subercaseaux [Errazurix], Luis. [Racing Club de France. Association Vélocipédique d'Amateurs, Paris.] Athletics—100 meters; 400 meters; 800 meters. Cycling—2,000 meter sprint; 10,000 meters; 100 km.; 12-hour race; Road race.

Denmark

Jensen, Alexander Viggo. Gymnastics — Horizontal bar; Horse vault; Parallel bars; Pommelled horse; Rings. Wrestling — Unlimited, Greco-Roman.

Nielsen, Holger Louis. Athletics — Shot put. Fencing — Foil. Shooting — Free rifle (300 meters). Swimming —100 meter freestyle; 500 meter freestyle; 1,200 meter freestyle.

Schmidt, Eugen Stahl. Shooting — Free rifle (300 meters).

Winckler, Charles Gustav Wilhelm. [Handelsstandens Athletklub.] (b.9 April 1967–d.17 December 1932) Athletics— Shot put; Discus throw. Swimming—100 meter freestyle; 500 meter freestyle; 1,200 meter freestyle. Weightlifting— One-handed lift; Two-handed lift. Wrestling— Unlimited, Greco-Roman.

France

Adler, Louis. [Stade Français.] (b.1875) Athletics—100 meters; Shot put; Discus throw.

De La Néziere, Georges. Athletics — 400 meters; 1,500 meters.

De Lafreté, Gustave. [Association Vélocipédique d'Amateurs, Paris.] Cycling—2,000 meter sprint; 10,000 meters; 100 km.; 12-hour race; Road race.

Defert, ––. Tennis — Men's doubles.

Delaborde, Henri. Fencing — Sabre.

Flameng, Léon. Cycling — Road race.

Gravelotte, Eugene-Henri. Fencing — Sabre.

Grisel, Alphonse. Athletics — Triple jump; Shot put. Gymnastics — Horizontal bar; Horse vault; Pommelled horse; Rings; Rope climbing. Swimming —100 meter freestyle; 500 meter freestyle; 1,200 meter freestyle. Weightlifting — One-handed lift; Two-handed lift.

Hatté, Jules. [Amiens-Cycle.] Cycling—2,000 meter sprint; 10,000 meters.

Masson, Paul. Cycling —100 km.; Road race.

Reichel, Frantz. Athletics — 800 meters. Swimming —100 meter freestyle; 500 meter freestyle.

Renaud, Jean-Joseph. (b.1876–d.7 December 1953) Fencing— Foil.

Tournois, André. [Racing Club de France.] Athletics—100 meters.

Tuffèri, Alexandre. Athletics —100 meters; 110 meter hurdles.

Vacherot, ––. [Racing Club de France.] Tennis— Men's singles; Men's doubles.

Vanoni, Charles. [Racing Club de France.] Athletics—100 meters; 400 meters; 110 meter hurdles; Pole vault; Shot put; Discus throw.

Germany

Böcker, Conrad. Athletics — Shot put; High jump.

Doerry, Kurt. Athletics — 800 meters; Pole vault; Long jump.

Flatow, Alfred. Athletics—100 meters; High jump; Pole vault; Long jump; Triple jump; Shot put. Gymnastics—Rope climbing. Weightlifting—One-handed lift; Two-handed lift.

Flatow, Gustav "Felix." Athletics—High jump; Pole vault.

Galle, Carl. Athletics—Pole vault; Long jump.

Goedrich, August. Cycling—100 km.

Hofmann, Fritz. Athletics—800 meters; 110 meter hurdles; Pole vault; Long jump. Gymnastics—Horizontal bar; Horse vault; Parallel bars; Pommelled horse.

Knubel, Bernhard. Cycling—2,000 meter sprint; 10,000 meters; 12-hour race; Road race.

Leupold, Theodor. Cycling—2,000 meter sprint; 10,000 meters; 12-hour race; Road race.

Manteuffel, Fritz. Athletics—High jump; Pole vault. Cycling—2,000 meter sprint. 10,000 meters; 100 km.; 12-hour race; Road race. Gymnastics—Rings; Rope climbing. Weightlifting—One-handed lift; Two-handed lift.

Neukirch, Karl. Athletics—Pole vault. Gymnastics—Rope climbing.

Rosemeyer, Joseph. Cycling—12-hour race; Road race.

Röstel, Richard. Gymnastics—Rope climbing.

Schuft, Gustav. Athletics—High jump.

Schuhmann, Carl. Athletics—High jump; Pole vault; Discus throw. Weightlifting—One-handed lift.

Traun, Friedrich Adolf "Fritz." Athletics—400 meters; 110 meter hurdles; Pole vault; Long jump; Triple jump.

Weingärtner, Hermann. Athletics—Long jump; Pole vault; Shot put. Gymnastics—Rope climbing. Weightlifting—One-handed lift; Two-handed lift. Cycling—2,000 meter sprint; 10,000 meters; Road race.

Great Britain and Ireland

Battel, E. Cycling—2,000 meter sprint.

Elliot, Launceston. Athletics—400 meters.

Goulding, Grantley Thomas Smart. Athletics—400 meters.

Keeping, F. Cycling—100 km.; Road race.

Levy, Edward Lawrence. [Birmingham Athletic Club.] (b.21 December 1851–d.1932) Gymnastics—Rings. Weightlifting—One-handed lift; Two-handed lift.

Marshal, Frank. [Panakhaikos Gymnastikos Syllogos.] Tennis—Men's singles; Men's doubles.

Marshal, George. Athletics—400 meters; 1,500 meters. Tennis—Men's singles; Men's doubles.

Merlin, Sidney Louis Walter. Weightlifting—One-handed lift; Two-handed lift.

Robertson, George Stuart. Athletics—Shot put.

Suter, H. F. [London Athletic Club.] Swimming—100 meter freestyle; 500 meter freestyle.

Greece

Antoniadis, S. [Podilatikos Syllogos Athinon.] Cycling—100 km.

Aspiotis, Georgios. Cycling—100 km.

Athanasiou, G. Swimming—1,200 meter freestyle.

Diamantopoulos, Ag. Swimming—100 meter freestyle; 500 meter freestyle; 1,200 meter freestyle.

Dontis, I. Swimming—100 meter freestyle; 500 meter freestyle; 1,200 meter freestyle.

Frangopoulos, D. Swimming—100 meter freestyle; 500 meter freestyle; 1,200 meter freestyle.

Gaitanos, Giorg. Swimming—100 meter freestyle; 500 meter freestyle.
Georgiadis, I.[7] Swimming—500 meter freestyle.
Grigoriadis, A. Swimming—500 meter freestyle.
Iatrou, Miltiades. Cycling—100 km.
Karagiannis, G. K. Swimming—100 meter freestyle.
Katravas, ––. Swimming—100 meter freestyle; 500 meter freestyle.
Kharilaos, Epamaindos. Cycling—Road race.
Khatzis, V. Swimming—100 meter freestyle; 500 meter freestyle; 1,200 meter freestyle.
Khristopoulos, D.[8] Swimming—500 meter freestyle.
Kolettis, Georgios. Cycling—2,000 meter sprint; Road race.
Komninos-Miliotis, Konstantinos. Fencing—Épée.
Konstantinidis, Aristidis. Cycling—2,000 meter sprint; 12-hour race.
Konstantinou, Konstantinos. Cycling—100 km.
Kontos, Theod. Swimming—100 meter freestyle; 500 meter freestyle; 1,200 meter freestyle.
Koukoudakis, P. F. Swimming—100 meter freestyle; 1,200 meter freestyle.
Kourakos, Nik. Swimming—100 meters for sailors; 500 meter freestyle.
Kourkoulas, K. Swimming—100 meters for sailors; 500 meter freestyle.
Lamprakis, Georg. Swimming—100 meter freestyle.
Laskaridis, Sav. Swimming—100 meter freestyle; 500 meter freestyle; 1,200 meter freestyle.
Lerias, Merk. Swimming—100 meter freestyle; 500 meter freestyle; 1,200 meter freestyle.
Mangourakis, V. Swimming—100 meter freestyle; 500 meter freestyle.
Markou, I. Swimming—100 meter freestyle; 500 meter freestyle.
Marnezos, G. Swimming—100 meter freestyle; 500 meter freestyle.
Mazoukas, G. Swimming—500 meter freestyle.
Mikhalopoulos, P. Swimming—100 meters for sailors; 500 meter freestyle.
Nastos, Pan. Swimming—100 meter freestyle; 500 meter freestyle; 1,200 meter freestyle.
Nikolopoulos, Alexandros. Weightlifting—Two-handed lift.
Nikolopoulos, Stamatios. Cycling—Road race.
Papasideris, Georgios. Weightlifting—One-handed lift.
Pathilos, Fil. Swimming—100 meter freestyle.
Pepanos, Antonios. Swimming—1,200 meter freestyle.
Petmezas, Aristovoulos. Gymnastics—Horizontal bar; Horse vault.
Petrou, Georg. Swimming—100 meter freestyle.
Pierrakos-Mavromikhalis, Periklis. Fencing—Épée.
Pothitos, Fill. Swimming—500 meter freestyle.
Poulos, Ioannis. Fencing—Épée.
Romantzas, A. Swimming—1,200 meter freestyle.
Salouros, K. Swimming—100 meters for sailors; 500 meter freestyle.
Santanis, D. Swimming—100 meters for sailors; 500 meter freestyle.
Stournaras, N. Swimming—100 meters for sailors; 500 meter freestyle.
Tryfiatis-Trypiaris, A. Cycling—Road race.
Valakakis, Georgios. Swimming—100 meter freestyle.
Valetsiotis, Emm. Swimming—100 meter freestyle; 1,200 meter freestyle.
Vanitakis, ––. Athletics—Marathon.
Vathis, ––. Athletics—Marathon.
Vlachos, Ir. Swimming—100 meter freestyle.
Xenopoulos, Sol. Swimming—100 meter freestyle; 500 meter freestyle; 1,200 meter freestyle.
Zanos, A. Swimming—500 meter freestyle.

Hungary

Dáni, Nándor. Athletics—100 meters; 400 meters; 1,500 meters; Long jump.

Hajós, Alfréd. Swimming—500 meter freestyle.

Kakas, Gyula. Athletics—High jump; Pole vault. Gymnastics—Rings.

Kellner, Gyula. Cycling—Road race.

Malcsiner, Gyula. [Magyar Testgyakorlok Köre.] Athletics—1,500 meters; Marathon.

Manno, Leonidasz. [Magyar Athletikai Club.] Athletics—100 meters; 400 meters.

Péthy, Pál. [Magyar Athletikai Club.] Athletics—110 meter hurdles; Long jump; Triple jump; Shot put.

Szabo Kisgeszeni, István. [Cercle d'Escrime, Györ.] Fencing—Foil; Sabre.

Szokolyi, Alajos. Athletics—High jump; Pole vault; Long jump.

Szöreny Reich, Ferenc. [Magyar Athletikai Club.] Swimming—100 meter freestyle; 500 meter freestyle.

Topavicza, Momcsilló. Athletics—Pole vault; Long jump; Shot put. Gymnastics—Horse vault; Parallel bars; Pommelled horse. Weightlifting—One-handed lift.

Wein, Desiderius. Athletics—High jump; Pole vault; Shot put. Gymnastics—Pommelled horse.

Zaborszky, István. [Magyar Athletikai Club.] Athletics—400 meters; 800 meters.

Zachar, István. [Magyar Athletikai Club.] Athletics—100 meters.

Italy

Airoldi, Carlo. [Società Pro Italia, Milano.] Athletics—Marathon.

Baroni, Vincenzo. [Circolo Internazionale di Scherma-Fini, Cantu.] Fencing—Foil; Sabre.

Caruso, Giuseppe. [Fechtclub Haudegen, Wien.] Fencing—Foil; Sabre.

Minervini, Roberto. [Tiro a Segno Nazionale, Napoli.] Shooting—Pistol (25 meters); Free rifle (300 meters); Military rifle (200 meters).

Porciatti, Angelo. [Veloce Club, Grosseto.] Cycling—2,000 meter sprint; 10,000 meters; 100 km.; 12-hour race; Road race.

Russia

De Ritter, Nikolaj. Wrestling—Unlimited, Greco-Roman.

Smyrna

Mouratis, Konstantinos. [Liskhi Ton Kynigon.] Athletics—100 meters; 400 meters; 110 meter hurdles; Long jump.

Sweden

Andersson, Harald. [Idrottsällskapet Lyckans Soldater.] (b.4 August 1867–d.31 July 1944) Athletics—100 meters; 110 meter hurdles; Long jump. Gymnastics—Horse vault.

Bergman, Johan. *[Upsala Simsällskap.] (b.6 February 1864–d.18 August 1951) Swimming—100 meter freestyle.*

Sjöberg, Henrik. Athletics —110 meter hurdles. Gymnastics — Pommelled horse.

Switzerland

Champaud, Charles. Athletics — Pole vault. Wrestling — Unlimited, Greco-Roman.

Zutter, Louis. Weightlifting — One-handed lift; Two-handed lift. Wrestling — Unlimited, Greco-Roman.

United States

Burke, Thomas Edward. Athletics — 800 meters.

Connolly, James Brenden Bennet. Athletics —110 meter hurdles.

Curtis, Thomas Pelham. Athletics — Long jump.

Derr, Ralph. *[Princeton University.] Athletics —100 meters; Long jump. Gymnastics — Horizontal bar.*

Edwards, John Stanley. *[Denver University.] Athletics — High jump.*

Garrett, Robert. Gymnastics — Horizontal bar.

Hellen, Fred. *[American School for Classical Study, Rome.] Fencing— Foil.*

Johnson, John. *[League of Amateur Wheelmen.] Cycling— 2,000 meter sprint; 10,000 meters; 100 km.; 12-hour race; Road race.*

Lord, Frederick W. *[Boston Athletic Association.] Athletics —110 meter hurdles.*

MacDonald, Ray. *[League of Amateur Wheelmen.] Cycling— 2,000 meter sprint; 10,000 meters; 100 km.; 12-hour race; Road race.*

Paine, John. Shooting — Free pistol (30 meters).

Waldstein, Charles. Shooting — Free pistol (30 meters); Free rifle (300 meters); Military pistol (25 meters); Pistol (25 meters).

NOTES

1. Some recent sources list this athlete as "Edward Battel." We are uncertain of this source, and Ian Buchanan, British Olympic historian, cannot confirm the first name by any sources.

2. Some recent sources list this athlete as "Frank Keeping." We are uncertain of this source, and Ian Buchanan, British Olympic historian, cannot confirm the first name by any sources.

3. Spelling may be "Mokchoinet."

4. The Greek name spellings have been derived by using the original Greek alphabet spellings and then applying consistently throughout a single system of transliteration, that of the *Encyclopaedia Brittanica*. While this may give some spellings different in the Latin alphabet than usually seen, it allows a consistency not seen in previous works.

5. Basically from Slovakia, then a section of the Austro-Hungarian Empire, this is the spelling always used and seen in the records. Czechoslovak Olympic records list him as "Alojz Szokol."

6. Topavicza was basically from Vojvodina in what would become Yugoslavia, then a part of the Austro-Hungarian Empire. "Momscilló Topavicza" is the spelling used in Hungary, while Yugoslav records have his name as "Momcilo Tapavica."

7. May be Ioannis Georgiadis, who did compete in Fencing.

8. May be Dimitrios Khristopoulos, who did compete in Athletics.

"The Olympic Games" — a Classical Greek Ode by George Stuart Robertson, 1896

(translated by E. D. A. Morshead)

Following is the Pindaric Ode which was given by George Stuart Robertson to the Greek crowd and the royal family at the Closing Ceremonies of the 1896 Olympic Games. Robertson was a Classics Scholar at Oxford. The poem was printed in Theodore Andrea Cook's book, *The Olympic Games: Being a Short History of the Olympic Movement from 1896 Up to the Present Day, Together with an Account of the Games of Athens in 1906, and of the Organisation of the Olympic Games of London in 1908* (London: Archibald Constable & Co., 1908), pp. 55–58. The translation, also given in Cook's book, is by E. D. A. Morshead.

Up my song!
　　An alien crowd, we come
　To this Athenian home —
Yet now like Persian plunderers of old,
But in frank love and generous friendship bold!

　　I too, who sing hereof,
I too, in strenuous sport, with sons of Hellas strove.
　　"All hail!" we cry, "All hail!"
Fair mother of the Arts! O violet-crowned
Home of Athena! Glory's sacred ground!
　　Onward, in love of thee, we spread our eager sail!

Up, comrades! Let your voice raise
The flower of song, the blossom or her praise —
And, as we fleet across a halcyon sea,
May the god gently waft our song to thee!

Love-smitten for the Maid, the loveliest birth
  That Heaven e'er gave to earth,
    We come, her grace to gain —
Ploughing with pinnace fair the bright auspicious main!

    O mother Athens! Ever from old time
The homeless wanderer found a home with thee —
  Bear witness Agamemnon's son, thy guest,
Whom awful Furies drove o'er land and sea
In stern requital of his glorious crime,
  Till Athens gave him rest!
Now unto us, O Land of fame divine,
Stretch forth thy hand in welcome! From afar
Let glory of the strife that is not war
  Commend us to thy shrine!

Lo, from the wide world manifold we come —
  From England's hearths and homes draw hither some,
Children of sires, who in the days gone by,
  Warred for thy liberty,
  Warred by the poet's side,

The Muses' child, who in Aetolia died!
And other some from gallant France draw nigh,
Lords of the peaceful strife, with thee to vie;
  And some from German forests, strong and bold,
Or where Hungarian cornlands wave their gold!
And some thro' Western ocean cleave their way —
  And fleet of foot are they!

Once, long ago — when Peleus to his side
  Drew Thetis as a bride —
Came gods and heroes to the palace-hall,
  For that high festival.
To-day, O happy Hellas, see him stand,
  Thy king, the nursing father of thy land,
Brother of one right dear to England's heart and mine!
  See form the North draw nigh'
    A star of Muscovy!
  See how, once more, from hills afar,
    Not now with arms and war,
An Alexander comes, of royal line —
  Quitting his land for thine!

Athens, all hail! Hail, O rejoicing throng!
And from our lips receive the tributary song.

Index